This is number two hundred and twenty-two
in the second numbered series of the
Miegunyah Volumes
was made possible by the
Miegunyah Fund
established by bequests
under the wills of
Sir Russell and Lady Grimwade.

'Miegunyah' was Russell Grimwade's home
from 1911 to 1955
and Mab Grimwade's home
from 1911 to 1973.

BARBARA TUCKER

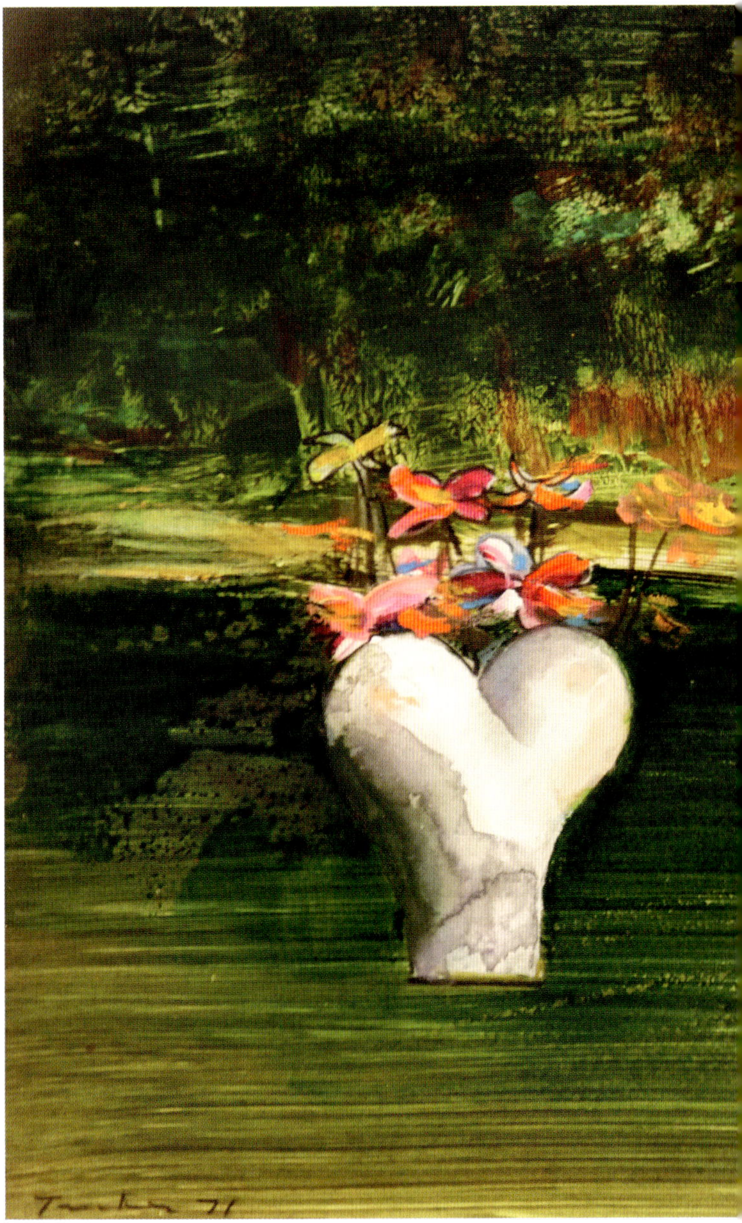

EDITED BY
HERMINA BURNS

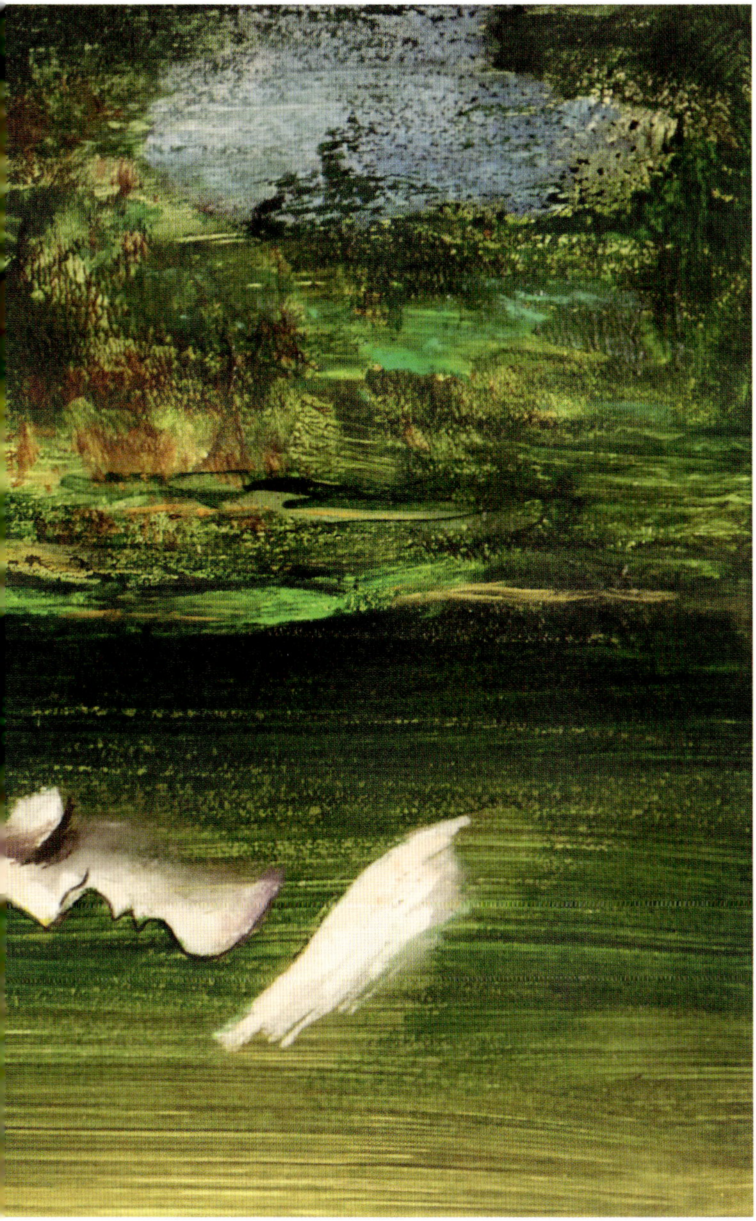

ALBERT TUCKER
RIVER DREAMING *1971*
SYNTHETIC POLYMER PAINT
ON CARD
24.5 × 33.8 CM
PRIVATE COLLECTION
© ALBERT & BARBARA
TUCKER FOUNDATION
COURTESY SMITH & SINGER
FINE ART

THE ART OF BEING

THE MIEGUNYAH PRESS

THE MIEGUNYAH PRESS
An imprint of Melbourne University Publishing Limited
Level 1, 715 Swanston Street,
Carlton, Victoria 3053, Australia
mup-contact@unimelb.edu.au
www.mup.com.au

First published 2024

This project was supported by
Albert & Barbara Tucker Foundation
Level 4, 600 Bourke Street, Melbourne, Victoria 3000
www.tuckerfoundation.org.au

ALBERT & BARBARA
TUCKER FOUNDATION

Cover image: Barbara Tucker, Hurstbridge, by Albert Tucker
Designed by Patricia Garner
Printed in China by 1010 Printing Asia Ltd

A catalogue record for this book is available from the National Library of Australia

9780522879094 (paperback)
9780522879100 (ebook)

for
BARBARA TUCKER

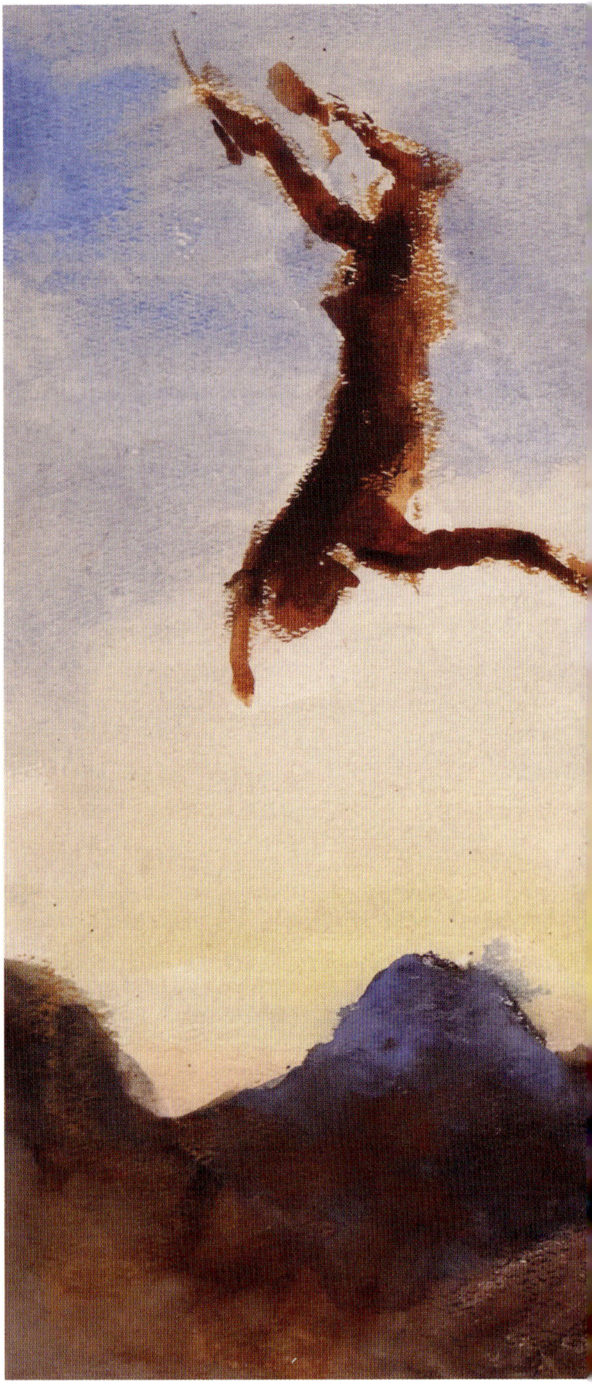

ALBERT TUCKER
BLAIRGOWRIE *1982*
WATERCOLOUR AND PASTEL ON PAPER
38 × 45.5 CM
PRIVATE COLLECTION

COURTESY SMITH & SINGER FINE ART

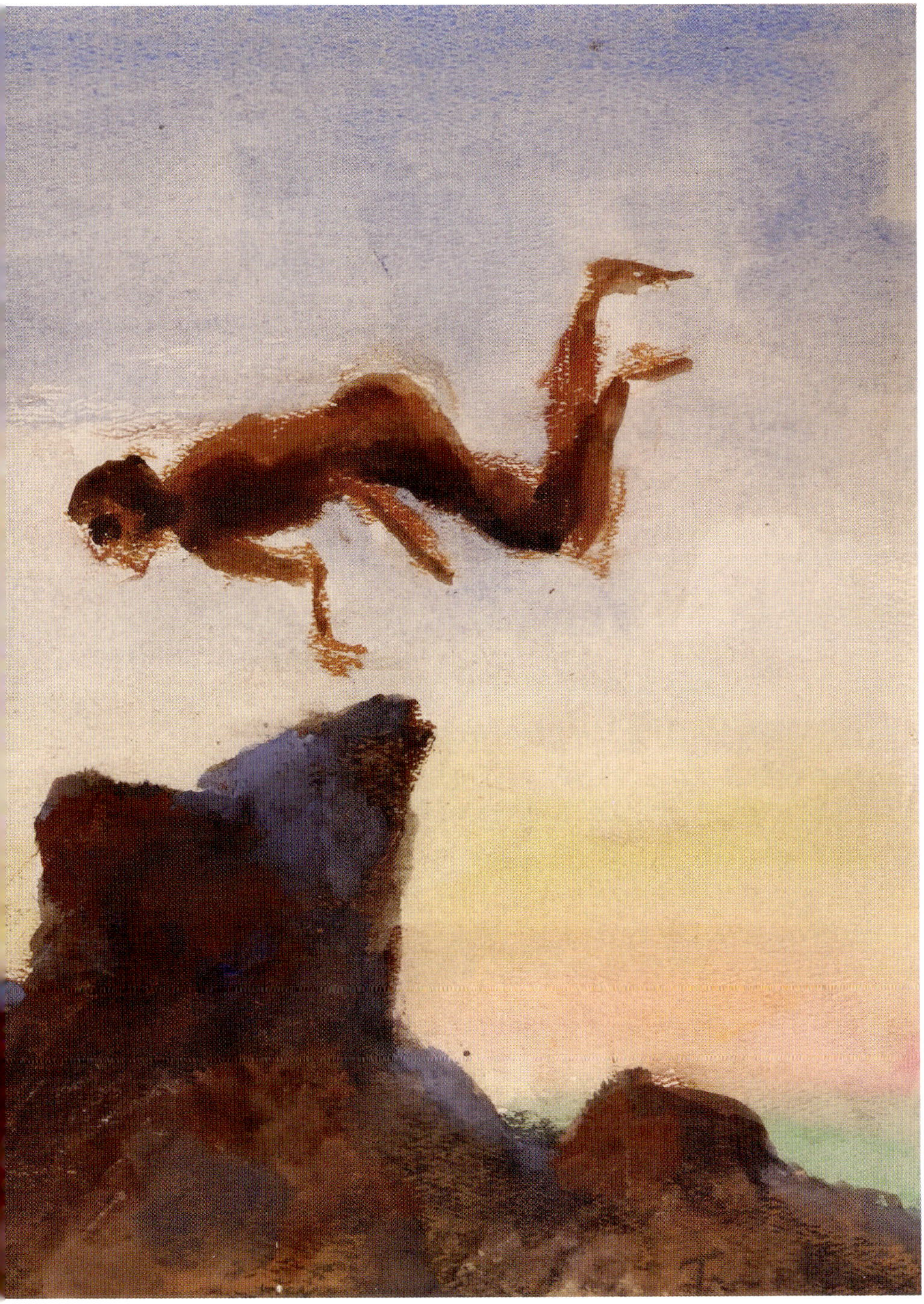

CONTENTS

PREFACE 1
HERMINA BURNS

PORTRAITS OF BARBARA 10
GEOFFREY SMITH

I | THE ART OF GIVING

BARBARA TUCKER AND HEIDE 45
LESLEY HARDING WITH KIRSTY GRANT

BARBARA TUCKER AND STATE LIBRARY VICTORIA 54
SHANE CARMODY WITH JOCK MURPHY

BARBARA AS CUSTODIAN 60
GEOFFREY SMITH

II | THE ART OF LIFE WITH ARTISTS

RECOLLECTIONS OF BARBARA TUCKER 67
LYN WILLIAMS

BARBARA'S VOICE 73
JUDITH PUGH

WORKING WITH BARBARA 81
GAVIN FRY

FROM A FAMILY ALBUM 90
RICHARD AND FLORENCE CRICHTON

FOUR LETTERS FROM BARBARA, POSTSCRIPTS BY BERT 114
BARBARA TUCKER AND ALBERT TUCKER

III | THE ART OF FAMILY

MY AUNT BARBARA ______130
DARREN JONES

MY SIREN AUNT______ 139
CAITLIN GRAHAM-JONES

FRAGMENTS OF BARBARA ______ 142
PETER BILCOCK

BARBARA: ALL THE DIFFERENCE______ 160
JUSTIN O'BRIEN

TALKING WITH BARBARA
LONG INTO THE NIGHT ______ 165
IAN JONES

BARBARAGANOUSH ______ 180
GARY SINGER

IV | THE ART OF FRIENDSHIP

CARROTS, ORANGES, BEES AND BOOKS ______186
FLORENCE CRICHTON

BARBARA TUCKER AND
THE GIFT OF FRIENDSHIP ______195
JILL REDNER

MISSING BARBARA ______ 206
JINX NOLAN

BARBARA AND THE RIDDLE OF THE UNIVERSE ______208
BRENDA SMITH

ELEGY FOR BARBARA TUCKER ______ 220
HERMINA BURNS

ACKNOWLEDGEMENTS ______ 223

INDEX ______224

FROM *AUSTRALIA FELIX* BY ETHEL RICHARDSON
[HENRY HANDEL RICHARDSON]

The first showy splendour of sunset had passed; but the upper sky was still aflush with colour. And in the centre of this frail cloud, which faded as he watched it, swam a single star.

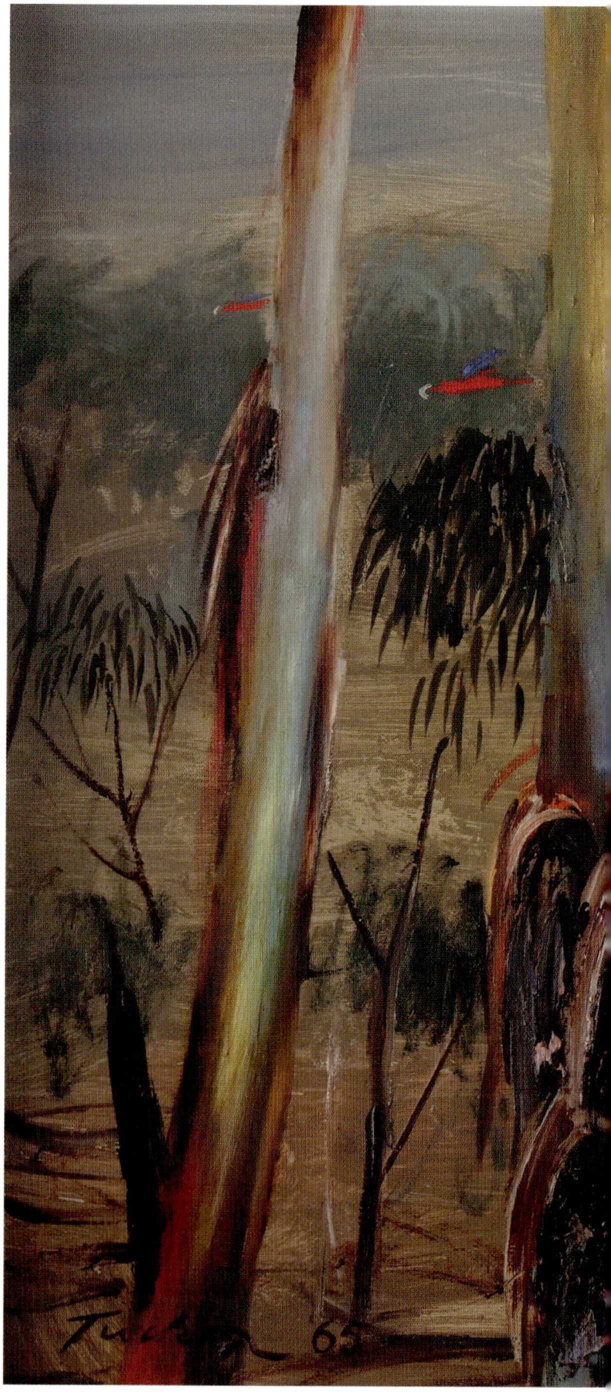

ALBERT TUCKER
TREES *1965*
SYNTHETIC POLYMER PAINT ON CARD
75.5 × 101.3 CM
PRIVATE COLLECTION

COURTESY SMITH & SINGER FINE ART

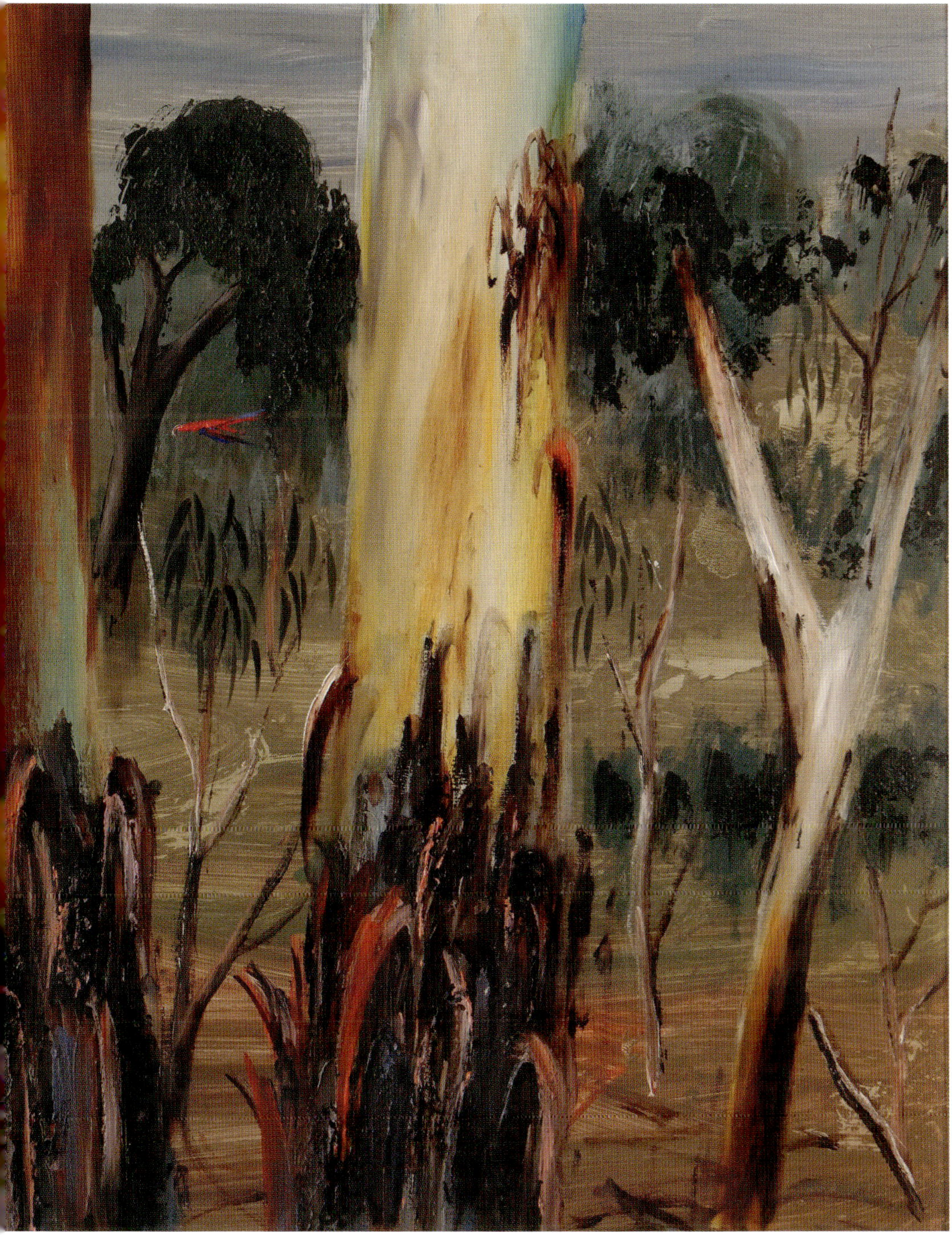

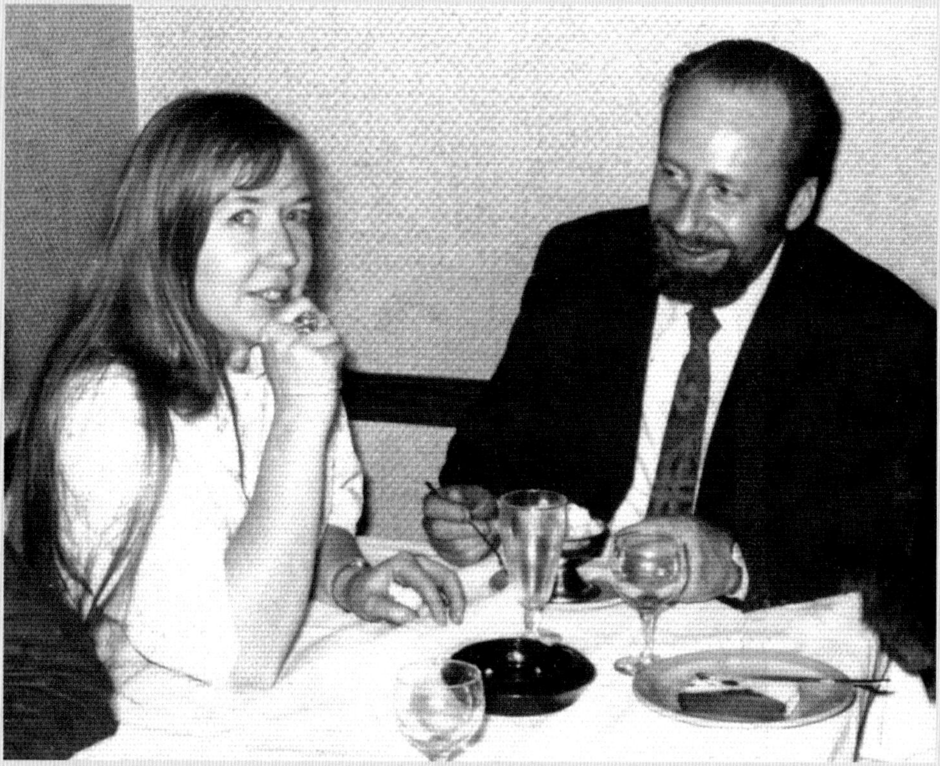

DINNER PARTY, BARBARA AND ALBERT TUCKER, 1961
Photographer unknown

PREFACE

HERMINA BURNS

Barbara Tucker grew up in Croydon, a rural suburb of Melbourne, in the 1930s, the third child of her profoundly deaf mother Jean, and David Bilcock, a pioneer Australian film-maker. She met the painter Albert Tucker in 1961 shortly after he'd returned from more than a decade in Europe. They married in a simple registry office ceremony in 1964 and lived together until Albert Tucker's death in October 1999. Barbara Tucker died in 2015. What was said in the tributes at her funeral and memorial service was so vivid and important that I raised the idea for the publication of a small volume which, with support from Darren Jones and Caitlin Graham-Jones of the Tucker Foundation and from friends and colleagues, grew into something larger—the book you now have in your hand.

The pieces in the book vary from tributes and eulogies given at Barbara Tucker's funeral, to memoirs, a journey through a family album, letters from Barbara with their postscripts from Albert, and articles by curators at institutions who speak of the significance of Barbara's generous donations and her advocacy of Albert Tucker's work, which has ensured ongoing exhibitions, often with contemporary painters, to foreground the continuing significance of his art. In the accounts of directors and agents you begin to understand the enormity of the gift to Australian culture that Barbara Tucker made in her choices and her actions as a woman, and as Albert Tucker's partner.

The first piece in this book, by Geoffrey Smith, is the first time that Barbara's figurative presence has been identified and acknowledged within Bert's work. Smith argues that Barbara 'infiltrated Bert's art in the broadest manner, often remaining subliminal and subversive'. It is a ground-breaking essay, sourcing and grouping paintings that have never before been assembled, considering the significance of Barbara in Albert Tucker's work.

The pieces in 'The Art of Giving' establish Barbara Tucker late in her life as a public figure, her important contributions to art in Australia taken into account and acknowledged. Lesley Harding and Kirsty Grant speak of Barbara being 'an important member of the Heide family'. They write about the Albert and Barbara Tucker Gift of over two hundred artworks worth more than $15 million at the time, a gift of national significance, of her support then during the evolution of the museum as Heide Fellow (2000), Life Benefactor (2004) and Co-Patron (2005). Barbara's vision has seen this collection complemented by her donation of Albert's personal library of art books and a rich archive of material that sits alongside his extensive art practice—sketchbooks, writing, catalogues, correspondence, photographs and press clippings—in all, an invaluable resource.

Shane Carmody and Jock Murphy deftly outline the important relationship Albert and Barbara had with State Library Victoria. They write about how, after Albert's death, Barbara developed that relationship, making critical decisions to ensure the preservation of documents, photos and paintings that speak for themselves about Albert's life and her own life and the cultural life of Melbourne.

Geoffrey Smith's second piece pays tribute to Barbara as custodian. It gives an account of Barbara's remarkable acumen with copyright issues and resale royalty legislation, taking decisions that were ground-breaking. Also acknowledged is her part in preventing fraudulent works entering the art market. The astute, active businesswoman of this article overlays and complicates the evocative images of Barbara in Smith's marvellous exploration of Bert's photos of Barbara.

Some of the pieces you can browse in this book are very aware of Barbara Tucker as both a friend and a figure of historical significance in the making of art. Lyn Williams' piece is a highly significant contribution to our understanding of Barbara. Written from a perspective of not-quite-close friend, more than acquaintance, and a fellow-traveller as an artist's wife, it is deeply empathetic. Her final paragraph should be compulsory reading. It acknowledges and confers agency and dignity to

Barbara's role and profoundly understands the difficulty and importance of the job Barbara took on and how effective she was in doing it.

Judith Pugh emphasises the unique quality of Barbara's friendship, but also conveys a sharp awareness of the difficulties of being an 'artist's wife' in those times, a difficulty they shared in making a place for creative art and spirit.

Gavin Fry documents his working relationship with Barbara when she approached him in the early 2000s to write what became the 2010 biography titled simply *Albert Tucker*. Fry writes of his growing respect for Barbara as he makes progress with the book. Fry informs us of the strength of Barbara's acknowledgement of the American Mary Dickson, Albert's partner after his relationship with Joy Hester had ended, which shifts the standard narrative about critical influences in Albert's earlier life. Barbara knew that Mary was agential in the New York Museum of Modern Art, acquiring *Lunar Landscape* (1957) and increasing Tucker's reputation. Fry notes that at every point Barbara is keenly interested in the production of the book, but also careful not to intrude on the work. This insight into Barbara as interested and independent, and fully respecting the independence of others, adds to the complex portrait of Barbara Tucker in this volume.

Flo and Dick Crichton's photo-essay provides a vivid pictorial sense of the lives of artists in Melbourne in the second half of the twentieth century, but also a sense of a long, important and rich friendship between the Tuckers and the Crichtons. Flo commented, as she selected from photos snapped in some shared moment round a table or on a picnic, or on overseas holidays, that a photographer can be an accidental historian.

Other pieces in this book are up close and personal, recollections that linger on the relationship they had with Barbara as a relative, and all offer insights. Barbara's nephew Darren Jones and his sister Caitlin both write eloquently of adoring their aunt. Peter Bilcock, Barbara's brother, offers a memory-filled account revealing love and pain at the loss of his beloved sister.

Justin O'Brien writes as Barbara's godson and is fiercely partisan, aware of her being under-acknowledged, and defending her against misrepresentation. He knows her as an almost-relative, but he also offers us an outsider's perspective, very aware of the Barbara Tucker who had to operate in the public sphere as well as in a historical context.

Barbara's brother-in-law Ian Jones remembers her in relation to his own life, and his piece inherently gives a sense of a time in which the lives of 'the wives' were not as important to take into account as the lives of husbands. Ian married Barbara's older sister Joan, who had taken the stage name Joan Bilceaux, a famous Australian singer and actress who gave up her career to marry. Ian Jones was an important television writer and director, and wrote a book about Ned Kelly. You will find references to trips that he took, accompanied by Joan, Barbara and Albert, to the Victorian Alps into bushranger and Ned Kelly territory. And you will find references to Ned Kelly's gun, a Sneider Enfield rifle, which Albert Tucker subsequently bought at an auction and

Barbara later gifted to State Library Victoria, where you can see it now.

Gary Singer's account is infused with enormous affection for Barbara. He writes of how incredibly warm and funny she was, a woman who enjoyed good food, good friendship and was marvellous company, even near her end.

The marvellously titled 'Carrots, Oranges, Bees and Books', by Flo Crichton, vividly creates what it was like to visit the world of Barbara and Bert. You could add 'Birds and Art' to the title, and perhaps it would sum up everything. The Tucker dog Gretel and David Bilcock's dog Ella get rare cameos, and their playfulness adds to the sense of Barbara's spirit, a welcoming and imaginative lightness and grace throughout the Hurstbridge house. Flo shows us Barbara as beekeeper and Bert as serious birdwatcher, binoculars to hand. The piece tells of a rich friendship, lives intertwined in travelling, camping, painting, talking and meals together, Barbara organised, adaptable and adventurous.

Jill Redner's account speaks of her friendship with Barbara, which began later in their lives, but is the more observant and evocative because of that. She writes of Barbara's resilience, decision-making and negotiating skills, evident especially during the years immediately after Bert's death.

Jinx Nolan writes briefly but eloquently of the loveliness of Barbara's friendship, which sustained her while she lived at the Chelsea with her parents Sidney and Cynthia Nolan. At the end she writes, 'I called her my sister. I will always miss her.' It is in these final sentences that you realise the depth of her feeling for Barbara and her gratitude.

Another friend, Brenda Smith, is both intrigued and bemused by Barbara's pursuit of the spiritual on a trip to India they take together with Barbara's sisters. It is a piece that shows the explorations we sometimes take in middle or later life to explore the meaning of being, and of being an independent self.

Barbara Tucker's life has too often in the past been reduced to that of being 'the wife' of a great artist—the woman in the background. That narrative needs to change. We need to see Barbara Tucker as a woman with a particular genius: for understanding the talent of the artist Albert Tucker; for encouraging and supporting his daily work and discovery; for understanding the context of the art establishment and then finding new ways of promoting his art; for encouraging the mounting of exhibitions of his work; and for ensuring that his art does and did not lapse into obscurity. We need to see her as a famous advocate in the Australian art world. The accounts in this book are part of changing the narrative around a remarkable woman: Barbara Tucker. ¶

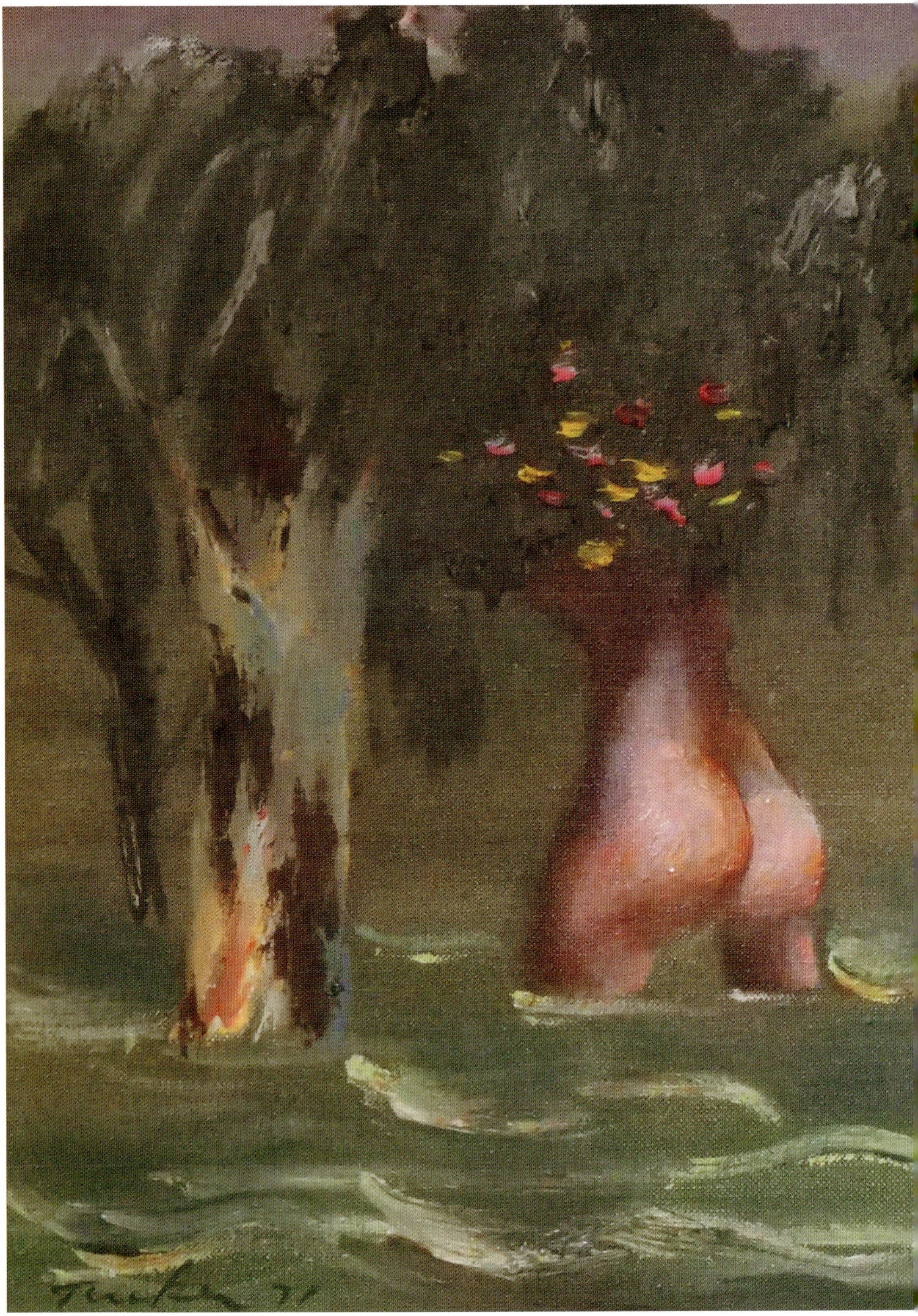

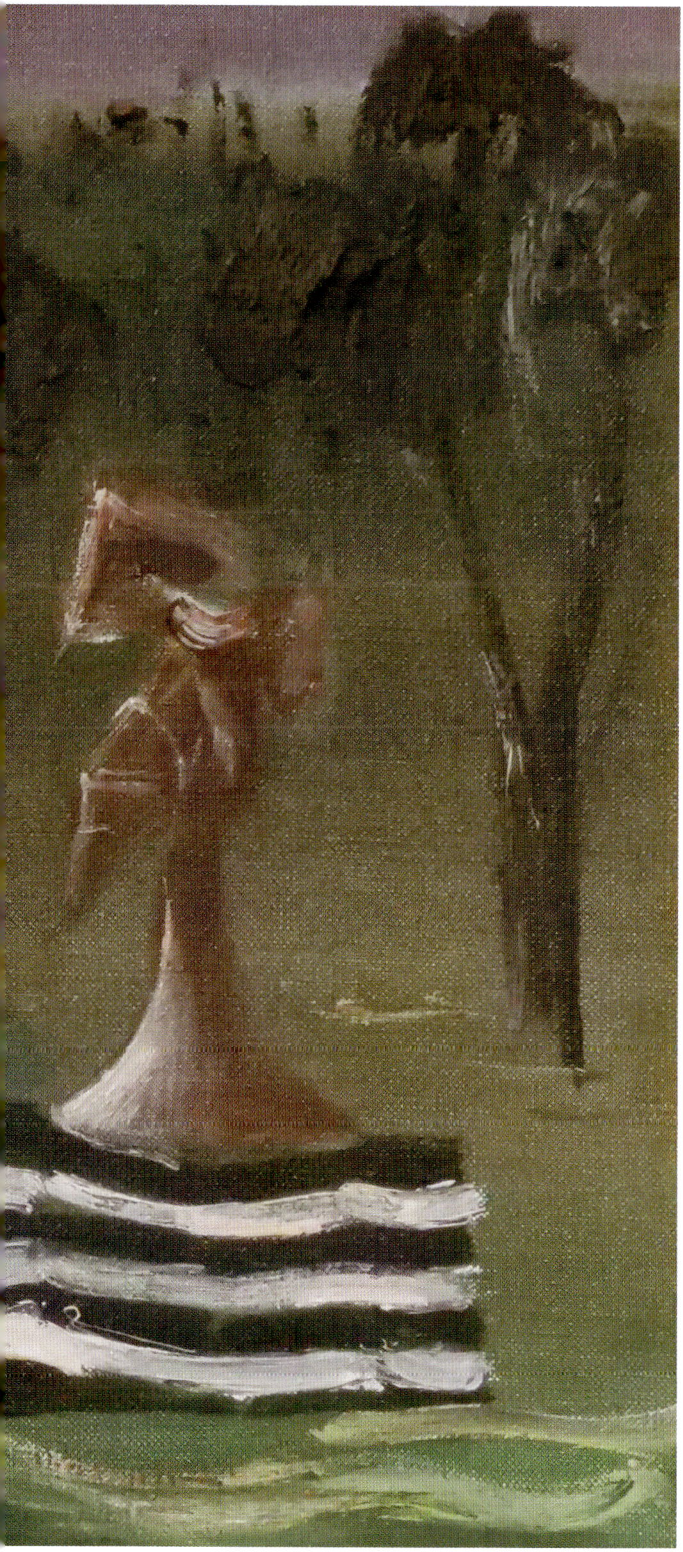

ALBERT TUCKER
CONVICT IN SWAMP *1971*
SYNTHETIC POLYMER PAINT ON COMPOSITION BOARD
39.5 × 50 CM
PRIVATE COLLECTION

COURTESY SMITH & SINGER FINE ART

PORTRAITS OF BARBARA

GEOFFREY SMITH

If there is an expectation to find a rich abundance of images of Barbara within the paintings and drawings of Albert Tucker, this search will inevitably lead to disappointment. Barbara does not feature in Tucker's numerous spontaneous life-drawings of the female form, nor in the proliferation of landscape subjects depicting the wildlife and local landmarks surrounding their domestic homes at Hurstbridge and later St Kilda, and beach house at Blairgowrie, located on the Mornington Peninsula.

Perhaps most conspicuously Barbara's profile is absent from the hauntingly powerful extended series of portraits, collectively known as *Faces I Have Met*, created by Tucker between 1976 and 1985. Bert's roll call of sitters included Yosl Bergner, Arthur Boyd, Noel Counihan, Joy Hester, Michael Keon, Adrian Lawler, Cynthia and Sidney Nolan, John Perceval, John and Sunday Reed, Sweeney Reed, Barrett Reid, John Sinclair, Bernard Smith and Danila Vassilieff—all luminaries of the Melbourne art world during the 1940s whose various and sustained contributions forever changed the course of twentieth-century Australian art.

Tucker's intense preoccupation with recording the physiognomy of his subjects is particularly evident in the oil paintings, watercolours and drawings of the most enduring and sustained motif of his career—that of himself. For more than sixty years, from the mid-1930s to the 1990s, Bert examined and scrutinised his own face in the greatest detail, in various forms and guises, from the benign to the anguished. At times his depictions verge on egotism. Mostly they remain unflinching, brutally honest and without vanity. Fundamentally they represent studies of the soul.

If Tucker's fascination (at times obsession) with the human form resulted in those closest to him—especially himself—appearing within his iconography, how then is the apparent absence of Barbara explained? The answer lies in a less literal definition of portraiture. Barbara's presence infiltrated Bert's art in the broadest manner, often remaining subliminal and subversive, and only rarely appearing in the most obvious of visual representations. If one scours Tucker's iconography from the time the couple met in 1961 and married in 1964, their shared experiences permeate each major composition. Their daily life at Hurstbridge, with its newly built home and studio, reflect a period of containment and contentment, bound together by a common affection for the native Australian landscape and for its protection and preservation for future generations. With each rendition of a bird (brolga, cockatoo, ibis, parrot, magpie, swan or wren) either wading, flying or attacking, Tucker reveals a subject or scene that is common to both him and Barbara. Their eyes collectively witnessed and experienced these images. They are scenes from their personal domestic space, from their window, door and verandah. Each painting of the luxuriant bush, with gum trees, ferns, gullies and creeks, shows their backyard.

When, on the rare occasion a female figure infiltrates Tucker's otherwise pure landscape compositions or seemingly male-dominated subjects of convicts, explorers, intruders and fauns, its slightly rounded and pale form is strikingly familiar. In *Woman and Parrot* (1965, Private Collection) the protagonist shares Barbara's features, however remains a somewhat generic and totemic emblem. Several years later in the two closely related scenes, *Woman Bathing* (1970, Private Collection) and *Woman Bathing* (1970, Private Collection), the subject is unmistakably Barbara, shown as a kind of classical goddess, an antipodean 'Diana' bathing in the deep recesses of the Australian bush.

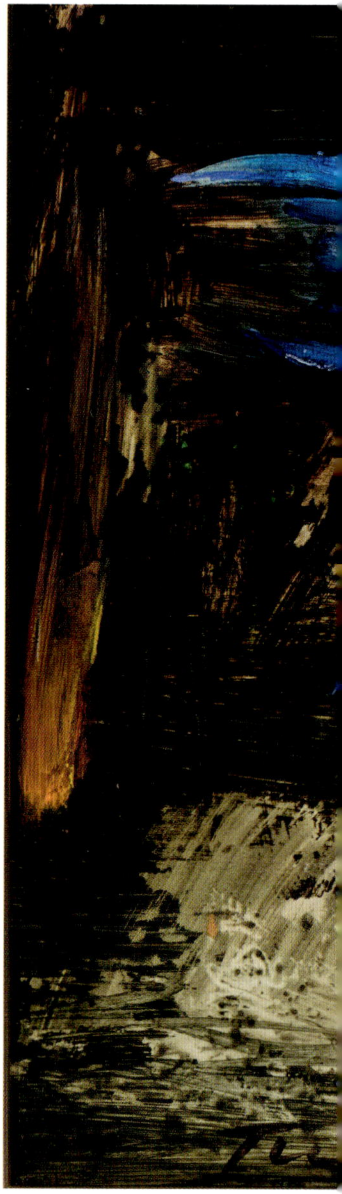

ALBERT TUCKER
WOMAN AND PARROT *1965*
SYNTHETIC POLYMER PAINT
ON COMPOSITION BOARD
30.7 × 40.7 CM
PRIVATE COLLECTION

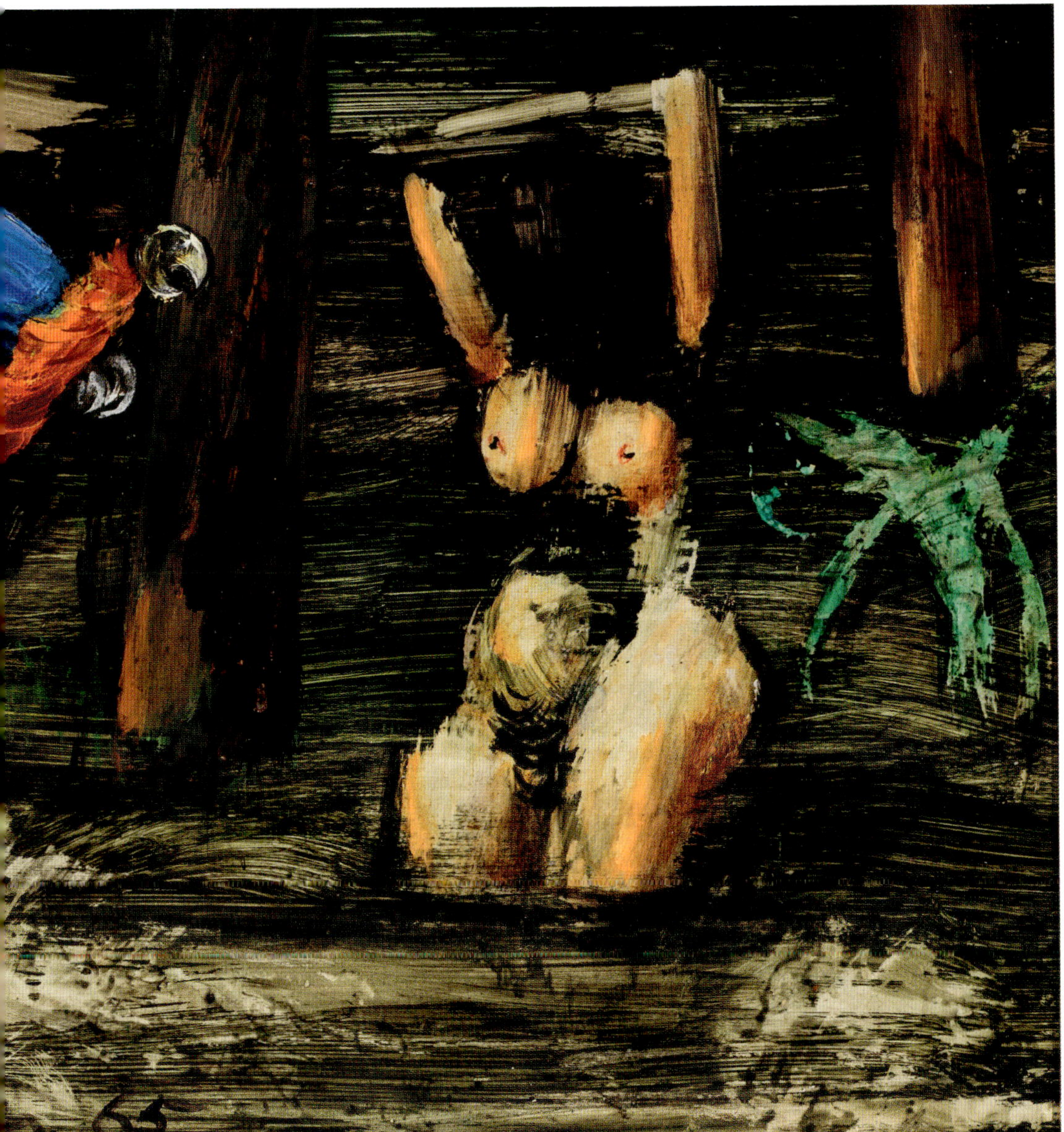

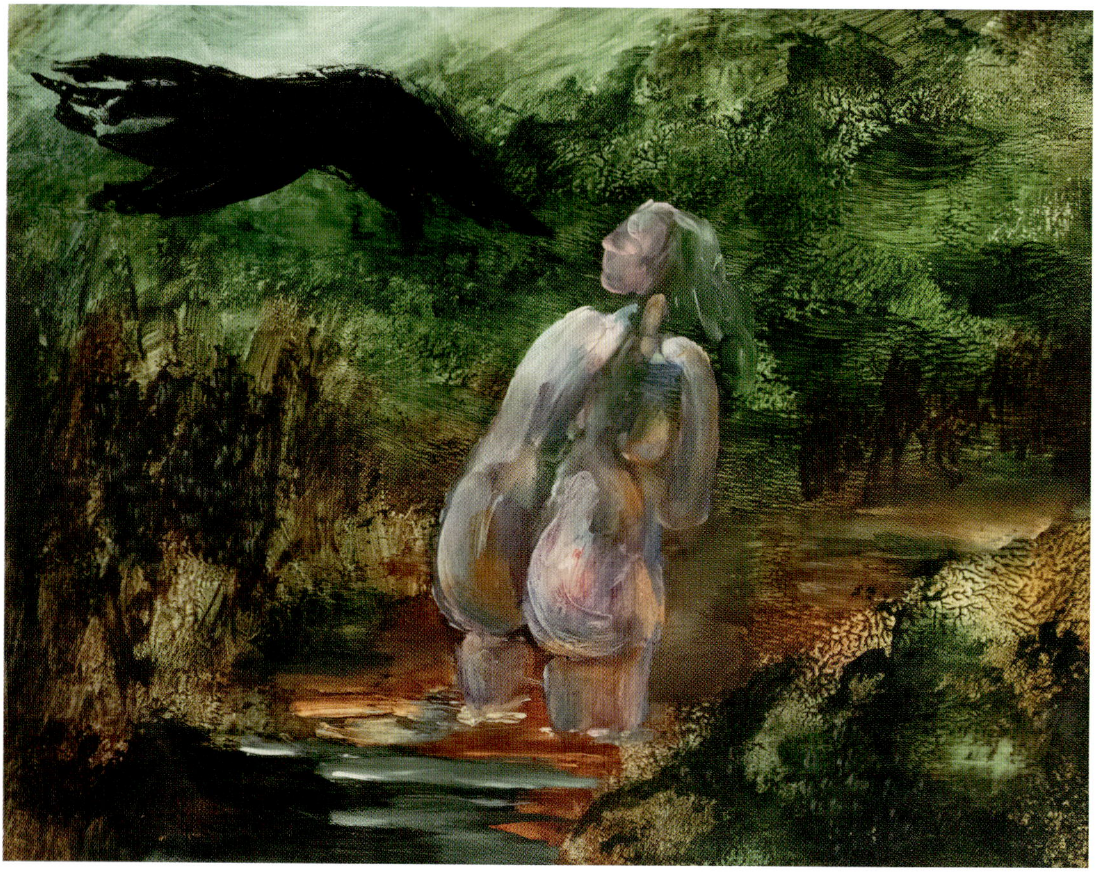

ALBERT TUCKER
WOMAN BATHING *1970*
SYNTHETIC POLYMER PAINT
ON COMPOSITION BOARD
35.8 × 46 CM
PRIVATE COLLECTION

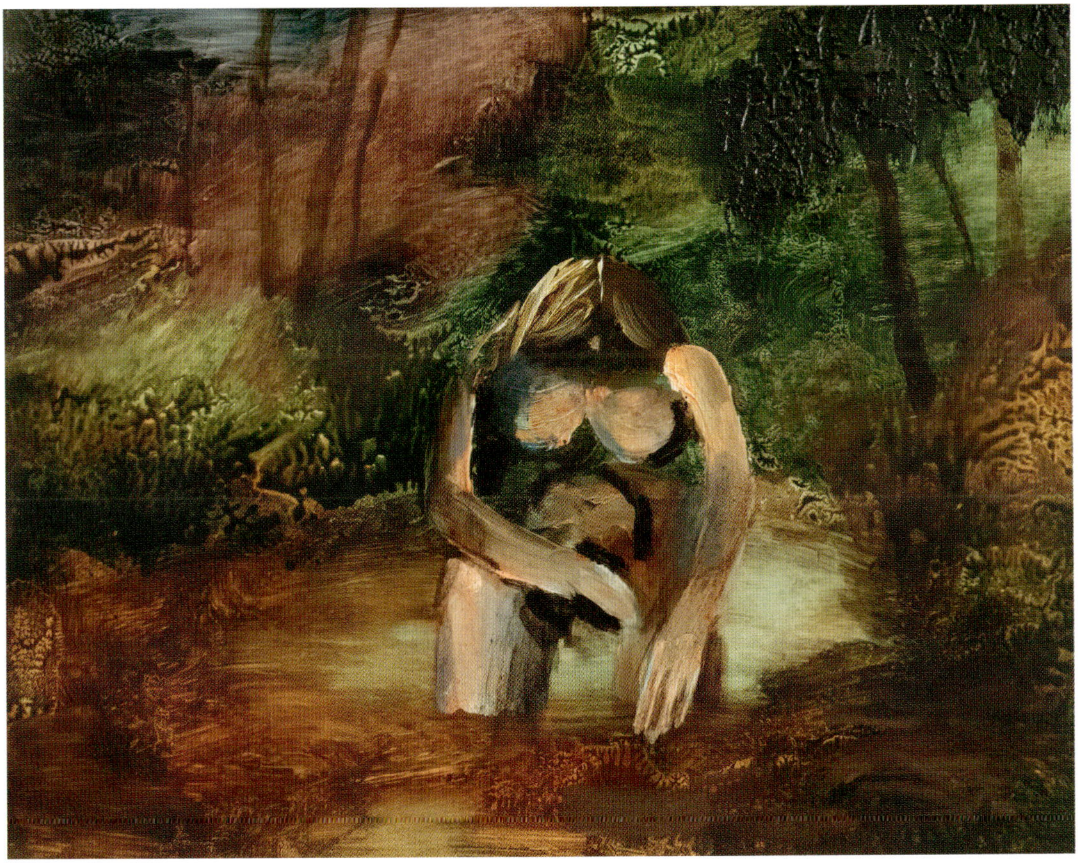

ALBERT TUCKER
WOMAN BATHING *1970*
SYNTHETIC POLYMER PAINT
ON COMPOSITION BOARD
36 × 45.8 CM
PRIVATE COLLECTION
© ALBERT & BARBARA TUCKER FOUNDATION
COURTESY SMITH & SINGER FINE ART

More frequently Barbara's figure morphs into the persona of Eliza Callaghan in Tucker's regaling of the historical narrative of John Batman, or as a more generalised female character from Australia's colonial and convict past. In works such as *Girl Fleeing* (1971, Private Collection) and *Girl and Convict* (1971, Private Collection), Barbara's presence assumes a striking and incongruous tone as her pale and naked form attempts to physically leave the confines of the scene depicted as well as the very composition itself. There is a vulnerability and preciousness connected with Barbara's appearance within these painted canvases that is fleeting and fragile. Perhaps in response to the decision to deflect from any perceived deeper meanings to such representations of Barbara by Bert from this period in their lives, we would in later years refer to such iconography in each other's company as representing the 'Barbara's bottom' series.

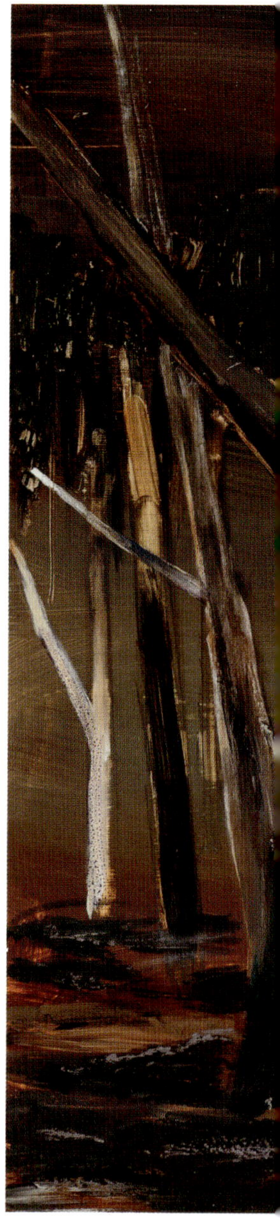

ALBERT TUCKER
GIRL AND CONVICT *1971*
SYNTHETIC POLYMER PAINT
ON COMPOSITION BOARD
70.8 × 91.1 CM
PRIVATE COLLECTION
© ALBERT & BARBARA TUCKER FOUNDATION
COURTESY OF SMITH & SINGER FINE ART

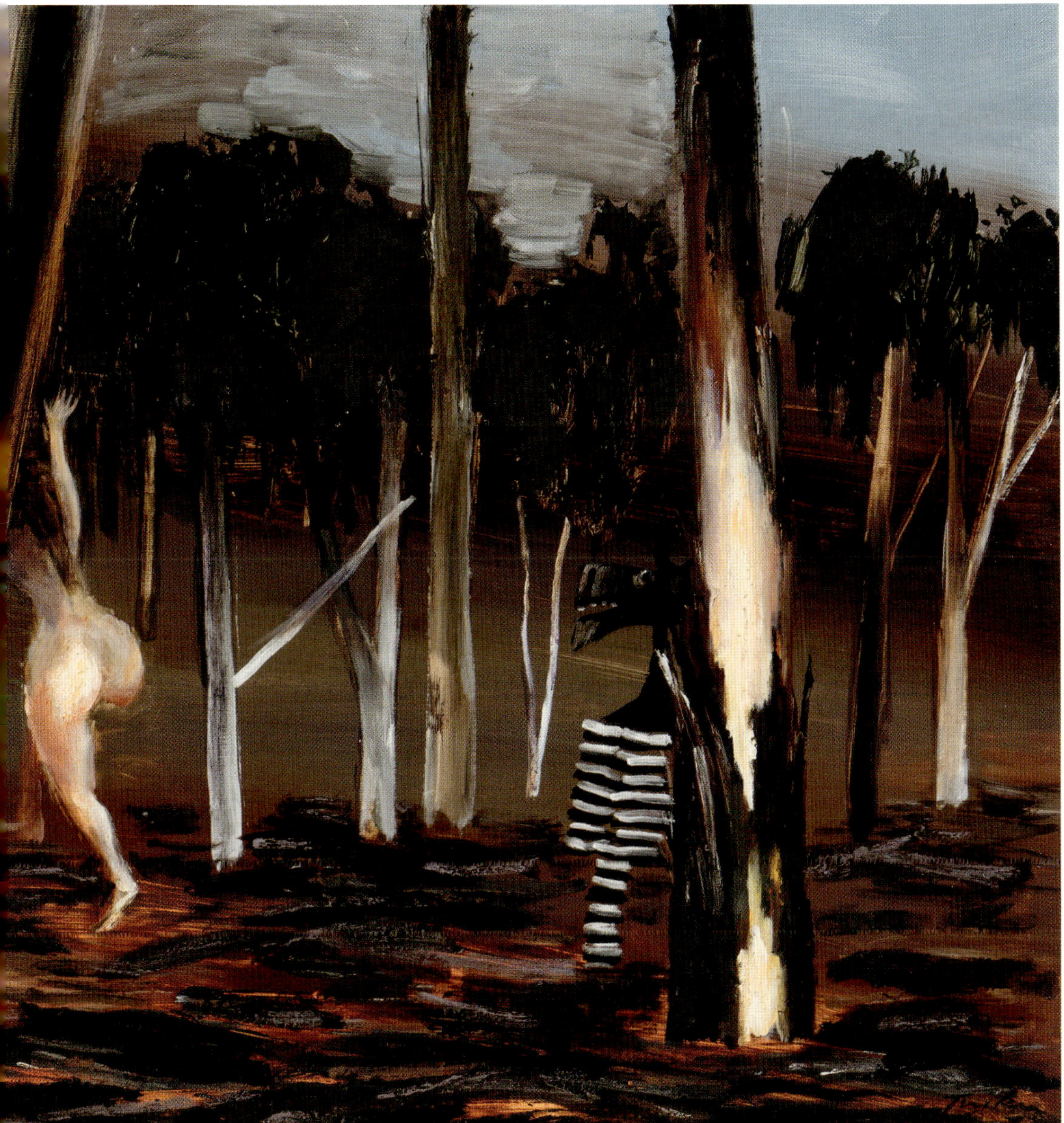

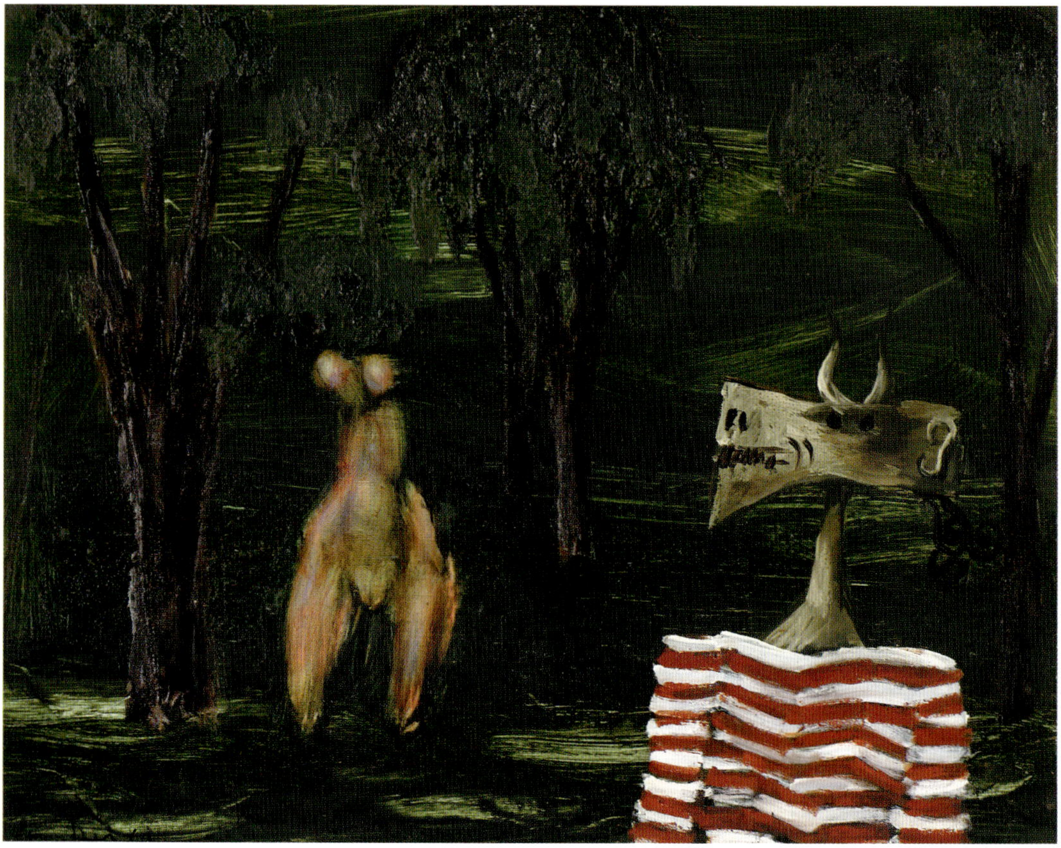

ALBERT TUCKER
CONVICT DREAMING *1969*
SYNTHETIC POLYMER PAINT
ON COMPOSITION BOARD 56.5 × 71.5 CM
PRIVATE COLLECTION
© ALBERT & BARBARA TUCKER FOUNDATION
COURTESY SMITH & SINGER FINE ART

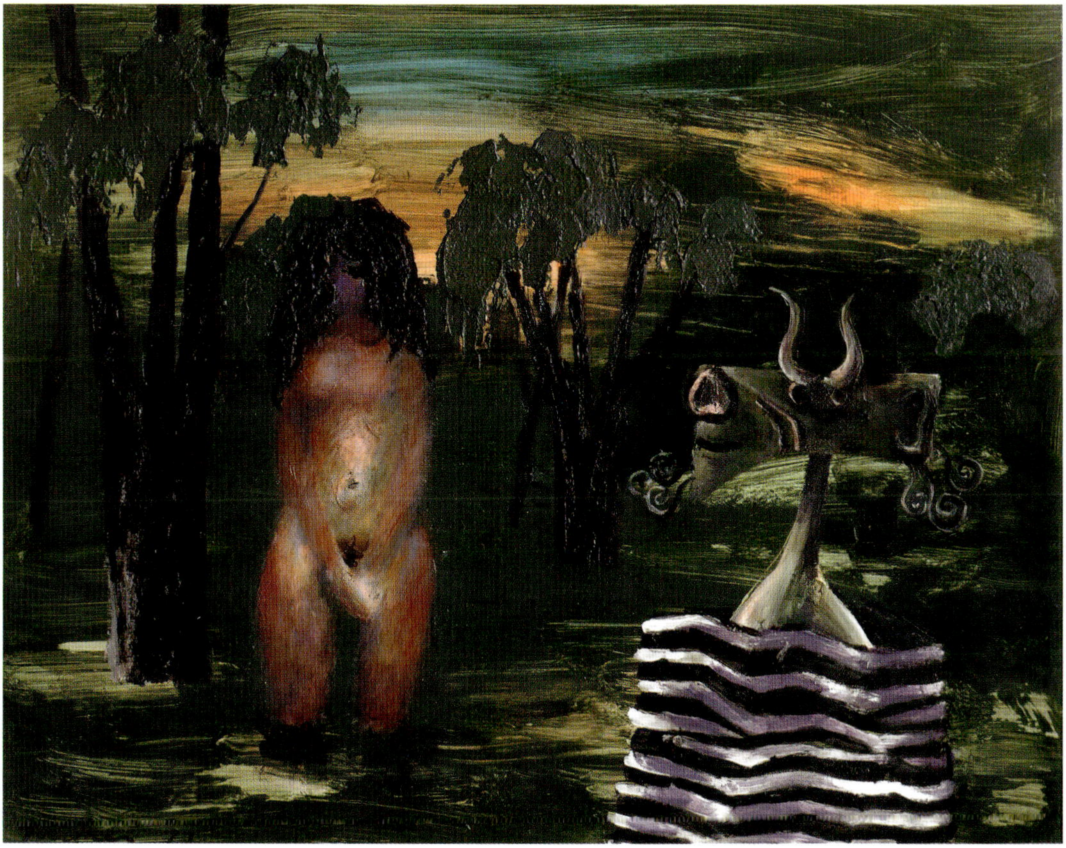

ALBERT TUCKER
CONVICT DREAMING *1972*
SYNTHETIC POLYMER PAINT
ON COMPOSITION BOARD
71 × 91 CM
PRIVATE COLLECTION

COURTESY SMITH & SINGER FINE ART

Barbara possessed a spirit of inner beauty and goodness that radiated within her being and extended beyond her physical boundaries. This feeling of light and wellbeing seeped into the room and filled the space. The world became calm, problems dissolved, and solutions became clear.

Prior to meeting Bert, Barbara's personal history had been one sprinkled with disappointment, displacement, disruption. There had been traumatic episodes of domestic violence with her first husband, buried but never forgotten. Such physical and psychologically damaging experiences generated introversion, circumspect, insecurity and caution; however, they also created acute empathy and compassion that engendered deep loyalty and kindness, as well as a desire to protect.

Barbara found love, solace and purpose with Bert. Together they forged a foundation of security, strength and resilience. They shared a commitment to lead meaningful lives that contributed to the general sustenance of society that was largely achieved through art and education. They recognised their place within the world and shared a deep desire to appreciate and conserve the natural environment. To tread carefully and leave a faint footprint on the forest floor. There were no children together. Legacy was achieved elsewhere.

* * *

Arguably the most ethereal, wistful and beautiful of all of Bert's depictions of Barbara in his painted genre is the delicate and exquisite *Springbrook* (1973, Private Collection). The image forms part of a small sequence of sensitive watercolours that celebrate the pristine beauty and primeval vegetation of their remote retreat nestled in the Queensland hinterland at Springbrook. Here Barbara is completely integrated into the bush, at one with nature, camouflaged yet partially visible, staring directly at the viewer. It is an image that perfectly captures and extols the powerful and pervasive presence that Barbara held within the iconography of Tucker's *oeuvre*—rarely seen but perpetually felt.

* * *

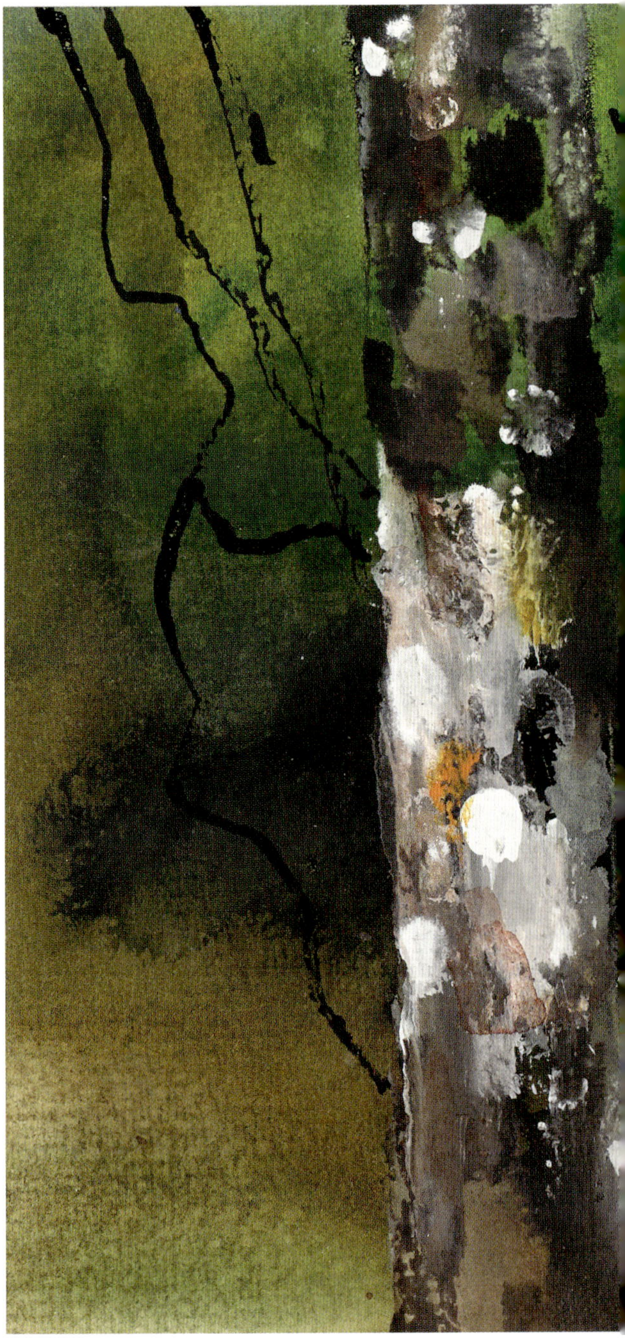

ALBERT TUCKER
SPRINGBROOK *1973*
WATERCOLOUR ON PAPER
19 × 27 CM
PRIVATE COLLECTION

COURTESY SMITH & SINGER FINE ART

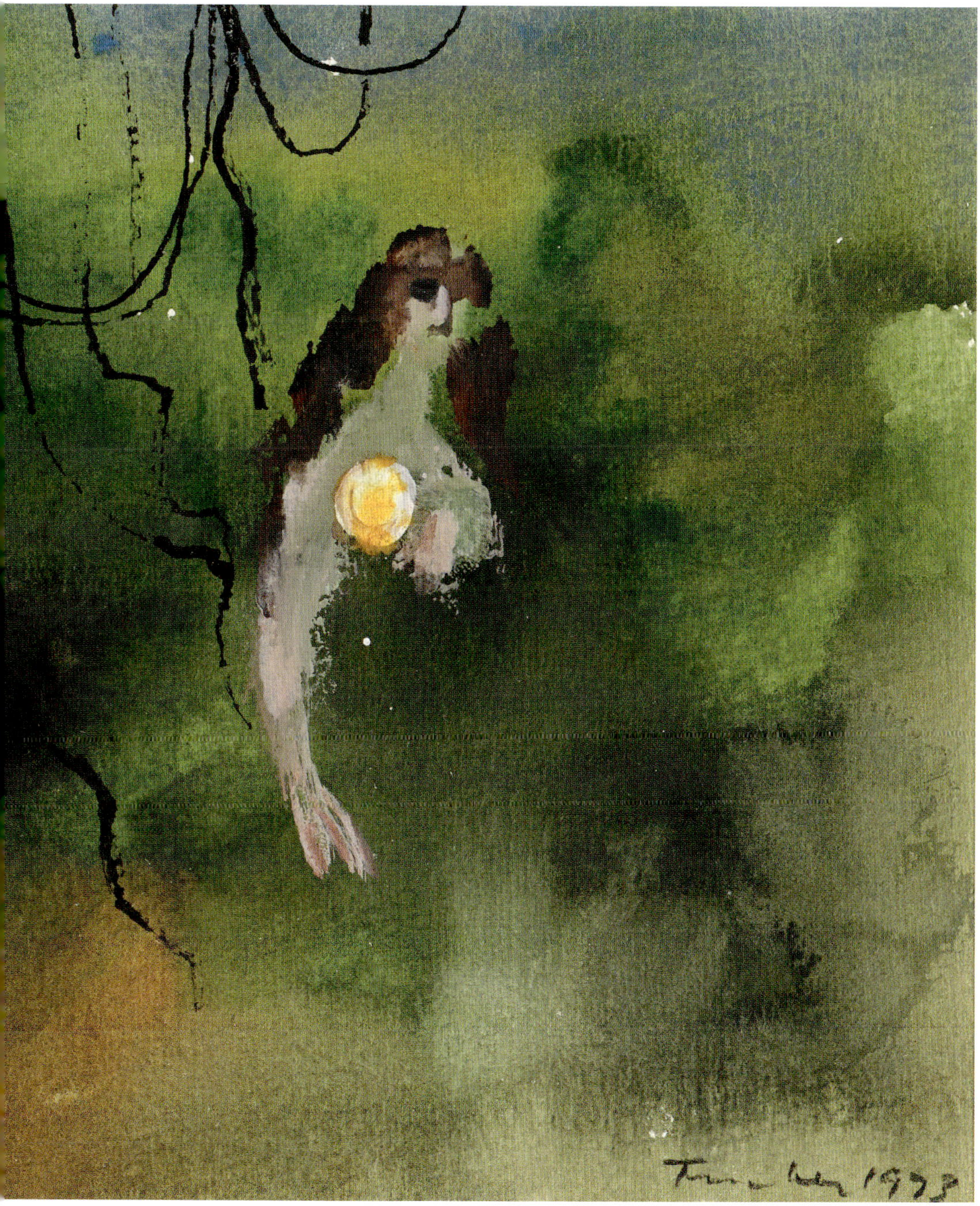

Portraits of Barbara are to be found in the photographic medium. The majority of these are intimate and personal, taken by Bert on various occasions as a record of their lives together. They were, like all of the photographs taken by Tucker from the 1930s, intended for private use rather than public consumption.

Photographs of Barbara reveal a sense of self and a sense of purpose. Some of the most evocative images convey Barbara's great love for the natural environment and her particular affinity with water. Barbara possessed a lifelong desire to live or be near water.

Her physical appearance remained largely unaltered over the course of the decades. Photographs taken in the 1960s show a similar physiognomy, expression and relaxed pose as those taken forty years later. Hers was not a life of invention and re-invention. Trends and styles passed Barbara by. She loved colours, patterns and textures that proved timeless in their expression and meaning.

Barbara showed no signs of being ambitious, jealous or avaricious. At times these qualities, which prove so destructive to the mind and soul, also failed to provide Barbara with a protective mechanism that left her vulnerable to the exploitative motives of others.

Above all, Barbara possessed a sense of fairness and a desire for accuracy. As a person who played a key role in a generation of Australians who created history, Barbara remained concerned by those who tried to re-write it and make it their own.

Barbara was sensitive and responsive to those who were marginalised and also to those who perhaps did not have the will, determination, strength and resources to rally against those whose voices were louder, and whose resources were deeper.

Barbara generally favoured the path avoiding conflict and maintaining harmony. Unless the ramifications to those closest to her—Bert, family and friends—were too brutal and damaging to condone and endure.

Images of Barbara are generally serene, peaceful and relaxed—especially when she is alone in the landscape. Photographs of Barbara in the rockpools at the back beaches of Blairgowrie and Sorrento show her at her most content and happy.

Portraits of Barbara are images of kindness and of love. The desire to provide a place of sustenance and security. A safe place where conversation, opinions and ideas could be freely expressed and shared. Where beneficial decisions could be made that reflected the desire to educate, protect and inspire.¶

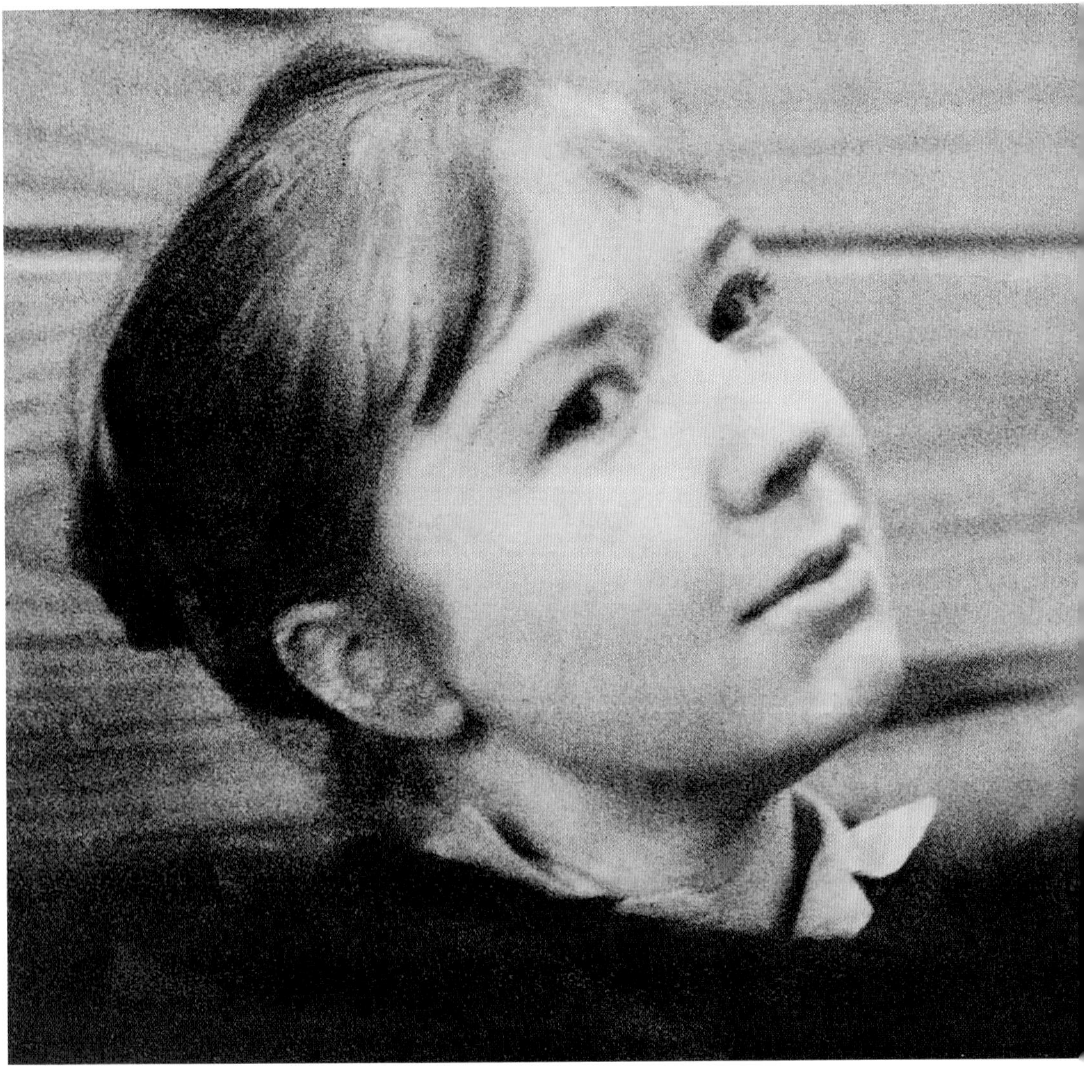

On her own, shown with her head titled slightly to the back and to the side and set against a backdrop of wide, plain, vertical timber panels, is Barbara. Her pale and delicate complexion, complimented by brushed-back, slightly plastered, fair hair, emerges from the neck up from the blurred mound of a coarse woollen jumper and a crisp white collar. Her rounded cheeks, full lips and kind eyes engage gently with the photographer, expressing perhaps, a slightly tender gaze.

Barbara is fully present, aware of the moment and of being observed by an observer. There remains, however, a sense of distance and introspection. She appears slightly guarded and aloof to the world at large, self-contained in her own thoughts, content and confident with herself, and comfortable with those within her immediate realm. It is an image of peace.

BARBARA TUCKER C. 1963
Photo by Albert Tucker

With a slightly bemused expression, lips pursed, barely suppressing a smile, gazing to the right off-camera, is Barbara. Her strawberry hair flows freely to her waist between slender arms, wrists and fingers that gently hold a note, a card, a photograph? She sits outside on a newly paved, cold, stone surface. There is a mound of rocks in the background nestled against the brick walls of a residence. She wears black fish-net stockings and thin skivvy. She is young and fresh-faced. It is an image of hope and possibilities.

BARBARA TUCKER AT HURSTBRIDGE C. 1970
Photo by Albert Tucker

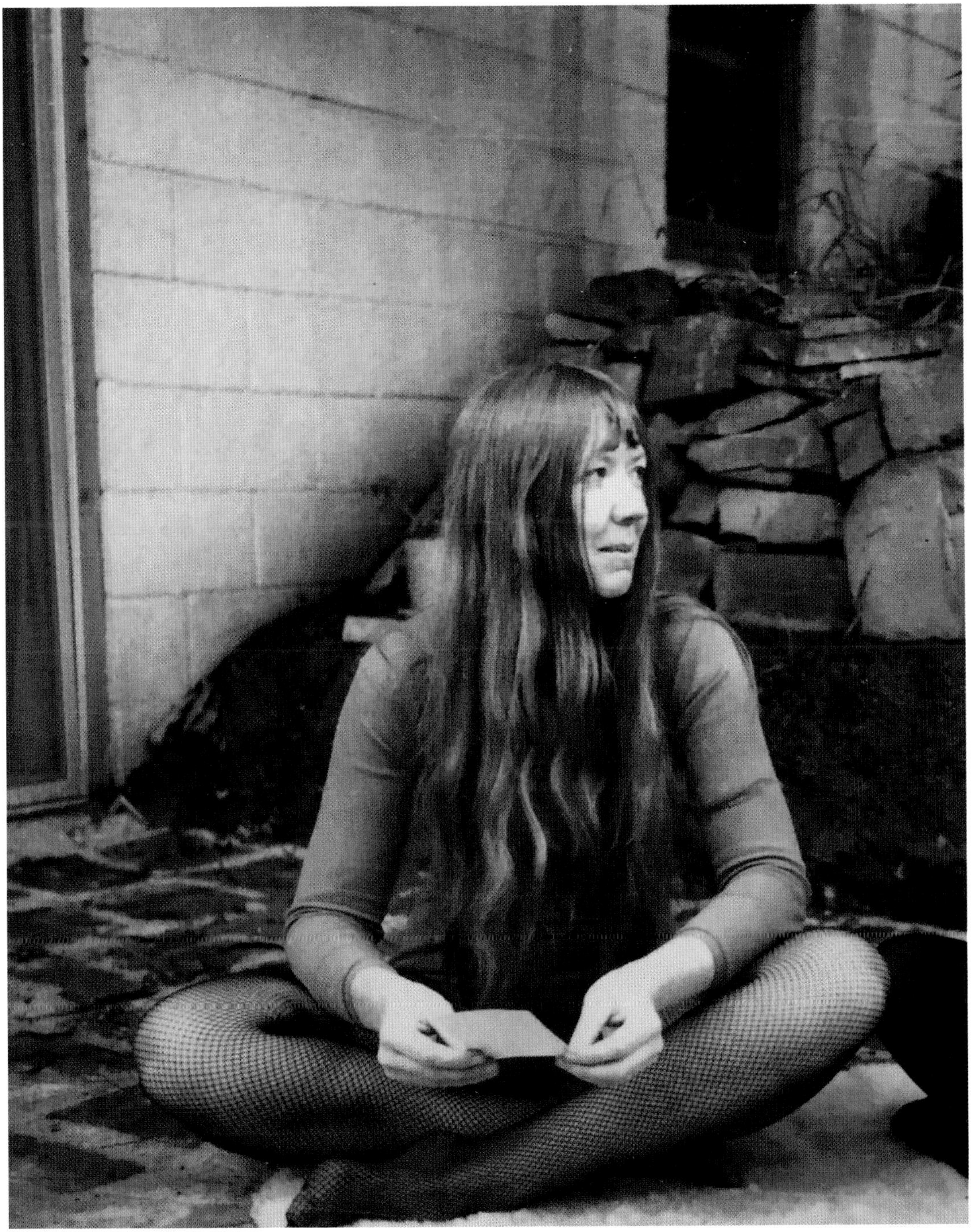

And seated in the half shadows of a dimly lit room, perched on the edge of a divan with eyes half closed, is Barbara. It is New York. The year is 1967 and Bert and Barbara are in residence at the infamous Chelsea Hotel. Barbara is working at the United Nations. The lamplight highlights the nape of her neck, a portion of her left cheek. Books, letters and photographs litter the room. A cup of tea rests on the side table. Barbara is withdrawn, almost oblivious to the photographer. She is barely there. There is a feeling of claustrophobia. Her world has shrunk rather than expanded. It is an image of displacement and exhaustion.

BARBARA TUCKER AT CHELSEA HOTEL C. 1963
Photo by Albert Tucker

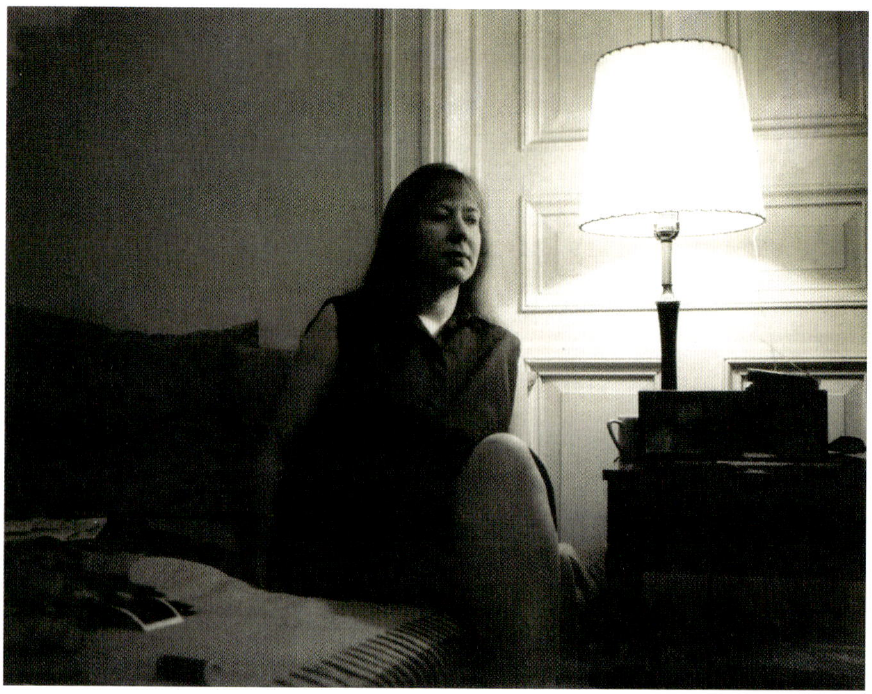

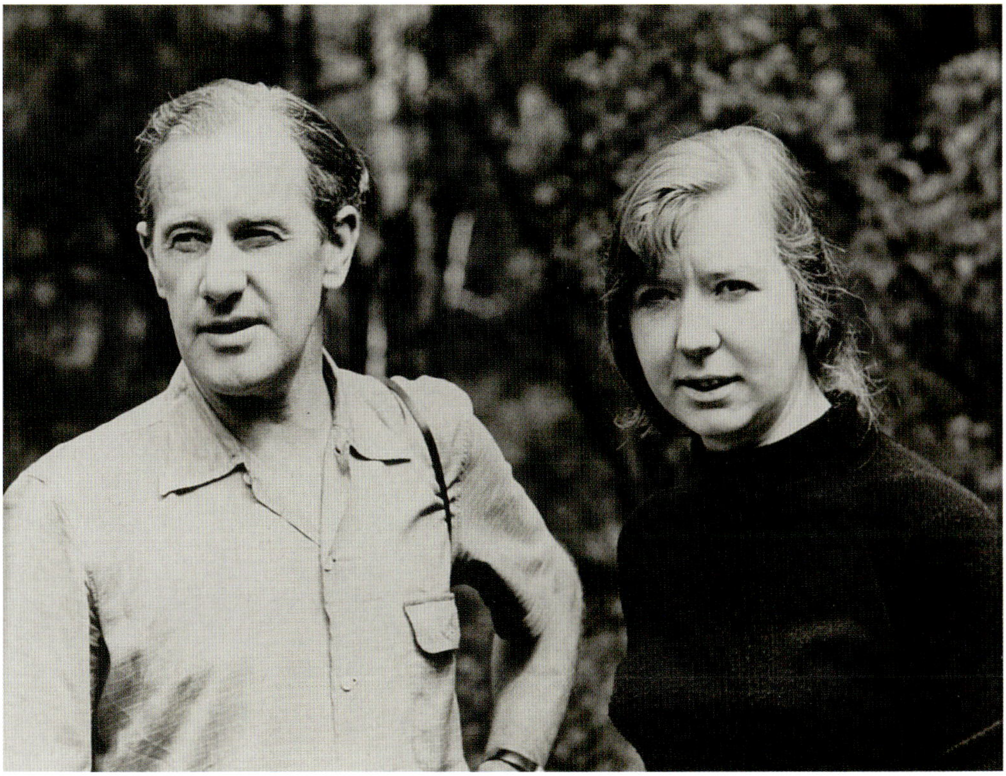

SIDNEY NOLAN AND BARBARA TUCKER C. 1965
Photo by Albert Tucker

On the right, wearing a dark turtle-neck jumper, mouth just open, looking into the light with eyes slightly squinted, is Barbara. This time, her hair is parted and tied back, fringe partly curled. Standing by her side is Sidney Nolan, Australia's most internationally famous artist; friend, confidant, pen-pal and occasional rival to Bert. Together they stand with shoulder and elbow almost touching, at home in the Australian bush at Hurstbridge. Living a world apart, they are united by parallel experiences, shared histories, singular visions, common friends and associates; inexplicably entwined, no single degree of separation.

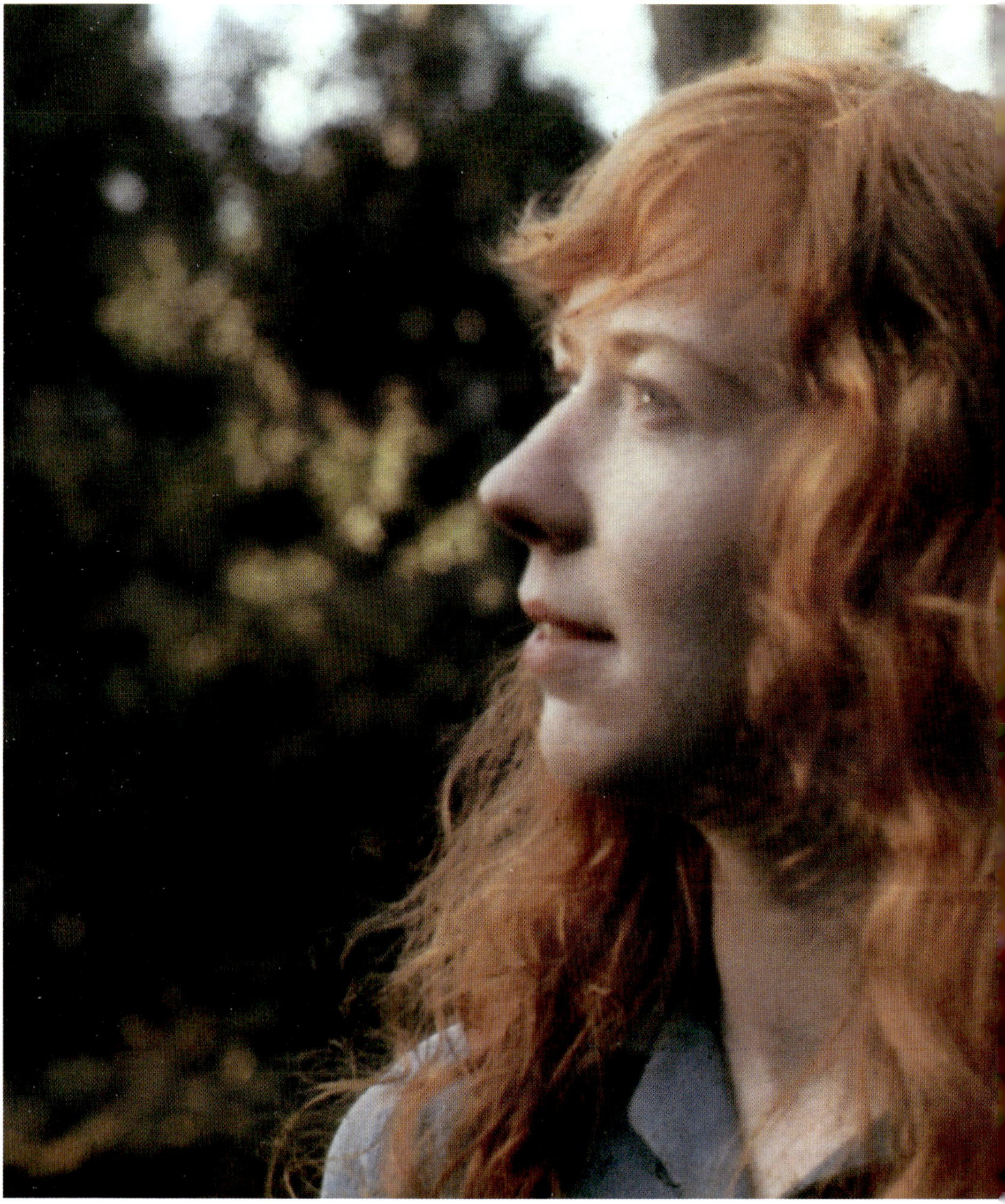

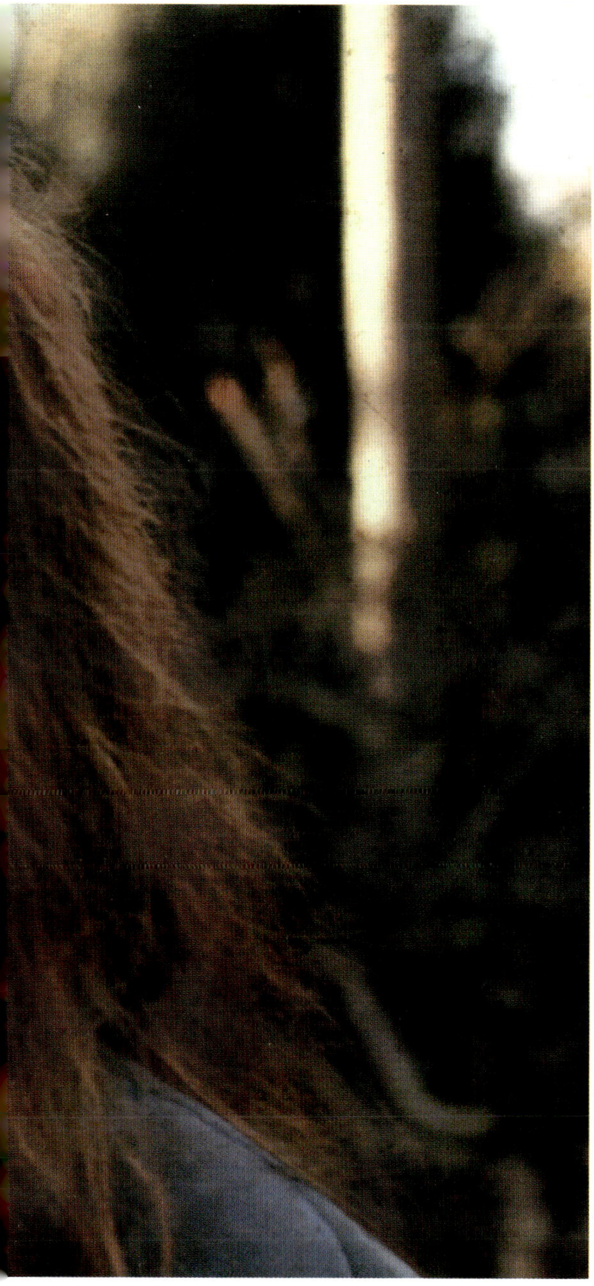

Bathed in the warm golden glow of the declining rays of light, ablaze with tenderness, love and hope, this is Barbara. A fiery vision of purity, simplicity, honesty and poise. An image of unabashed beauty and one of the most memorable, life-affirming, and exhilarating portraits created by Albert Tucker.

BARBARA TUCKER, HURSTBRIDGE C. 1962
Photo by Albert Tucker

Reminiscent of the French sculptor Aristide Maillol's classical bronze compositions of the female body placed in landscape settings, sits Barbara. Her right hand outstretched and firmly placed on the ground, her left hand cusps her head, her left elbow resting on her left knee. Her compressed and composed form creates a tightly contained shadow on the sandy riverbank. The texture and palette of her complexion and clothing harmonise with the surrounding vegetation. Light filters through the densely wooded background and glistens on the water's surface. It is an image of contemplation and exaltation, strength and resilience.

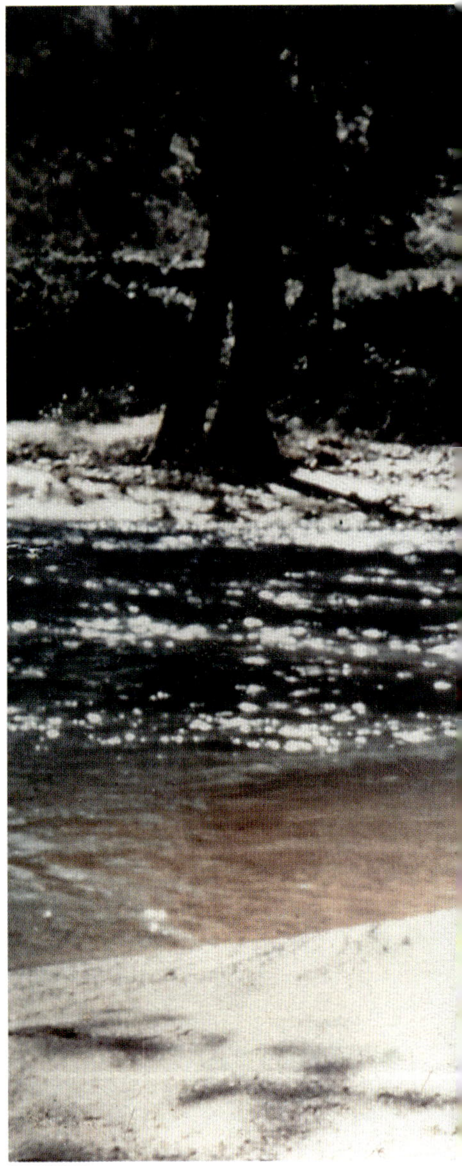

BARBARA TUCKER 1966
Photo by Albert Tucker

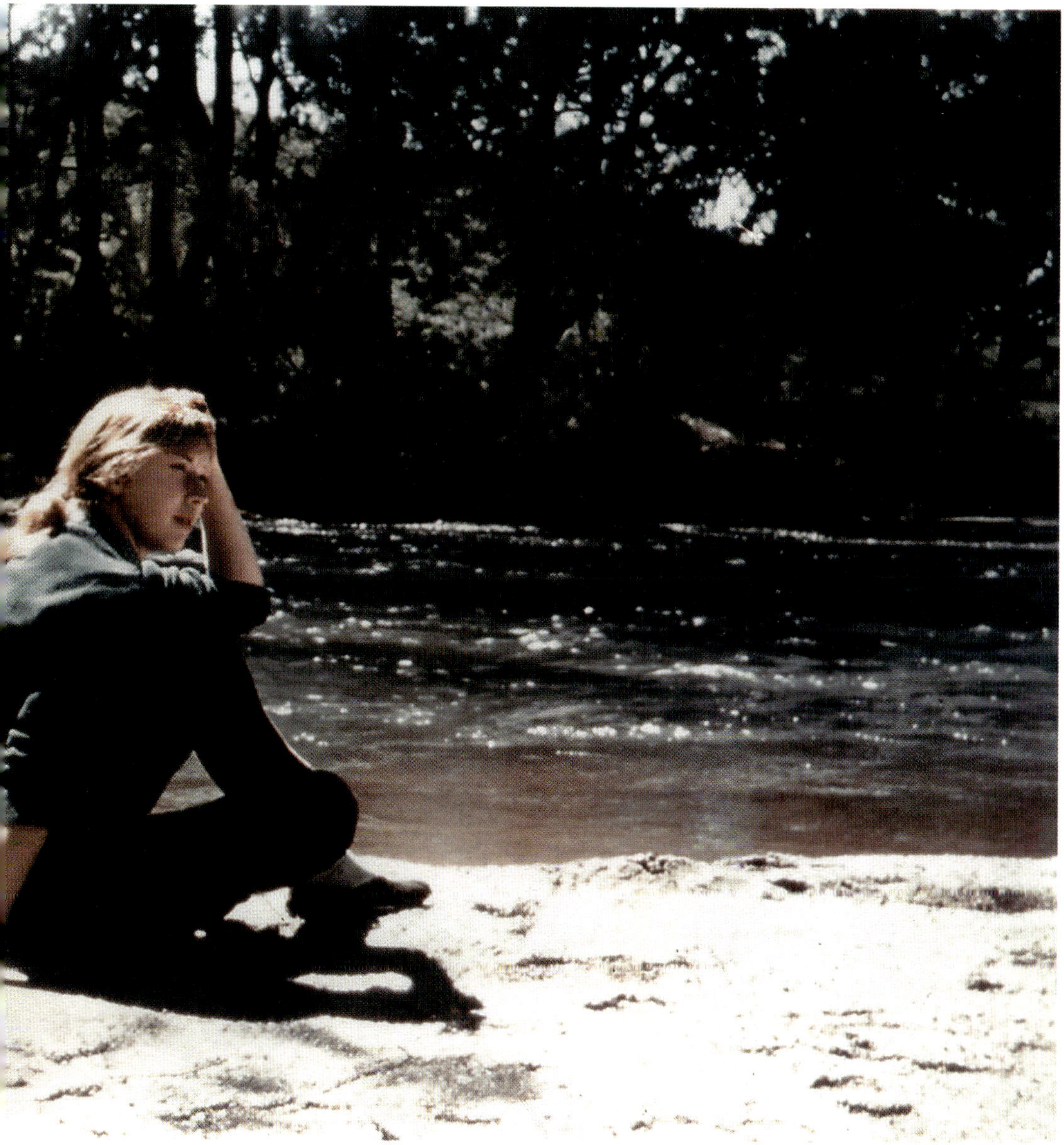

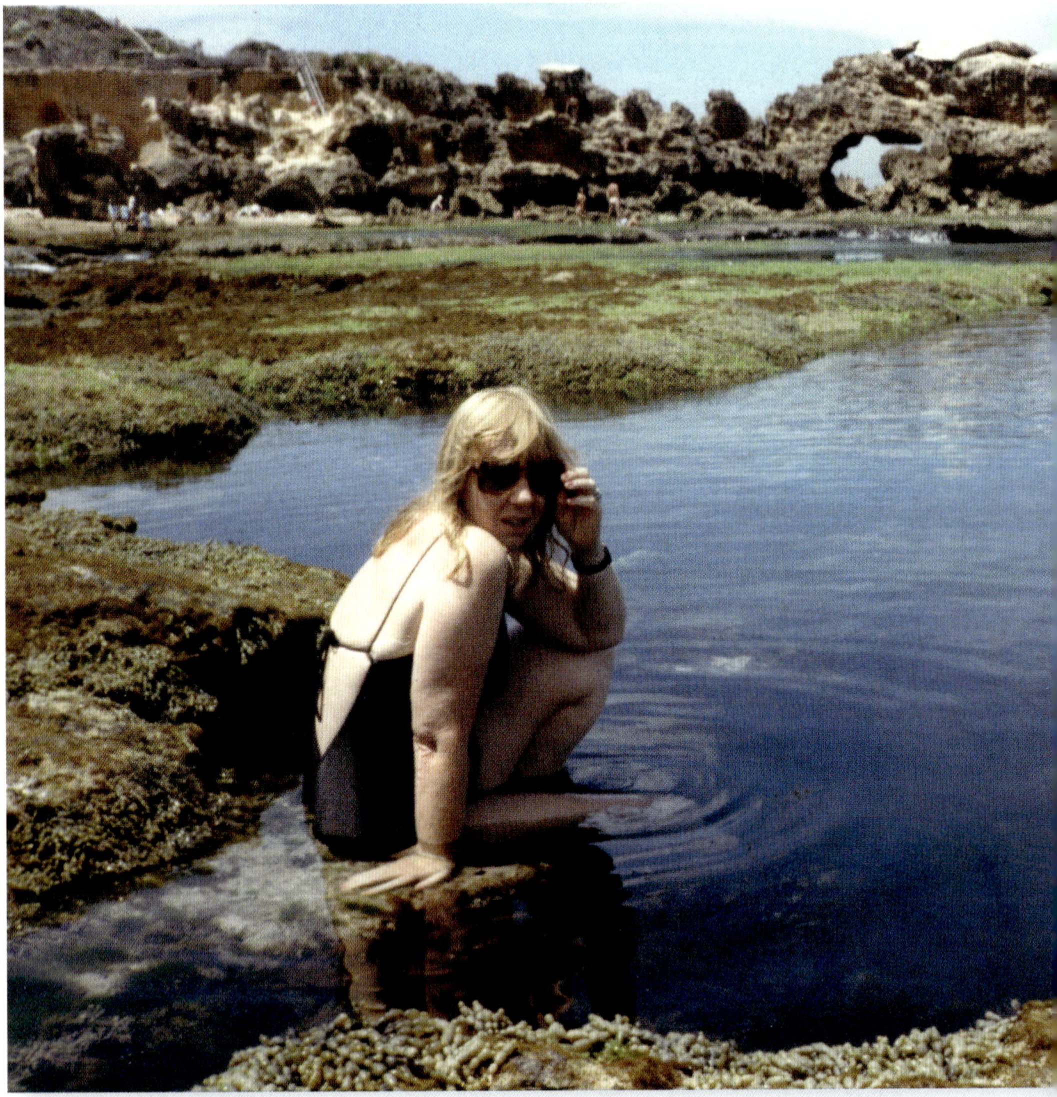

BARBARA TUCKER C. 1977
Photo by Albert Tucker

Whilst the years may have elapsed, the pose and poise of Barbara remains consistent. Relaxed and content, her limbs lie partially submerged beneath the still waters of the rockpools that scatter the back beaches of Portsea, Sorrento and Blairgowrie, areas that possessed a deep and special significance for Barbara. Pools of tranquillity for healing and pleasure.

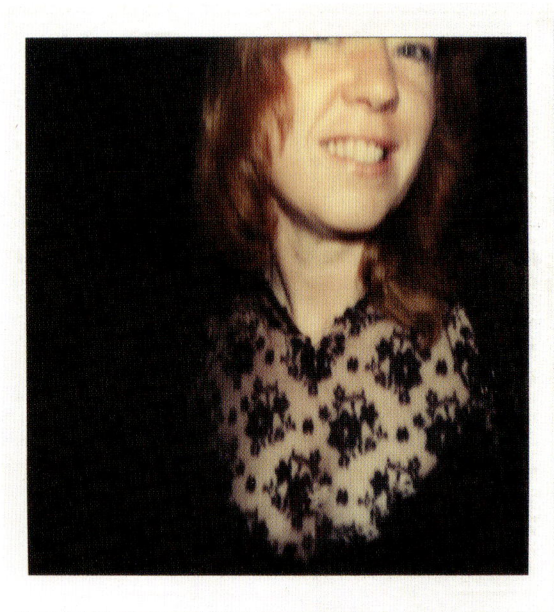

BARBARA TUCKER C. 1970s
Photos by Albert Tucker

With eyes almost slipping beyond the edge of the composition, yet still managing to hold the full attention of the photographer and the viewer, gazes Barbara. Spontaneous, candid and splendid, with an energy and radiancc that cxudes warmth and joy, her shining eyes, smiling mouth. The abstracted pattern of the lace sits tautly above the skin's surface, creating a double cleavage that is simultaneously sensual and demure. It is an image of enduring beauty and vitality.

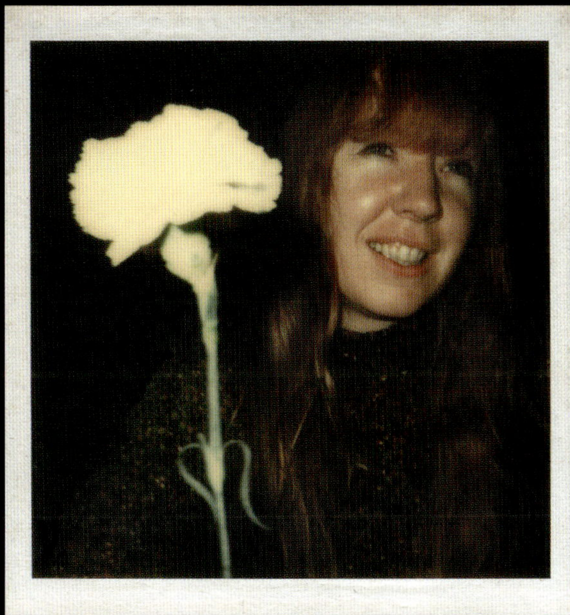

Portrait of Barbara with a carnation. Where nature pales b

I

THE ART OF GIVING

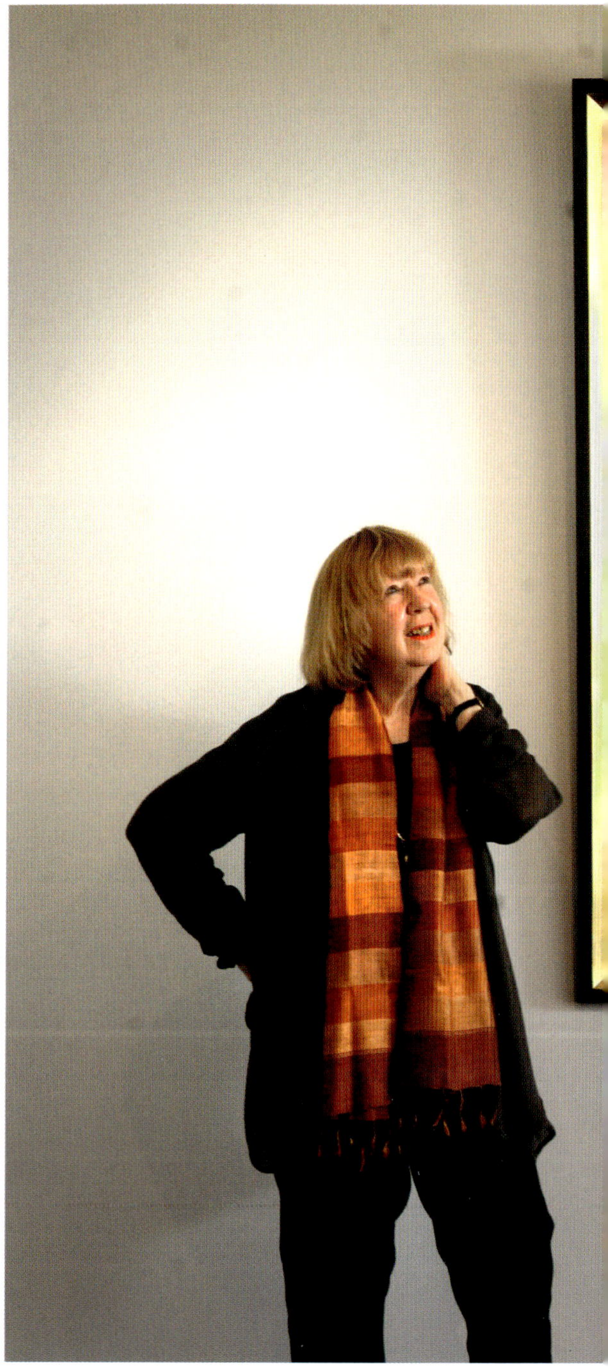

BARBARA TUCKER WITH
ALBERT TUCKER'S EXPLORERS
(1967, PRIVATE COLLECTION) 2008
Photo by David Gerathy/Newspix © News Ltd

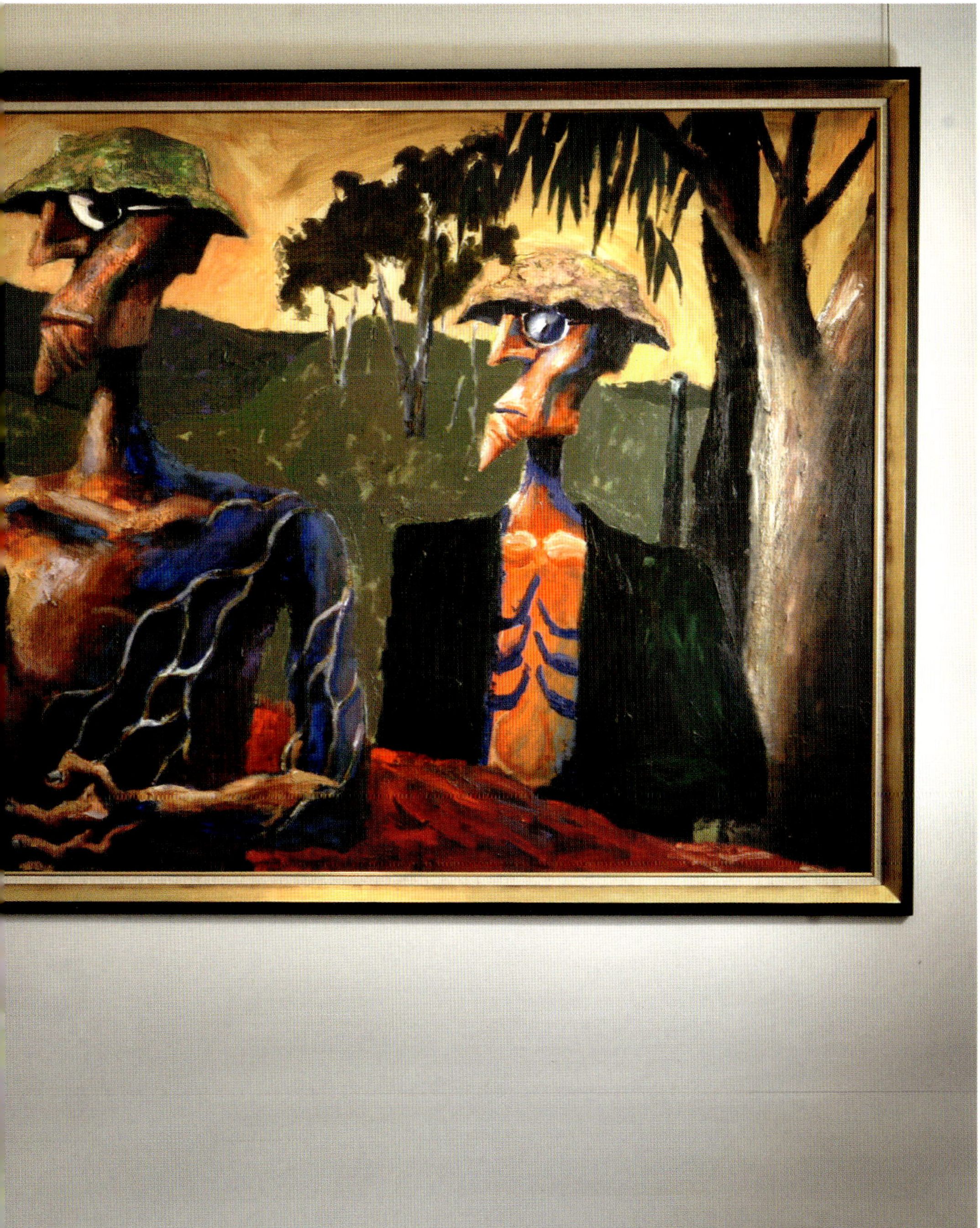

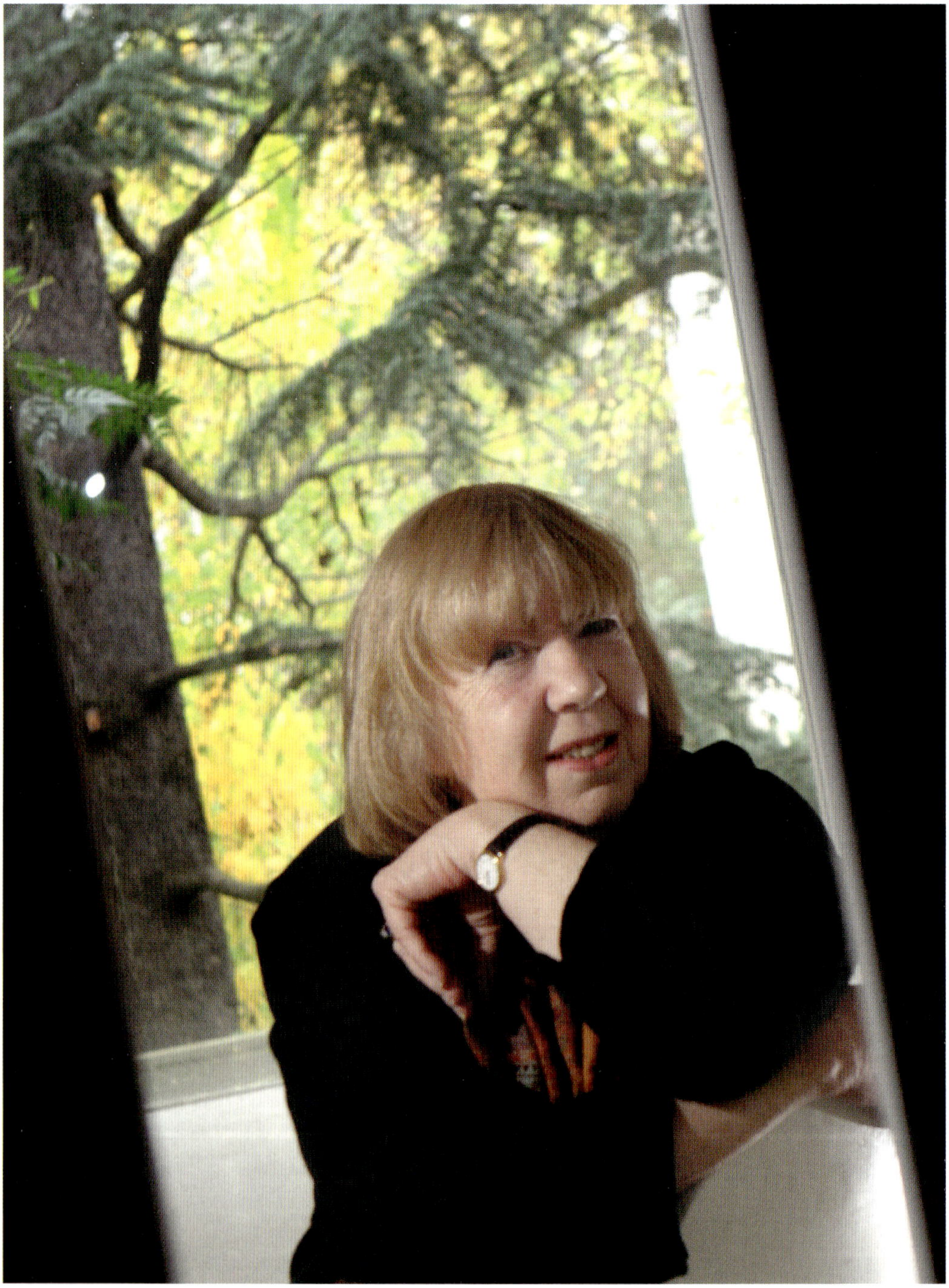

BARBARA TUCKER AT A PREVIEW OF
THE TUCKER GALLERY AT HEIDE 2006
Photo by Norm Oorloff / Newspix © News Ltd

BARBARA TUCKER *AND* HEIDE

LESLEY HARDING
with KIRSTY GRANT

In the late 1990s Barbara and Albert Tucker made the magnanimous and bold decision to donate a significant proportion of their personal collection to the nation. While this generous gesture included a select number of gifts to state institutions and the National Gallery of Australia in Canberra, they determined to transfer the major part of the collection to Heide Museum of Modern Art in their hometown of Melbourne. It was the culmination of a decade of deliberation, discussions with the Victorian Government and a series of false starts. The Tuckers had preserved a strong and representative group of paintings and related material spanning the depth and breadth of Bert's career and they felt it was 'vitally important' that these works stay together and be made available for public viewing.[1]

The Albert and Barbara Tucker Gift, on long-term loan to Heide from 2000 and progressively donated since 2005, was to the Tuckers' thinking a fitting acknowledgement of the role

1 Barbara Tucker, speech at Heide Museum of Modern Art upon the appointment of Albert and Barbara Tucker as Heide Fellows, 22 May 2000, Heide Museum of Modern Art Archive, transcript, p. 2.

John and Sunday Reed had played in Bert's nascent career. As Barbara related, he had 'a sense that the proper destination had been reached ... that the body of work would be housed in a place inextricably involved with that surge of creative energy of which in his youth he had been so much a part'.[2] Bert was one of a number of artists in Melbourne who received the Reeds' encouragement and support in the late 1930s and 1940s, and benefited richly from the stimulating environment and congregation of like-minded people at their property near Heidelberg. The Heide years had been for him a period of great personal development and creative growth, and though there were times of conflict, turmoil and even heartbreak, Heide was a place where a life in art was made possible. With this gift the museum would be the recipient of nearly two hundred artworks. 'I'm very pleased,' he told his biographer Janine Burke. 'I've done the right thing. My works have gone to the right place.'[3]

Along with paintings and drawings by Albert Tucker dating from 1938 to 1995, the Tucker Gift also represents his close colleagues Yosl Bergner, Arthur Boyd, Joy Hester, Sidney Nolan and Danila Vassilieff. Collectively these artists had begun their maturation during the Depression and had nothing to lose by taking artistic risks and committing to avant-gardism. As Robert Hughes pointed out from the relative proximity of the 1960s, 'Commitment returned to painting; such vitality in a group had not been seen since the Heidelberg school'. They staged 'not merely an aesthetic revolt, but a revolt of ideas'.[4]

At a time when Bert and artists in his milieu found their work commercially and critically at odds with convention and public taste, the Reeds' openness and generosity was, if not

2 Ibid.

3 Janine Burke, 'From Tucker with Love', *The Age*, 28 October 2000, p. 4.

4 Robert Hughes, 'Albert Tucker', *Art and Australia*, vol. 1, no. 4, February 1964, p. 253.

essential, then at the very least affirming and sustaining. While Nolan had his own arrangements, living at Heide on and off for seven years during the 1940s, Bert and his first wife Joy Hester received practical assistance from John and Sunday by way of a weekly stipend—just enough to keep the wolf from the door during the privations of World War II. For Bert this assistance continued for more than a decade, until 1953. This was not mistaken by either party as charity, but neither was it loaded with tacit expectation—'I never had to sing for my supper,' Bert said.[5] He wrote articles and edited the Sociological section of the Reed-financed *Angry Penguins* journal during the mid-1940s as one way of earning his living.

The Reeds also purchased his art at a time when there were few buyers, though in truth their investment was much more than financial. They believed in the ambitions and aesthetic and intellectual challenges Bert and his peers had set themselves. As John Reed described, 'Prior to 1938–39 the whole atmosphere was one of stagnation and death, and to be able to share in the activity which so utterly and irreversibly changed this situation, was a truly beautiful and exciting experience.'[6]

After living overseas between 1948 and 1960, Bert came back to Melbourne. It was a triumphant homecoming; having left Australia as a self-described 'refugee' from his own culture, he returned with new perspectives and accomplishments. John Reed, by now the director of the Museum of Modern Art of Australia, arranged both an exhibition and a bursary to support Bert's return. The exhibition toured nationally in 1960–61 and at its close Bert was able to use the proceeds

5 Janine Burke, 'From Tucker with Love', p. 4.

6 John Reed, unpublished biography, Reed papers, MS 13186, Australian Manuscripts Collection, State Library Victoria, box 9b, file 10, p. 59.

from sales to purchase outright a 3-acre property in Haleys Gully Road, Hurstbridge. After marrying Barbara in 1964 he entered a productive and settled phase of his life. For the best part of the next twenty years he painted almost exclusively the raw, untempered landscape of his immediate surroundings, populating his images with fauns from classical mythology or the darting, sometimes menacing parrots of the Hurstbridge environment. Barbara purchased indigenous plants from the Forestry Commission for the garden and turned her green thumb to growing vegetables, while the rest of the property was preserved in its natural state. She later talked fondly of their immersion in that locale—not far from Heide—drawing strength and inspiration from their walks in the bush nearby, and how during this time Bert helped her to 'see'. Writing for a Heide exhibition catalogue in 2008, Barbara explained that he forever changed the way she viewed the natural world, describing it as 'the greatest gift one person can give another'.[7]

Although Barbara had met the Reeds on several occasions and visited Heide a number of times, she knew them best from Bert's incisive stories. While he was grateful for John and Sunday's early support, his relationship with them was as complex as it was longstanding, especially after the Reeds formally adopted Sweeney, his and Joy Hester's son, in 1953. It was a binding, painful and emotionally fraught situation and when Barbara talked with us about it—knowing she could not speak for Bert but wanting to uphold his version of events—she remained loyal and consistent in her accounts, wanting the facts to prevail but with the proviso that the handling was sensitive.

7 Barbara Tucker, 'Introduction', in *Hinterlands: Albert Tucker's Landscapes 1960–1975*, Heide Museum of Modern Art, Melbourne, 2008, p. 24.

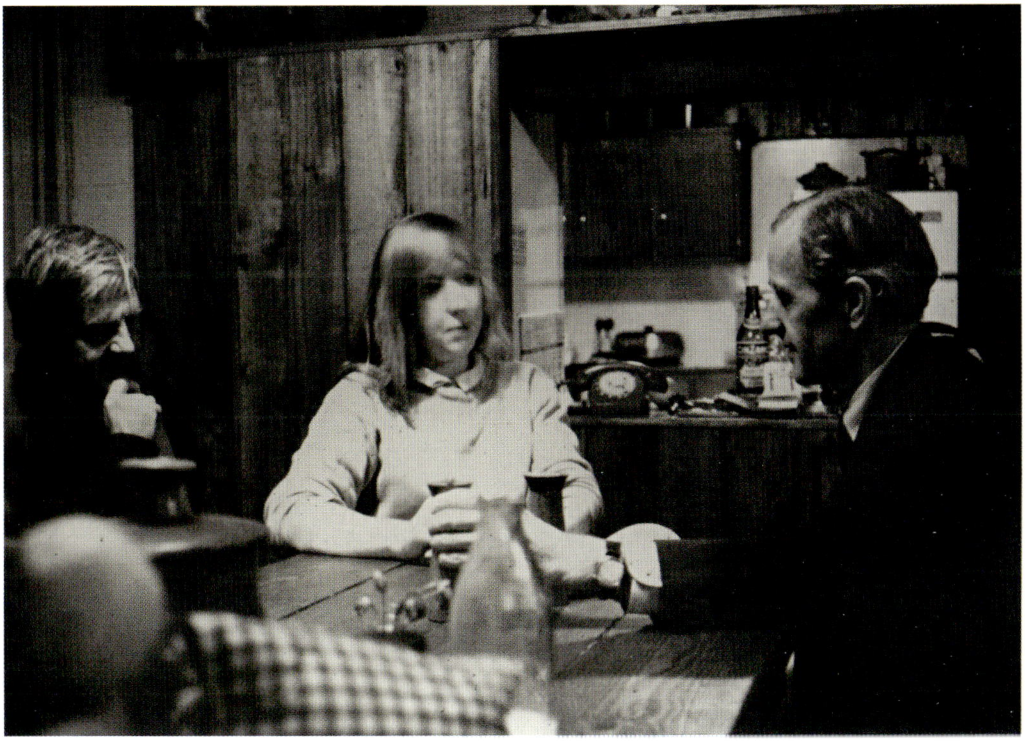

ARTHUR BOYD, BARBARA TUCKER AND SIDNEY NOLAN, HURSTBRIDGE 1968 Photo by Albert Tucker

The milestones and achievements of Bert's career were much easier to speak to, and so she did enthusiastically and sincerely. Many of these have been explored and celebrated in Heide's ongoing program of exhibitions over the past ten years in the Albert & Barbara Tucker Gallery, the cornerstone of the museum's 2005–06 redevelopment and purpose-built in acknowledgement of the Tucker Gift. Barbara was unflagging in her support of the program and the research that accompanied it, ever patient with the curators' myriad and sometimes obscure enquiries. She made everything in her own collection available for loan—even if that meant rehanging her living room—and was warmly generous with her guidance, encouragement and bottomless cups of tea.

Alongside his paintings, Bert's photographs hold a special place at Heide; they are the *aperçu* through which we have come to know the people associated with its rich heritage, particularly the vibrant years of the 1940s. Although the Reeds have since been duly recognised for making their indelible mark on Australian cultural history, it is largely through Bert's intimate, unposed photographs that John, Sunday, Heide, their friends and associates and the remarkable stories of their lives and times have a contemporary visibility and familiarity.

A selection of Bert's photographs from the 1940s and beyond were enlarged as exhibition prints for the hugely successful *Eye of the Beholder* exhibition that toured Australia in 1998–2000 and for a related show at Lauraine Diggins Fine Art in Melbourne. Barbara subsequently donated more than a hundred of these editioned photographs to Heide in 2001, including some beautiful portraits Bert took of her at Hurstbridge and Springbrook and a number of more spontaneous images of her with friends.

Fully understanding the cultural value of the material, in 2008 Barbara donated the original contact prints—then still housed in an old cigar box—together with many hundreds of photographs and negatives in her possession jointly to Heide Museum of Modern Art and State Library Victoria. To her thinking this was an ideal solution: the curators at Heide would be able to work with, exhibit and publish the photographs freely, while the library had the capacity to preserve the original material in cold storage and digitise the images, making them available to the wider public.

Barbara's magnanimity continued in 2011 with the gift to Heide of a substantial visual and literary archive comprising Bert's sketchbooks, early paintings and drawings, manuscripts for articles and lectures, photographs, press clippings and catalogues, together with some of his and Barbara's fascinating library of books. The archive has, needless to say, been essential to the generation of new scholarship on the art of Albert Tucker and the wider group of artists associated with Heide. But for Barbara there was a further, more personal motivation for her largesse, which extended over many years:

> *The gift of Tucker's works and those of his friends, is not only a matter of these important art works finding their natural home. The gift should be seen as the completion of a circle in human affairs. It is Bert's, and my, heartfelt gesture for the healing of wounded relationships within that circle. It is a gesture intended to reconcile the estranged spirits of John Reed, Sunday Reed, Albert Tucker, Joy Hester and Sweeney. It is a gesture that demonstrates Bert's personal resolution of, and ease with, that historical moment in his long and immensely productive life.*[8]

8 Barbara Tucker, speech at Heide, p. 4.

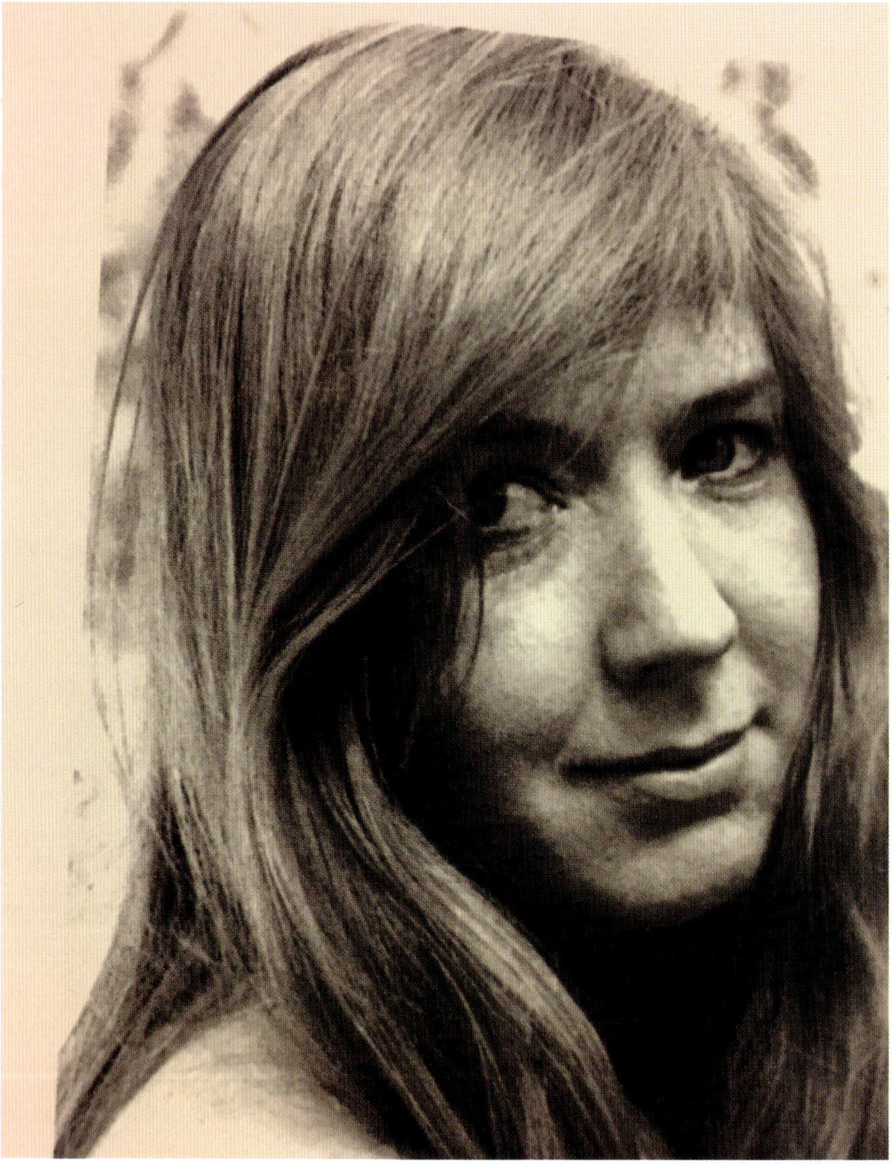

BARBARA TUCKER Photo by Albert Tucker

These donations are an apposite tribute to Albert Tucker, who thought that the past was always omnipresent, but they also speak volumes about Barbara. An important member of the Heide family, Barbara's legacy will live on at the museum—through the Gift that continues to be shared with visitors, and through the friendships she established with Heide staff, past and present. The walnut tree that was planted in the Heide gardens in her memory in 2015 stands as a permanent and personal reminder of Barbara, her love of the natural world, and her great support of all the museum's activities. ¶

This essay is based on a previously published text by Lesley Harding, 'The Albert and Barbara Tucker Gift', in The Heide Collection, *Heide Museum of Modern Art, Melbourne, 2011.*

BARBARA TUCKER *AND* STATE LIBRARY VICTORIA

SHANE CARMODY *with* JOCK MURPHY

On one of the desks in the La Trobe Reading Room at State Library Victoria there is a plaque that reads:

FOR ALBERT TUCKER,
WHO FOUND KNOWLEDGE IN THIS ROOM,
AND FOR BARBARA TUCKER
WHO HAS GIVEN SO GENEROUSLY.

The plaque commemorates a remarkable relationship between Albert Tucker, Barbara, his wife and widow, and the library. Albert Tucker never forgot his debt to the library, to the way it allowed him to travel a world of art in his imagination at a time when his world was constrained to Melbourne. Tucker spent hours under the dome reading, completing his education in a way that great public libraries allow. After his death it was left to Barbara to repay that debt, which she did with grace and good humour, and a touch of sadness that never quite left her.

All great stories have an author and this one begins with Nancy Underhill, who in the late 1990s was working with Barrett Reid on an edited collection of letters from the archives of John and Sunday Reed. Her work involved talking with artists and others who knew the Reeds and among them was Albert Tucker. Nancy learned that Tucker had kept many letters and other items documenting his life and in time introduced Albert and Barbara to the librarians managing the Australian Manuscripts collection at the State Library. In early 1998 the Tuckers visited the library and were shown through the collection by Gerard Hayes. Following the visit Bert donated to the library a portrait of Barrett Reid, painted while Reid lived at Heide, and part of the *Faces I Have Met* series from 1985, together with a watercolour portrait of Reid and ten photographs.

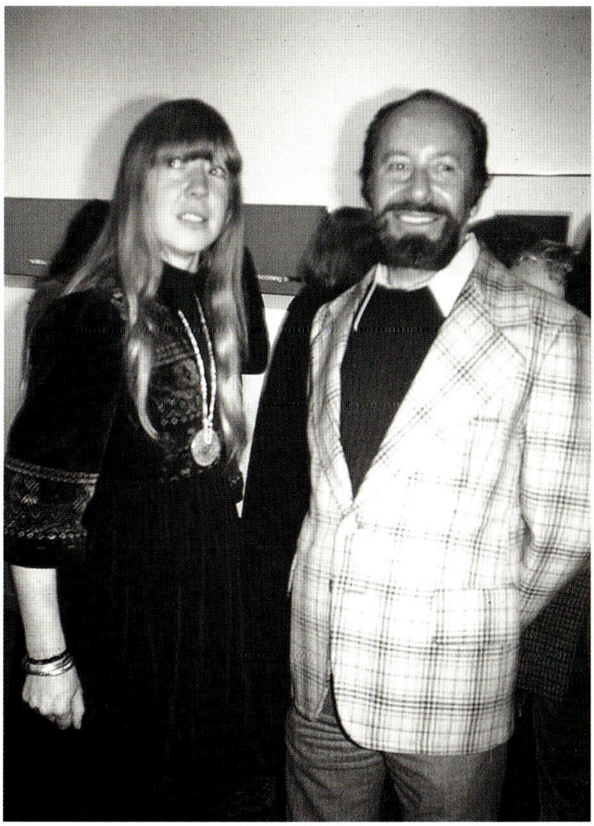

BARBARA & ALBERT TUCKER AT A GALLERY EVENT IN MELBOURNE 1977
Photo by Rhonda Senbergs

Tucker's death in October 1999 briefly halted this growing relationship. In December, with the tact and diplomacy for which she is famous, the then La Trobe Librarian, Dr Dianne Reilly, wrote to Barbara to reaffirm the library's interest in her late husband's papers. Barbara responded warmly, remembering with fondness the visit to the library, but said that it would take some time for decisions to be made about her husband's papers and possessions. In fact, her decision crystallised soon after. Warwick Reeder approached Barbara to enquire as to whether the papers might be well placed at Heide. Barbara sought advice from Nancy Underhill, who advocated for the library as a place best suited to the management and use of such archives, and Barbara, feeling a promise had already been made, decided for the library. In June 2000 the papers were placed there, adding to a rich collection of archives about Victoria's artistic heritage.

Barbara's relationship with the library was very personal. She had formed friendships with Dianne Reilly and Jock Murphy, and in the back and forth of negotiations a real bond of affection was formed. The next expression of this friendship was truly remarkable.

In her meetings with Jock Murphy, Barbara revealed that her husband owned a rifle reputed to have belonged to Ned Kelly. The conversation over the rifle with Jock Murphy continued over some months. Anxious not to have an unlicensed firearm in her possession, Barbara first offered it on loan to the library. Jock deftly explained that loans were often problematic, especially when the lender passed away, and Barbara agreed with this, making it a donation. As soon as he could, Jock drove to Hoddles Creek to collect the gun, returning with it on the back seat of the car, and driving very carefully for fear of being detected by the police.

Soon after commencing at the library as Director of Collections, Shane Carmody met with Barbara over lunch at the

Lyceum Club, hosted by Dianne Reilly and with Jock Murphy. Discussion ranged widely, over how best to cook lamb shanks (Barbara's cooking tips were always worthy of attention) and the potential of a book that might reunite correspondence between Albert Tucker and Sidney Nolan.

As a significant donor to the collection, Barbara became a regular and welcome guest at social events at the library, often with her friend Leisl Singer. In November 2003 Barbara attended the opening of the Cowen Gallery in the State Library. Impressed by the beautiful display of colonial paintings of Victoria, she promised Carmody the gift of *Jackson's Creek Sunbury*, painted by Henry Gritten in 1867. The painting used to hang over the fireplace in the house at Hoddles Creek. Barbara visited the library soon after to see the painting in its new location. Delighted with how well it looked surrounded by works from a similar era, she took a seat in the dome and calmly and generously wrote a cheque for $50,000 as a gift to support the library.

By now the idea discussed alongside recipes for lamb shanks had taken concrete form in the person of Patrick McCaughey. After delicate negotiation with Lady Nolan, permission was obtained to publish the correspondence of Albert Tucker and Sidney Nolan and Melbourne University Press, then in an expansionist mood, agreed to publish the title. Patrick McCaughey accepted the role of editor and during one of his return visits to Melbourne spent days in the library piecing the story together. Published in 2006, *Bert and Ned* achieved an ambition of Barbara's but also helped to heal a rift between two artists who together defined mid–twentieth century Australian painting. Barbara told the story of how Nolan took umbrage at seeing Tucker's *Images of Modern Evil* displayed in the same space as his *Ned Kelly* series at the opening of the National Gallery of Australia and how they never spoke again. Now in a book that documented their friendship and close collaboration, the depth of their friendship was revealed. The library took advantage of McCaughey's presence to invite him to open the permanent exhibition *Mirror of the World: Books and Ideas*.

On a subsequent visit to the exhibition with Carmody, Barbara was entranced by the display of Japanese wood block print books and offered another gift. During his time in Japan in 1947 with the Australian Army, Tucker had obtained four 'pillow books'—wood block books illustrating erotic tales. Barbara made sure that the library knew that they were already very worn before Albert acquired them!

At about the same time, Barbara was moving from the house in Blessington Street, St Kilda, and had uncovered more archival material relating to Heide and the Reeds. One item was a slim folder containing correspondence between Albert Tucker and John Reed on the ownership of paintings that he had left when he went to Europe. It revealed a bitter fight that saw the paintings returned to Tucker and ended the relationship. This was crucial to understanding the history of Tucker's relationship with the Reeds, and Barbara, while conscious of the sensitive nature of the material, understood its significance and placed it with the rest of the archive in the library.

A second item recorded a happier time. In a cigar box were dozens of tiny contact prints of photographs taken by Tucker recording life at Heide, at the beach house at Aspendale and in Melbourne in the 1940s. This was a major discovery, and after long discussion they were jointly gifted to the State Library and Heide, with the library taking responsibility for their care.

Barbara had mentioned on several occasions her desire to give to the library posthumous portraits of John and Sunday Reed. From the same series of the first gift from Albert Tucker to the library, *Faces I Have Met*, Barbara explained that they were criticised at the time as being grotesques. Dramatic and gothic, the portraits show the Reeds in old age. We agreed that they would be well placed in the library, which has housed so much of the historical record of Heide and its artists. In 2013 the library celebrated the centenary of the opening of the Dome Reading Room. Barbara, along with others, made generous gifts to mark this milestone and the portraits now hang in the Cowen Gallery.

Barbara's care in placing so much of the record of Albert Tucker's life in the library was an act of love for her husband. She was always very conscious of his place in history and very modest about her role. Different interpretations of that history could upset her, but she knew that the best way to ensure an accurate record was to have the original material safely in the library. The record of her generosity is tucked away in the accession records and on catalogue notes, leaving Albert Tucker as the hero, exactly as Barbara would wish it, and only readers who happen to sit under the great dome at the desk that is adorned with the plaque may have a hint of her part in preserving his story. ¶

BARBARA *AS* CUSTODIAN

GEOFFREY SMITH

Barbara memorably said, 'I had no training for *this*.'

'*This*' referred to the responsibility of caring for the legacy of her partner and husband of four decades, Albert Tucker.

When Bert died in 1999, Barbara faced the challenges of dealing with the loss and her grief. As Bert was a highly significant figure in the history and development of Australian art, these challenges were compounded by the complexities that surrounded Barbara's responsibility to nurture and perpetuate this legacy. Issues relating to appropriate documentation, conservation, exhibitions, publications, donations and sales, together with copyright and authenticity, all became paramount to Barbara's daily existence.

Barbara faced these challenges with strength, determination, wisdom, compassion, fortitude and, at times, bravery. All of these attributes were sprinkled with her unique wit and sense of humour. She lived and worked modestly and achieved remarkable results. I have a lasting vision of Barbara with a cup of tea in one hand and one of her own home-made scones with her own raspberry jam and cream in the other hand, asking questions, expressing opinions and providing direction on what needed to be done to support and strengthen her own and Bert's legacy.

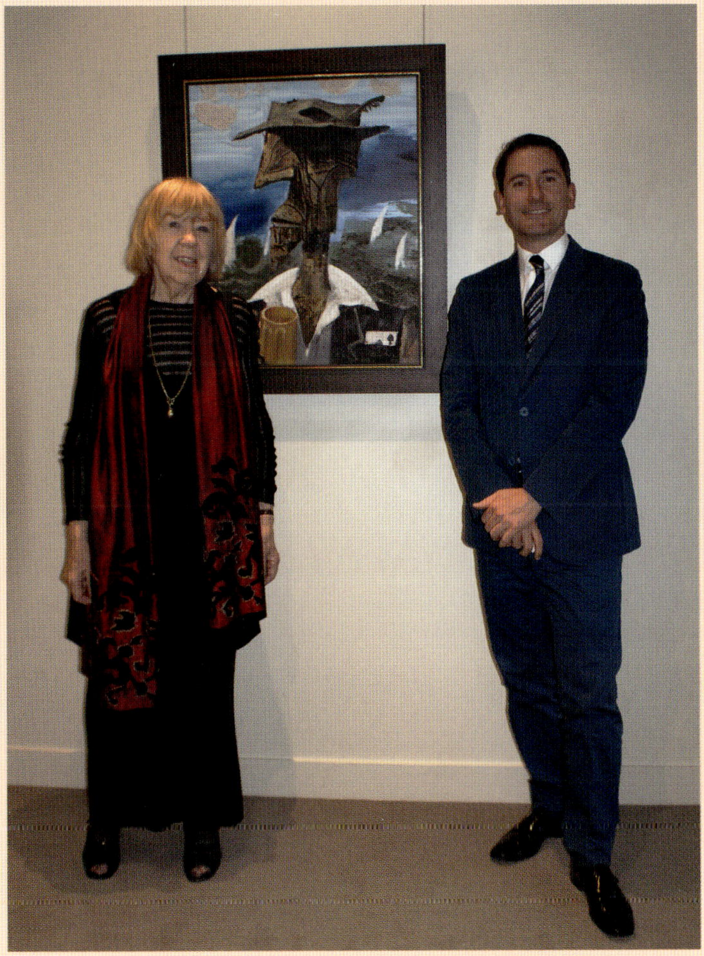

BARBARA TUCKER AND GEOFFREY SMITH WITH ALBERT TUCKER'S LUCKY COUNTRY *(1964, PRIVATE COLLECTION) 2013*
Photo courtesy Geoffrey Smith

Barbara's philosophy remained strong and consistent and she often made decisions based not on personal gain, but on moral and ethical principles. Two issues that particularly stand out for me are her views on copyright and resale royalty.

Barbara, at all times, controlled copyright. As the appointed custodian she did not relinquish this responsibility to a third-party agency, although this would have presented the easier option. It was her inherent belief that those who were closest to an artist were in the best position to determine the manner and context in which their work was to be reproduced and recorded.

Requests for copyright occurred on a daily basis: from galleries, museums, auction houses, universities, schools, libraries and literary agents, to the sometimes more obscure medical journals and music publishers. Barbara was continuously uplifted by the keen interest shown in Bert's work and was never more enthusiastic than when an international request was submitted to reproduce a painting, drawing or photograph.

Barbara almost without exception granted copyright permission and without ever charging a fee, on the basis that the work was not compromised from the artist's original intention. In this manner Barbara acutely respected and protected the charge to which she had been given.

By personally guarding this custodianship, Barbara was able to prevent 'problematic' works of art from entering the market. In the past ten years Barbara and I, working together, were able to detect and identify several fraudulent works that were circulating within the marketplace. As works of art could not be reproduced without Barbara's prior consent, we were able to identify a handful of paintings and works on paper *before* they were published. This was preventive rather than remedial action and remains the most effective way an artist can deal with problematic works.

This process was at times extremely confronting and distressing, especially if it led to litigation, and caused Barbara great anguish. However, it was through this fearless process that we were able to protect the authenticity and integrity of the art of Albert Tucker.

Barbara also held strong views on the introduction of resale royalty, which became legislation in 2010. Although she understood its merits for impoverished and disadvantaged artists and their families, she was challenged by the ramifications it held for successful artists and their beneficiaries. She personally felt guilty for receiving a royalty on a work of art that had been acquired by a collector in good faith, regardless of whether it had increased, and particularly if it had decreased, in value.

At the very first opportunity, Barbara led by example in refusing the fee. When Bert's record-breaking *Flirtation* became subject to resale royalty, Barbara promptly instructed the agency that she would waive the fee. This bold action of waiving her right to collect tens of thousands of dollars was undertaken privately and discreetly. However, it had significant ramifications within the industry.

Barbara often said that the transference of one person's way of seeing to another was 'the greatest gift one person can give to another'. Gary Singer and I share and cherish Barbara's great gift to us.

We have listened, learned and understood from Barbara and we feel particularly close to her as we collaborate with family, friends and colleagues to perpetuate Barbara's wishes and her legacy, not only to the visual arts, but also to the much wider community, for the benefit and welfare of future generations. ¶

II

THE ART OF LIFE WITH ARTISTS

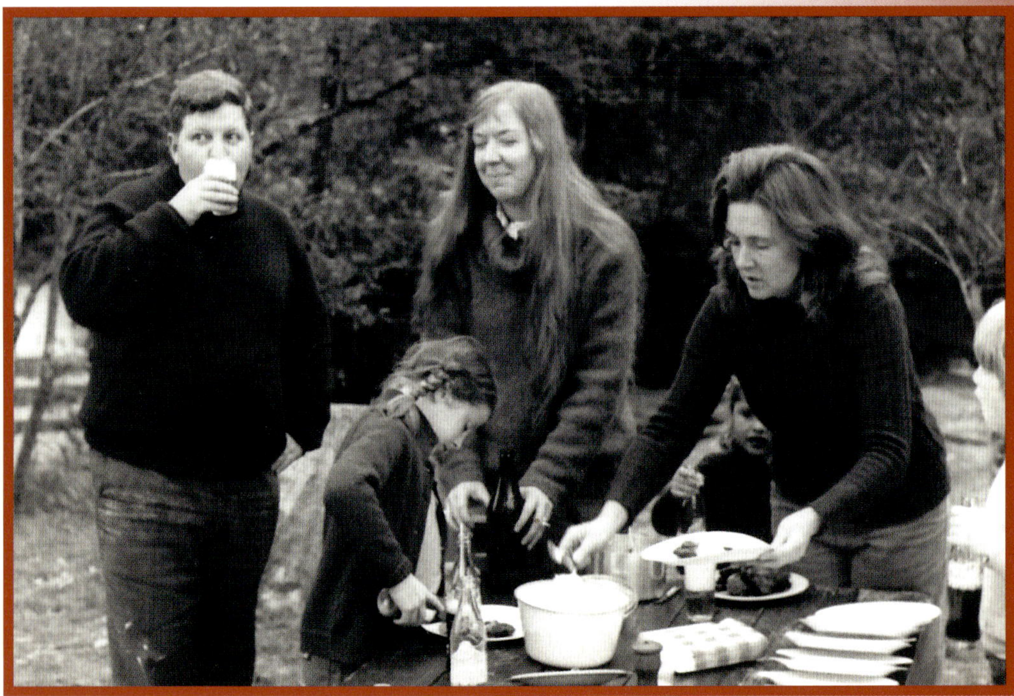

FRED WILLIAMS, BARBARA TUCKER,
LYN WILLIAMS AND CHILDREN
Photo by Richard Crichton

RECOLLECTIONS OF BARBARA TUCKER

LYN WILLIAMS

Barbara and I met in the early 1960s through our husbands, who were both artists in the Australian Galleries stable at the time. Although we were probably much the same age, Albert Tucker was Fred's senior by about fifteen years and the same age as my parents. He belonged to the earlier generation of the artists around Heide. Barbara married Bert when he returned from living overseas for many years.

Bert was quite a commanding figure, while Fred was still very much an emerging artist. He was not an easy person socially and we were in awe of him personally. He had a reputation for being abrupt and outspoken. Little did we realise at the time that he was actually quite insecure.

In 1963 we had moved to a modest bungalow at Upwey in the Dandenong Ranges with our little daughter Isobel. To get to know each other they suggested coming for a visit. As Bert had lived in France for so long Fred, not knowing he had lived very humbly, assumed he would have very sophisticated tastes. We were at great pains to make a special meal, only to discover that Bert rarely drank and was quite scathing about the cheesecake I had made to impress him. It was a disaster, until Barbara, with her easy manner, rescued the evening. She managed Bert's moods with confidence and ease. During those years we had little contact with the Tuckers. We did not have a car and it was an hour and a half by train to the city.

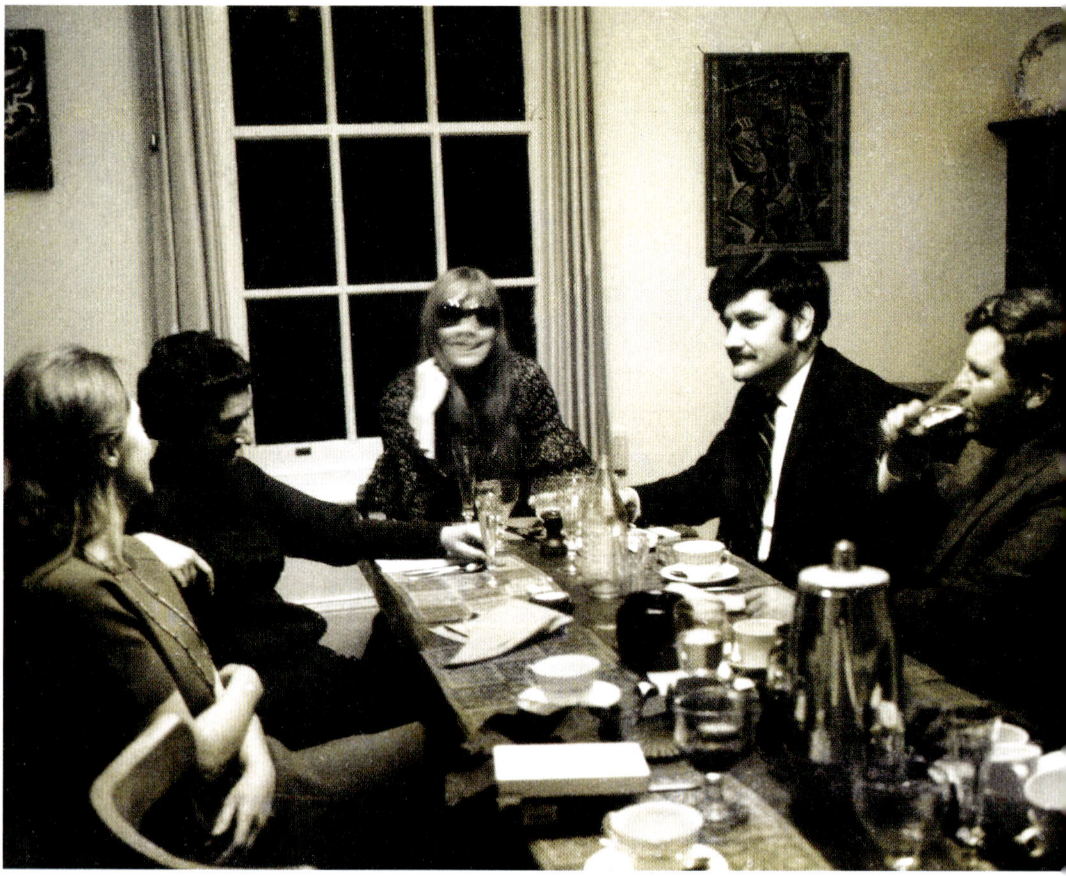

BARBARA TUCKER (CENTRE), WITH BARRY JONES AND FRED WILLIAMS TO HER LEFT, HAWTHORN C. 1974
Photo by Albert Tucker

Our lives were at very different stages, ours with a young family and theirs with overseas travel was more sophisticated. Given our very different lifestyles, we were not close friends.

When we moved back to Hawthorn in 1969, Bert and Barbara would visit on occasion with other artists: the Pughs, the Olsens, Len French. Fred would visit Clif Pugh at Dunmoochin to paint and Barbara and Bert, who lived at Hurstbridge, would often be there, especially when Clif lived with Judith. She and Barbara became very close. As I had three small children I did not have as much time to visit.

At some point Bert and Barbara bought land at Springbrook in the rainforest above the Gold Coast. It was infested with lantana and other noxious weeds. They intended to restore it to its natural state, with its beautiful waterfalls, magnificent tree ferns and rainforest vegetation, even a rare Antarctic beech tree. They were both passionate about the project. Barbara continued with the conservation after Bert's death, I believe.

We visited in the September 1971 school holidays with a view to possibly buying an adjoining block. While it was not feasible for us at that time, I believe Arthur Boyd and Sid Nolan bought blocks subsequently.

You asked if Bert mentored Fred. That was not their relationship. If you mean Fred's *Sapling Forest* series, he painted and exhibited them before Bert returned to Australia. In 1961 or 62 Bert did suggest Fred try painting with acrylics, which he did. He found with works on paper that while the surfaces dried very quickly, it remained sticky underneath, causing stacked works on paper to stick together. As for work on canvas, he found it quite a lifeless medium.

I was widowed many years before Barbara and saw little of them in the intervening years before Bert's death. Later we talked about our partners, managing properties and estates.

Barbara was close friends with Geoffrey Smith and Gary Singer, who supported her with matters to do with Bert's art. We both had holiday houses on the Mornington Peninsula and did have an occasional visit.

My position was quite different from Barbara's. When Fred died, he was in middle age and I had three daughters in their teens. We were not as organised with our affairs as they were when Bert died. I did develop closer associations with the art world through roles on boards of galleries, which has helped me keep in touch in managing his estate.

Barbara gave Bert's life as an artist the stability that he had not had prior to their marriage. His public life from the 1960s onwards was made to work because of her unfailing support and understanding. It could not have been easy to accommodate the constant reminder of the life at Heide and his earlier marriage to Joy Hester. She was generous and looked after his legacy impeccably. We do not see that written up. ¶

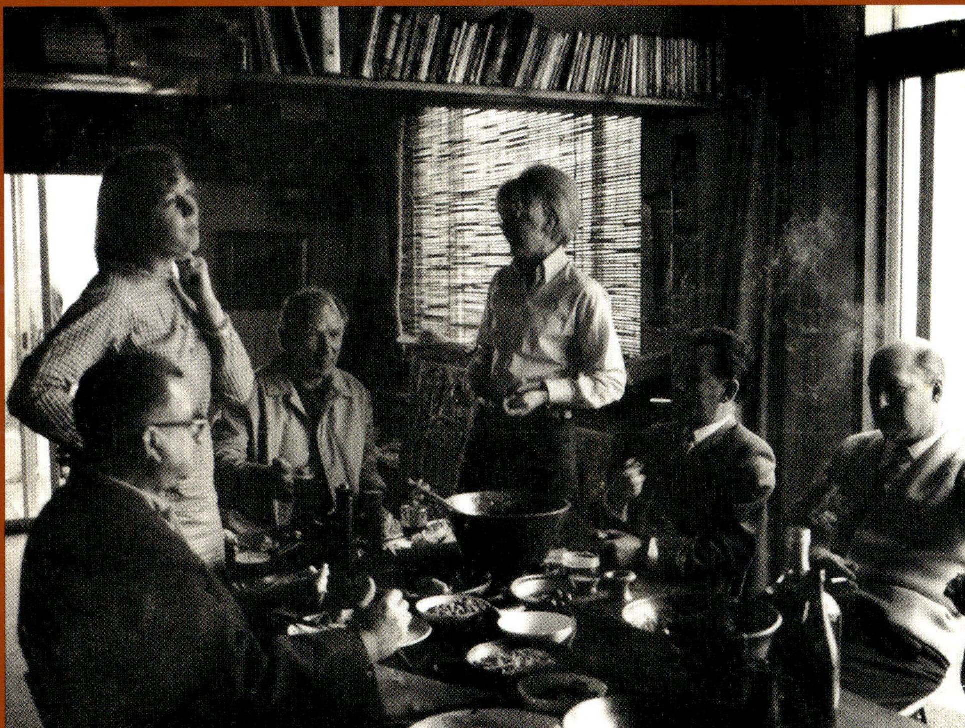

BARBARA TUCKER WITH DAVID BILCOCK SNR (TO HER LEFT) AND LINDA BILCOCK (CENTRE) AT HURSTBRIDGE C. 1972
Photo by Albert Tucker

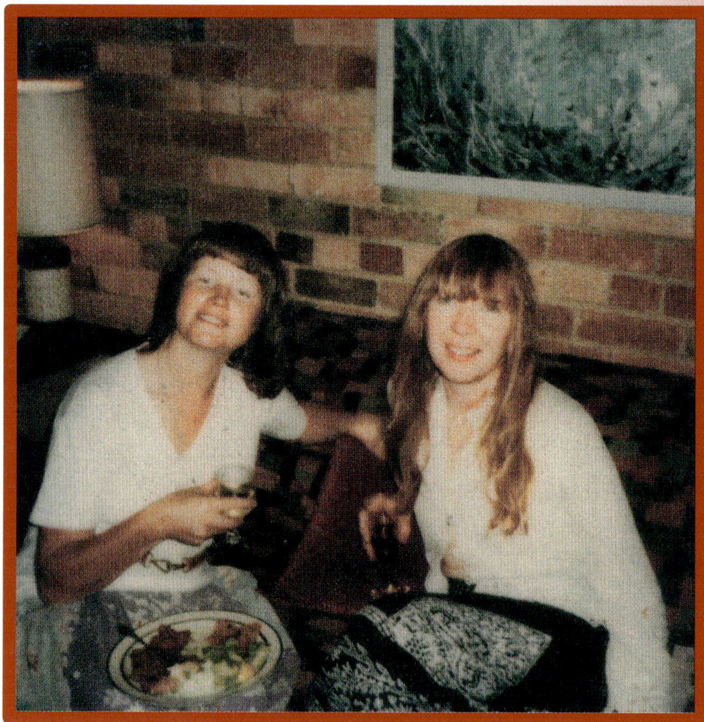

BARBARA TUCKER WITH JUDITH PUGH
Photo by Albert Tucker

BARBARA'S VOICE

JUDITH PUGH

When I begin to write—an article, a speech, an essay—I use specific visual memories of significant or telling events that will illuminate the story. But as I thought about speaking at her memorial, I kept hearing Barbara's voice. Not articulated phrases, not words; just the sound of the voice itself.

If I thought of her beside Bert, I could see him clearly: he transacted in images; we are, in the Heide Museum of Modern Art, surrounded by his images. I could picture him at the table, or letting our orphaned baby wombat nuzzle his beard, because his beard felt like its mother.

But I had no images with which to begin to talk about Barbara alone. Just the sound of her voice, and her laugh.

I tried all the usual writer's remedies: watch a film, read something distracting, go from keys and screen to pen and paper. To no effect.

So I decided to state my problem aloud.

'I want to do you justice,' I said. 'To remember you formally, to analyse your place in history, what you did while you were with Bert, in the United States and in Australia, at openings, at dinners, with me, and how you carried on after he died. What shall I say?'

And the sound I heard—imagined, if you like—the memory that was triggered by my question, was Barbara's laughter. Perhaps she was laughing at the very concept of this memorial: she was always self-deprecating, never pompous. Perhaps it was delight, that we'd all be here to remember her. I realised that always, even when she was upset, or very serious, she also sounded just a little amused.

So I decided: I will begin with that beautiful rounded voice, full of laughter and enthusiasm and humour, and see if she materialises.

Her voice was light. When we met in 1970, ten minutes from each other but an hour from Melbourne, we travelled across half a dozen suburbs to Blackburn for fresh yeast and buttermilk to make our bread, and to Preston and Prahran markets, where the range of herbs, meats, cheeses, vegetables was just beginning to expand into the cornucopia now available. Barbara had recipes from Mary Dickson, with whom Bert had lived in Italy, and I'd watch the Italian stallholders appreciate Barbara's understanding of their wares, enjoying the clarity of her voice. Light, but confidently strong.

Light, easy, it was the voice of a mature woman. It was never urgent, even when she was serious, explaining to me the need to wear a blindfold while I climbed the ladder to get the possum trapped in the ceiling of Bert's studio. The blindfold was necessary so I wouldn't see and therefore sap the energy of Bert's unfinished pictures.

She had a huge repertoire of jokes, at a time when women did not tell jokes, and she was witty, when women were rarely witty. Her voice never jarred, even when she laughed out loud.

When we discussed ideas about society, events, individual politicians, her comments were incisive, questioning, shrewd; they had that distance one admires in really clever commentators. Always the voice was ironic, reminding her hearers that current politics are in history and history is a continuum.

There was something so reassuring, so sweet, in her voice, that one felt, or assumed, her attitudes: but they were never contentious. The four of us—Clif, Bert, Barbara and I—spent most evenings together for a couple of years. On those nights we watched the news, shared the news, knew the news-makers, discussed the news. Barbara and I were friends for forty-five years, more than half of my life and hers, but I cannot tell you how she voted.

Her voice could sound hurt: by people who failed to understand the tasks she undertook, the value of her work at the Australian Consulate in New York, as academic liaison officer at La Trobe University, as bookshop owner. But most when people undervalued her success as Wife to Bert.

There are hardly any wives of any kind now among intellectuals or artists: the term is politically incorrect. Reproductive choice, feminism, economic realities have made women partners and individuals. But the role of artist's wife was very real when Barbara met Bert.

In New York, in the Chelsea Hotel, Bert was fed and watered, with a studio and plenty of stimulating companions, so after a couple of weeks in the city Barbara wanted something to do. I can hear her on the verge of laughter, telling me that she approached the Australian Consulate for work, and was asked if she knew anything about editing film. 'Well, my family are film-makers,' she answered. 'I feel sure I could.' With efficiency and panache, Barbara supplied the image of Australia to the American media. And financial support to Bert.

Barbara and Bert returned from the thrilling bohemia of the Chelsea Hotel to sleepy rural Hurstbridge. The village lacked coffee shops or restaurants, let alone the intellectual variety of New York. This was not a problem. When he came out of the studio, Bert had Barbara. I can hear her amusing him as she made tea and cakes and served meals, talking about books, about music, telling him news she'd heard on the radio, passing on phone messages, making arrangements for dinners and lunches where friends and dealers and curators and clients were welcomed and entertained.

Once Bert had a routine in Hurstbridge, Barbara became academic liaison officer at the La Trobe University bookshop. The role was to liaise with academics to make sure that their books, and those they were prescribing or recommending for their courses, were stocked. Barbara took this further. She contacted secondary schools near and far. The warmth and enthusiasm in that voice was so persuasive: the La Trobe bookshop income boomed.

Bert was an intense man, and he dug deep for his work. Barbara's light touch and high intelligence balanced his passionate denouncement of the 'psychopaths, waiting in the wings, armed to the teeth' who found their way into many political discussions. She told me with that amused lilt in the voice about the social scientist whose interview with the exasperated Bert ended when he exclaimed: 'I could express this better by playing it to you on a piano.' 'I tried to warn her,' said Barbara.

When she persuaded Bert to co-operate with Richard Haese in the project that became the book *Rebels and Precursors* her most difficult task began. In the 1940s Bert had not been able to afford to develop his photographs of the Heide denizens. Barbara pointed out that the photographs might assist Haese, and hundreds of the thirty-year-old images were printed. Bert was of course a masterful photographer, and seeing the vivid prints—of Joy Hester, of Sweeney as a boy, the Reeds—affected Bert profoundly. They reproduced a time when everything was felt at the extreme, when he drew the stages of surgery of servicemen with faces blown apart, when Joy betrayed him, and he could hardly cope. Many wives could not have stood the strain, but Barbara saw Bert through this time and he emerged gentle and contented.

I want to convey the resilience, the sinewy confidence this took: how somehow her complete womanliness was present in that capacity to meet any challenge and deal with it. She could be tactful and direct, warm and tough: never bothering with social clichés, she was diplomatic. She did not seek the limelight, but she warmed the room.

As I wrote this tribute, thinking of her voice, I realised why it was hard to visualise her. We didn't face each other; we were beside each other. When I lost a baby and was quite numb, Barbara came to Dunmoochin. She didn't enquire how I felt: this was obvious. She put me in the car, and we went to the market. We cooked and we washed up together.

While Bert was very troubled, Clif would take him to paint in the landscape or they would get a model with some other artists, and I would collect Barbara and we would drive off together. On a road trip, you are beside your companion's voice. When I moved interstate the telephone became our link: that rich sound—'Judith, it's Barbara'—and she'd have a joke to tell, or a story to share. As she began to drift a bit from the present, we reminisced about our lives, went over our memories over the phone. So the voice became the link through the past to our present.

I have talked about the voice, but I can leave you with an image. On one occasion, Clif and Bert had flown to Sydney, and Barbara and I decided to drive up to meet them. We'd planned our second night in Omeo, but there were no beds.

We looked at the map and decided to drive overnight down the track over Brown Mountain. I can see Barbara now. I can see us both. We are out of the sedan, looking at a sign by the dirt road. It is a warning sign. It says 'Four-Wheel-Drive Only, Dangerous in Wet Conditions'. We are both wearing sandals and those long Indian cotton dresses that made the 70s so colourful and comfortable. The light rain that is muddying the track begins to drift, and I realise it is about to snow. Dusk is falling. I am seized by a moment's doubt. I say, 'You can change a tyre, can't you?' And ... I can hear her now: confident, warm, that sound of laughter, 'Well I haven't, but I feel sure I can.' ¶

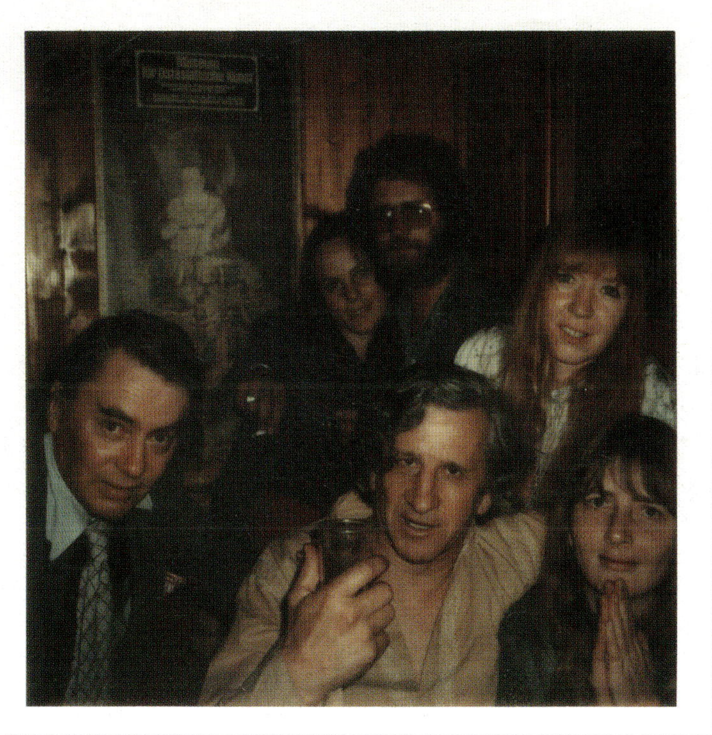

JOHN PERCEVAL (LEFT) WITH
BARBARA TUCKER AND FRIENDS C. 1974
Photo by Albert Tucker

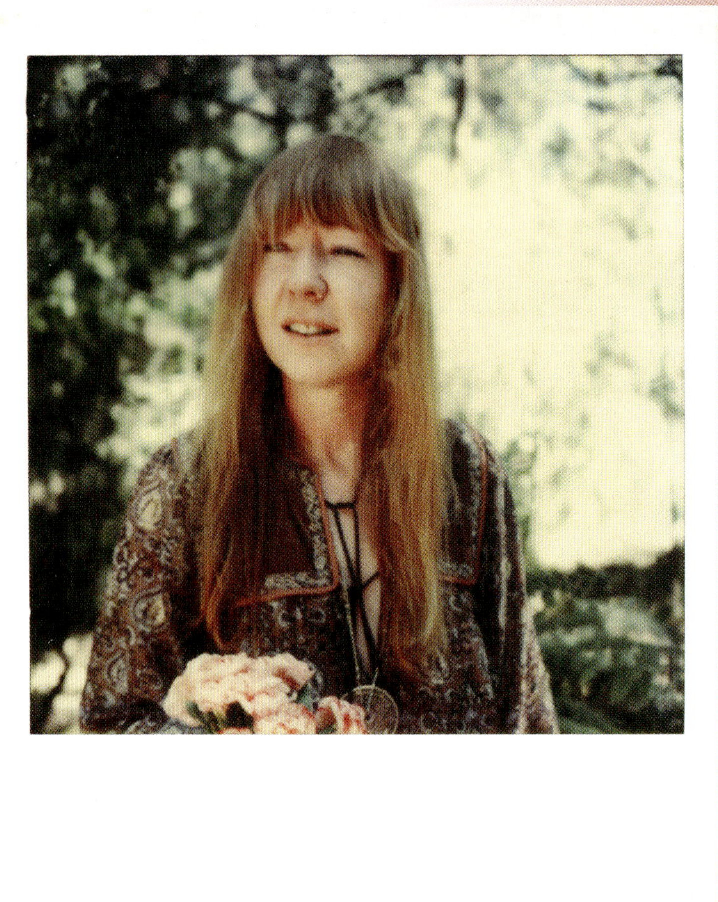

BARBARA TUCKER AT HURSTBRIDGE C. 1979
Photo by Albert Tucker

WORKING *WITH* BARBARA

GAVIN FRY

I first met Albert and Barbara Tucker early in 1979 when I was working on my Master of Arts thesis at Monash University. The subject of my work, Adrian Lawlor, had been a major influence on many of the younger modernists in the late 1930s. Tucker was mentioned in a number of Lawlor's letters and Adrian was the subject of many photographs he had taken at the time. One of those images, taken at Lawlor's new house in Warrandyte after the fires of 1939, became the basis of one of Tucker's most important paintings. *Portrait of Adrian Lawlor* introduced the crooked smiling mouth that became the defining motif of the famed *Images of Modern Evil*. I was a little reluctant in approaching Tucker, as he had a somewhat forbidding reputation, but the introduction was made through Sweeney Reed and a meeting arranged. We met at the Tuckers' house in Hurstbridge and I spent a very pleasant and informative afternoon documenting memories, people and places. Barbara was a helpful presence, bringing refreshments but remaining in the background—this was, after all, a professional meeting about times past and she left us to it.

My meetings with Tucker became more regular in the 1980s when, as senior curator of art at the Australian War Memorial I entered negotiations with Tucker towards the acquisition of his wartime works for the AWM collection. Again, Barbara was there, but always as a background figure rather than a participant in the meetings. They had recently moved to *Woodside* in Blessington Street in St Kilda, a substantial Victorian house with a studio built in the converted stables at the rear of the property. Visitors would usually be met at the door by Barbara, who would then take you through to where her husband waited in the large lounge room at the back of the house. We would exchange pleasantries, and then be left to carry out the business of the day. A decade and a half later, I was approached by Craftsman House in Sydney to undertake a book on Tucker, which meant conducting a round of interviews, probably on five or six occasions over a twelve-month period. Barbara became a participant in these discussions, providing much of the background material for the latter thirty years of the Tuckers' life. It was not a matter of inserting herself into the story, but an acknowledgement of the fact that we were dealing with many shared experiences, and her husband was by this time in his eighties and needed reminding of various things. The project advanced well, but the stresses caused by the infamous robbery and the subsequent trial meant that the book had to be put on the backburner. Sadly, Tucker died before the project could be resurrected.

In the run-up to 2000, my publisher in Sydney, Lou Klepac, decided to produce a substantial commemorative book entitled *Australian Painters of the Twentieth Century*. He asked me to write an essay on Tucker, and having undertaken the interviews not long before, it was a task I enjoyed greatly. As a consequence of that work Warwick Reeder, then director of Heide, invited me to speak at the opening of a special exhibition mounted for the announcement of the Albert and Barbara Tucker Gift to the gallery. Again, the timing was crucial as, not long before, Janine Burke had published *Australian Gothic*, her new book on the life and work of Albert Tucker. The publication proved controversial as there had been disagreements between Barbara and the author, with the consequence that copyright images of the artist's work could not be included in the publication. As Barbara had explained at the time, she had requested some changes be made to the text to correct what she saw as inaccuracies, which the author had declined to accept.

At the Heide launch I was approached by Barbara and Lauraine Diggins, who asked if I would be interested in producing a new book on Tucker's work, to be published by Lou Klepac. I was, of course, honoured to be asked and we came to an agreement on the spot to get the work underway. This was a major vote of confidence in my work and I was determined to produce a book worthy of the subject.

The writing and publication of *Albert Tucker* became a very different project from that originally envisaged for Craftsman House. The scale and scope of the work was enlarged and Barbara was effectively the client. I returned to Blessington Street on many occasions, meeting with Barbara and going through the huge collection of material in her possession. This included a great many early drawings and studies for later works, photographs and personal material. Barbara was fully engaged with the project and I came to know her as a strong and charming personality. It was important that I be able to tell the Tucker story in my own way, and yet have Barbara firmly on side, especially with regard to the more controversial elements.

I had my own views of the story, based on thirty or more years being a close but not intimate observer of many of the main characters. I had met Sweeney, Bert's son, in the 1960s when he married Pamela Westh, a close friend of my sister Jeanette. Over the years I had visited Heide when Pamela and Sweeney were in residence and had absorbed all the stories about the early days there—the associated myths, the half-truths and speculations that swirled around the main players and their many acolytes, who came and went like the cast of characters in a drawn-out soap opera.

I was particularly conscious of the subtleties and sensitivities in the personal relationships, especially with women, that had been part of Tucker's long life. I was dealing directly with the artist's widow and wanted to respect her feelings, while not giving any impression that I was beholden to her in what was hopefully going to be the definitive work on Albert Tucker. Unlike many of my colleagues in the art world, I did not subscribe to the belief that Joy was the under-recognised genius behind Tucker and his circle, and that everything about his life and work needed to be reflected through the prism of her art and experience. As put to me, both by Tucker and others that I knew, Joy was important at the time, but that influence was relatively brief and not the over-riding core of the narrative.

When it comes to the women in Tucker's life, I suggest that Mary Dickson, Tucker's American de facto partner from the early 1950s until his return to Australia in 1960, was of equal, or perhaps greater import in the Tucker story. I discussed Mary at great length with Barbara and she too agreed that, in Tucker's story, her role had been of crucial importance to Tucker's existence and success as an artist. In most of the early work on Tucker, especially Uhl's book of 1969, Mary was completely absent. In all the tellings of Tucker's travels through Europe—the famous homebuilt caravan, the flat in Germany and the houses in Italy—it was never acknowledged that Mary

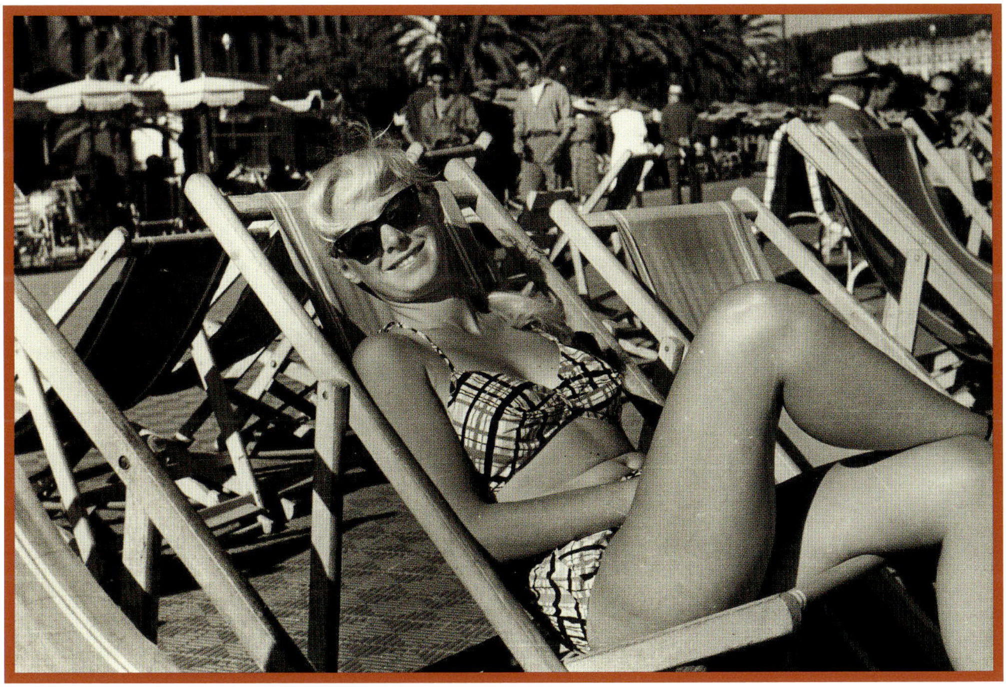

MARY DICKSON ON THE
PROMENADE DES ANGLAIS, NICE C. 1951
Photo by Albert Tucker

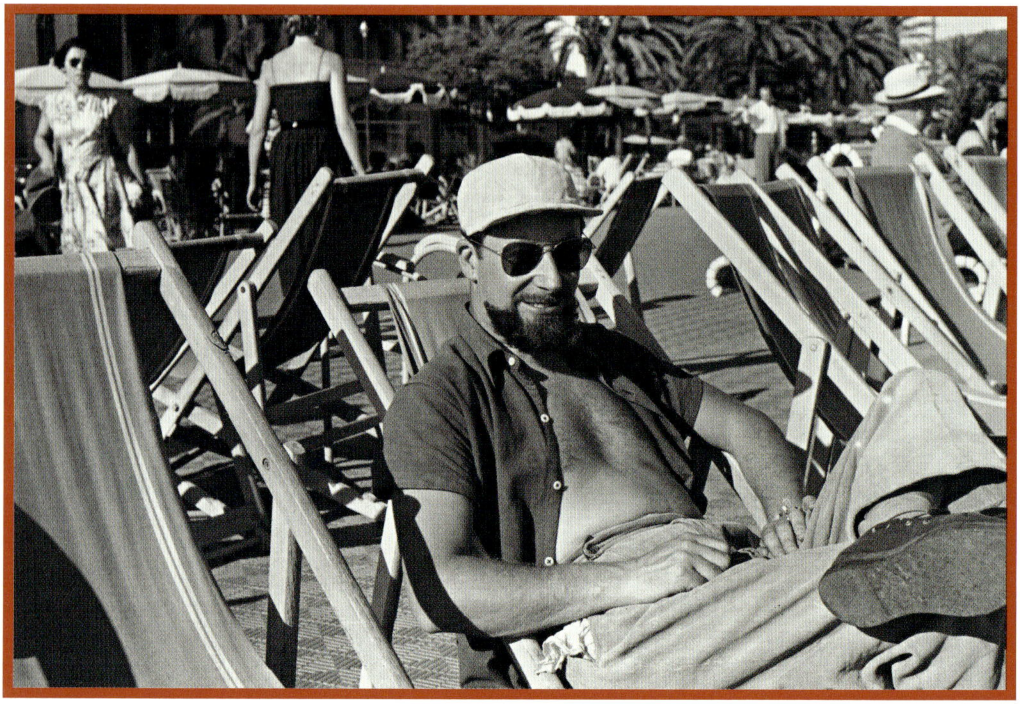

ALBERT TUCKER ON THE PROMENADE DES ANGLAIS, NICE C. 1951
Photo by Mary Dickson

provided the money, owned and drove the car that towed their caravan and paid for their accommodation and travel. She used her work for the US Government to smooth their way, worked as the translator and guide and allowed Tucker to continue his work as an artist. His paintings at the time were effectively unsaleable and Mary kept him going, his only other source of income being the funds provided by John Reed. Tucker's refusal to divorce Joy, supposedly on financial grounds, became the final tipping point as, when they planned to travel to America, Mary wanted to do so as a married woman, not as the unwed partner of an Australian artist.

Importantly, it was Mary who took Tucker's paintings to America and led to his work being acquired by the Museum of Modern Art. Barbara had great sympathy for Mary Dickson's place in Tucker's life and was happy to accept her as a friend when Mary came to stay in Australia not long before her death. Barbara knew well that her husband had a strong dependency on the women in his life and that he had relied on her to keep things together for more than thirty years.

Barbara was keenly interested in the work I was doing, answering my questions, looking for documents and checking dates, but she was also careful not to intrude into the work. She arranged meetings with people who might help and was supportive in every way. When my part of the project was complete, with not a little trepidation, I handed over the manuscript for her to read and comment upon. I was greatly relieved when, out of some 37,000 words, she suggested changing just two. The book was published in 2006 and it was the largest, grandest and most successful publication I had undertaken to that time. Barbara had taken over management of the project from Lauraine Diggins and soon we had two launches planned, one at the Melbourne Town Hall and one at the Art Gallery of New South Wales. Barbara was delighted with the project and she ensured the book remained in print and freely available.

I was not surprised when Barbara decided to move from Blessington Street—it was a grand residence, but I always found it a dark and somewhat dour place. Bert had left Barbara well set up financially, as he made a point of buying property and never selling, but I felt at times he had not really allowed her to blossom as a person. She had run her own business and, effectively, managed the Tucker enterprise and its legacy, yet while he was alive, he was always front and centre in everything. Bert was self-absorbed and somewhat self-indulgent, as seen with the pile of new cameras, never even taken out of their boxes, and the stocks of art materials that would have supplied a whole art school. He was a child of the Depression and carried that parsimonious streak throughout his life.

The one thought that defined Barbara and her role in the relationship came with the matter of her being depicted in Tucker's paintings. While she does appear almost recognisably in a couple of works, she never sat for a formal portrait, even when Tucker made portraiture a major part of his work in the 1980s. I did ask her quite directly as to why this had never happened and she answered, quite unambiguously, that she 'didn't trust what he might do to her'. She was acutely aware that Bert could be quite cruel and cutting in his depictions of people, and especially of attractive women. We had discussed one particular work, which was specifically included in the book to illustrate that point. Everyone knew Yvonne Lennie, the wife of Arthur Boyd, as a bright and vivacious person, in her youth a beautiful young woman in every way. Tucker painted her portrait in 1945, showing her as a sour-faced and petulant girl, barely recognisable as the person in life. Tucker always maintained that his role was not to make people feel good, to create pretty images—he did not believe in the maxim that beauty equals truth. Barbara was not prepared to put herself through the angst of being depicted through what she feared could have been the distorted vision of her husband's cold eye.

Like many wives of highly successful artists, Barbara's latter years were spent managing her late husband's legacy, ensuring his work was placed in the right public collections and being a force for good in the local art world. Her special relationship with the Heide gallery was important to both parties and Australian art is a better place for her discretion, good sense and thoughtful management of the Tucker legacy. ¶

FROM *A* FAMILY ALBUM MEMORIES *OF* BARBARA *AND* BERT

RICHARD AND FLORENCE CRICHTON

The kitchen table at Dick and Flo's house in Eltham is spread with photographs.

'And we were friends over years—how many years?' Dick smiles. 'There we were, arguing and talking, Bert at the head of the table—' He pauses. 'He always took the head of the table. Friends since 1962, sometime after Bert came back to Australia. And we met Barbara soon after that, up at Bert's little old cottage. Bert was doing it up with occasional help from Stephen May and me when he met Barbara. She was welcoming, and fitted in with us all. But she and Bert didn't live there long. Bert had quite a bit of land at the Hurstbridge property and they built the big house and studio up on the hill for the view of the huge manna gums that Bert loved. We'd go up there regularly and they came to our house at Eltham a lot. It was almost every weekend, eating here or eating up at Hurstbridge, kids running around, lots of laughter. Barbara had a wry sense of humour, enjoyed company, Bert, the talk, the children. She made marvellous stews and roasts, gravy and pickles. The visits went long into the night. The kids would go to the beds and couches, bundled in blankets up there.'

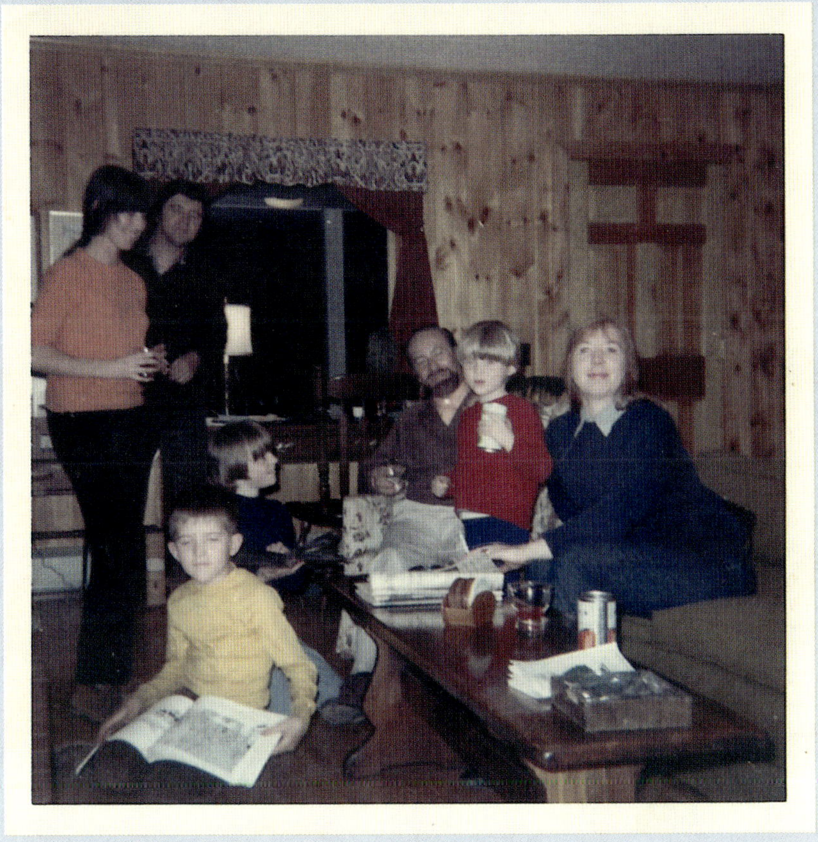

FLORENCE AND RICHARD CRICHTON, THEIR CHILDREN, BERT AND BARBARA TUCKER AT THE BIG HURSTBRIDGE HOUSE Photo attributed to David Bilcock

Dick talks of how bitterly cold it was when they carried the kids out to the old Rover that he'd got cheap.

While the kids slept, Bert and Dick watched television. Bert liked the wrestling and Dick would watch it with him, getting tired and grumpy watching Chief Little Wolf, Bonny Muir and others. Dick says, 'We shared all sorts of stuff back then.' The artist talk was central to the friendship, Dick emphasises, though he suddenly comments that over all the years, he was hardly ever in Bert's studio ... except he remembers one time when Bert asked him to look at a suitcase filled with Joy Hester's drawings and sketches. Bert wanted to photograph them. He told Dick that he felt her work had been neglected and wanted to ensure its survival.

Dick lifts another photo, one that shows a young Bert, taken right there in the Eltham house. Flo says it was taken in front of one of Dick's paintings, not long after Dick first met Bert.

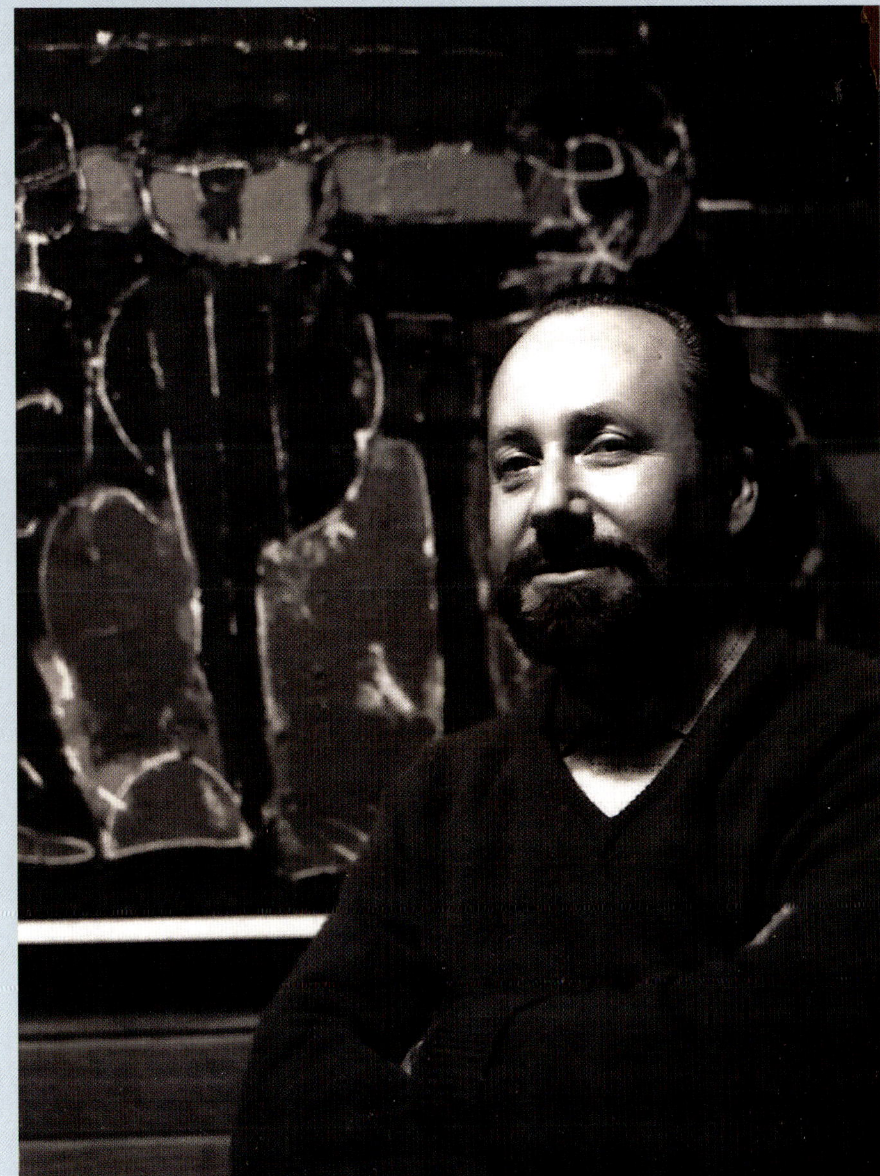

ALBERT TUCKER SITTING AT THE DINING TABLE IN FRONT OF RICHARD CRICHTON'S PAINTING IN THE CRICHTONS' ELTHAM HOUSE *Photo by Richard Crichton*

Dick met Bert at a party at the Zikaras' house in Eltham. 'It's a Lithuanian name,' Flo says.

'He was a sculptor. Bert was there, and he and I just got on from the start,' Dick says. Flo wasn't there, because the children were still small. 'Bert visited us frequently during the next few months and that's also about the time when he first met Barbara. We met her a little later, after she moved in with him. Before long, a site was cleared for the house and studio on the hillside next to the cottage, which they built together over the next year or so. They called in one day and surprised us by telling us they had been married at the Registry Office. It was a lovely surprise, but typical of Bert to keep it to himself until the mission was accomplished.'

'Our son Matthew was born in 1963, and Barbara was the first person to visit at the hospital,' Flo says, 'bringing a huge bunch of flowers. They were busy, happy times, and Barbara became a good friend.'

Dick turns over one black-and-white photo of Barbara and him with one of his children, taken at the Chelsea Hotel in New York in the late 1960s.

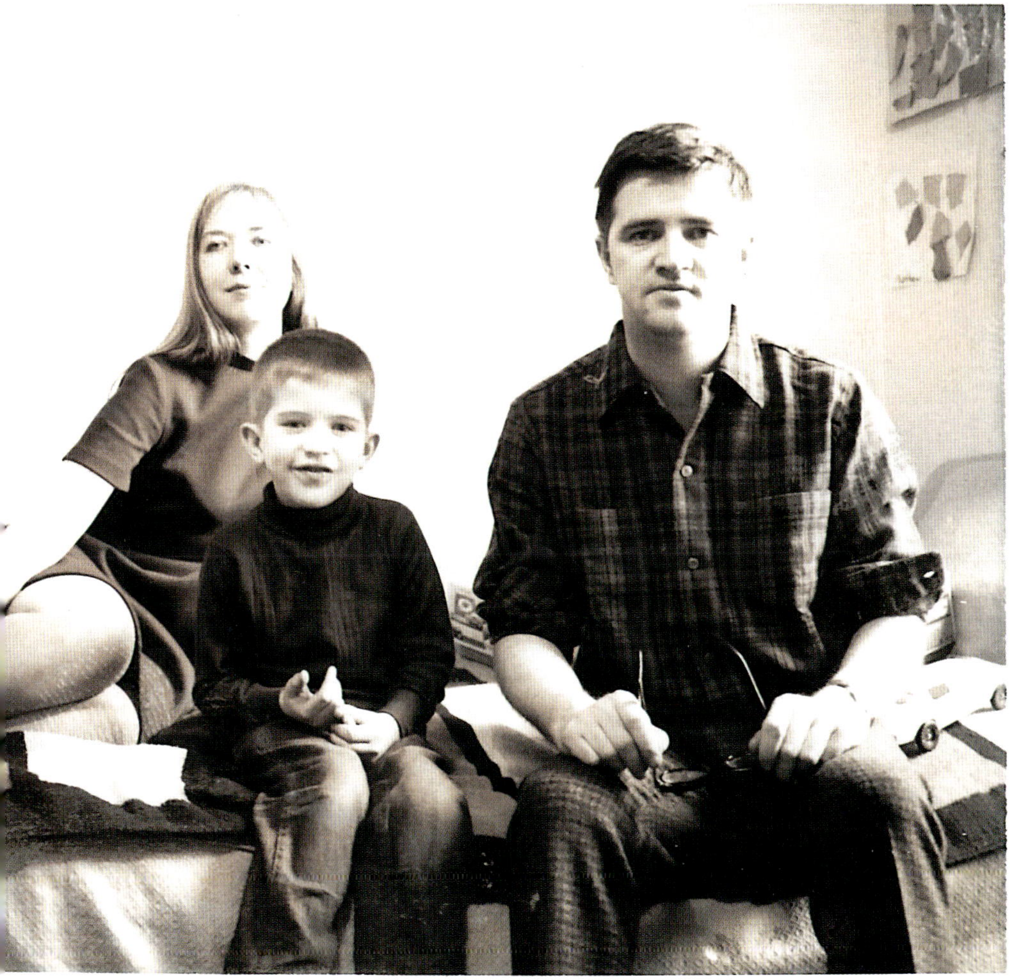

BARBARA TUCKER, ANDREW CRICHTON AND RICHARD CRICHTON AT THE CHELSEA HOTEL
Photo by Florence Crichton

He skims the pile and picks up a later colour photo of himself with Stanley Bard, the hotel's part-owner and manager. It was taken in the early 1980s by his daughter, Robyn.

'We returned to stay there a number of times after that first stay,' Dick says. 'It was a marvellous place for us and other artists.'

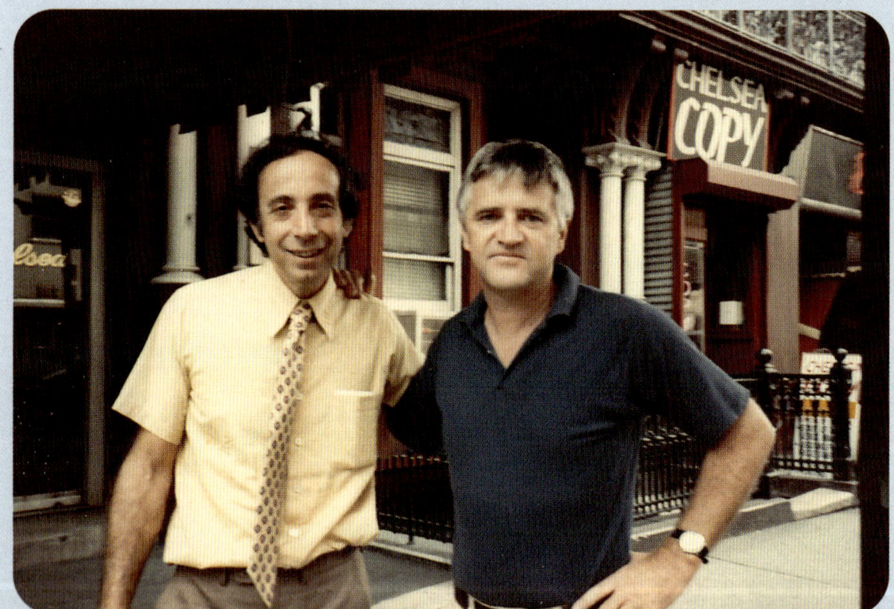

STANLEY BARD AND RICHARD CRICHTON
Photo by Robyn Crichton

Dick picks up some photos taken in 1967–68 at their apartment during the year they were based at the Chelsea.

Flo explains that Bert and Barbara stayed there for a number of months when Brett and Wendy Whiteley were in the penthouse above the Crichtons' apartment. During that year, they often looked after Arkie Whiteley, who loved being with the Crichton children. One black-and-white photo shows Barbara and Bert and the Crichton children and Arkie in the Crichton's apartment.

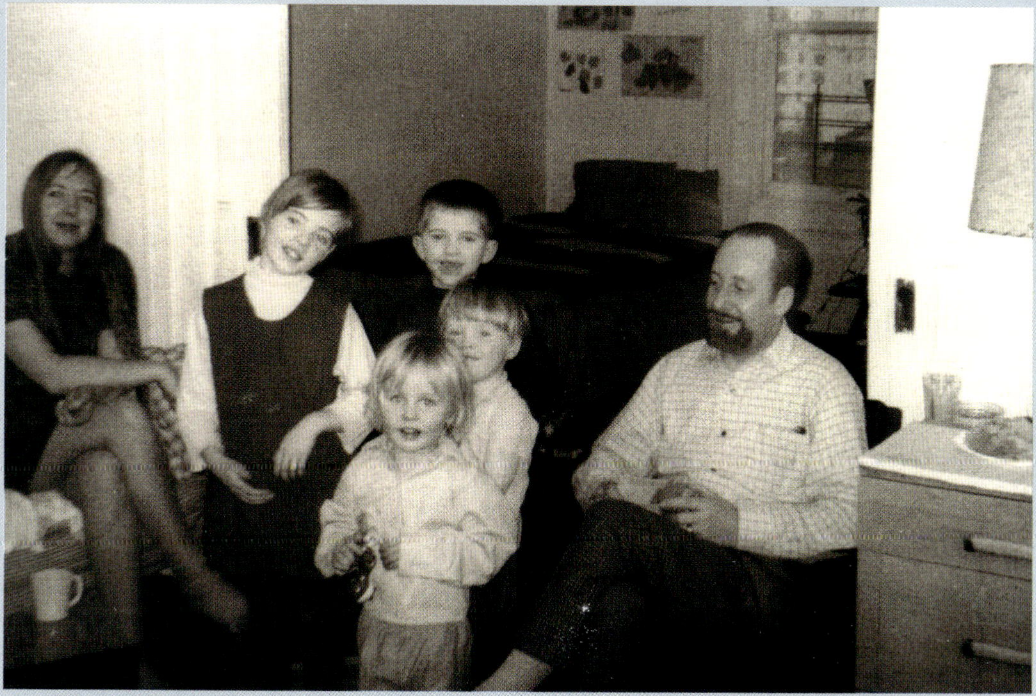

[BACK ROW] BARBARA TUCKER, ROBYN CRICHTON, ANDREW CRICHTON AND ALBERT TUCKER [MIDDLE ROW] MATTHEW CRICHTON [FRONT ROW] ARKIE WHITELEY Photo by Richard Crichton

Flo remembers that Matt and Arkie played together either at the Crichtons' or up on the rooftop outside the Whiteleys' apartment.

Flo laughs, caught in the memories, saying the Whiteleys had the penthouse, 'which is a posh name for it, but it did have a door that opened out on to a roof space and there were lots of potted shrubs and trees, so it was quite nice—and very safe! That's what it was like,' she says with a smile in her voice, pointing to a couple of photos. 'Brett would fly the kite with the kids up on the roof,' she remembers, showing a dancing Brett holding the kite string, with Arkie and Matt running away.

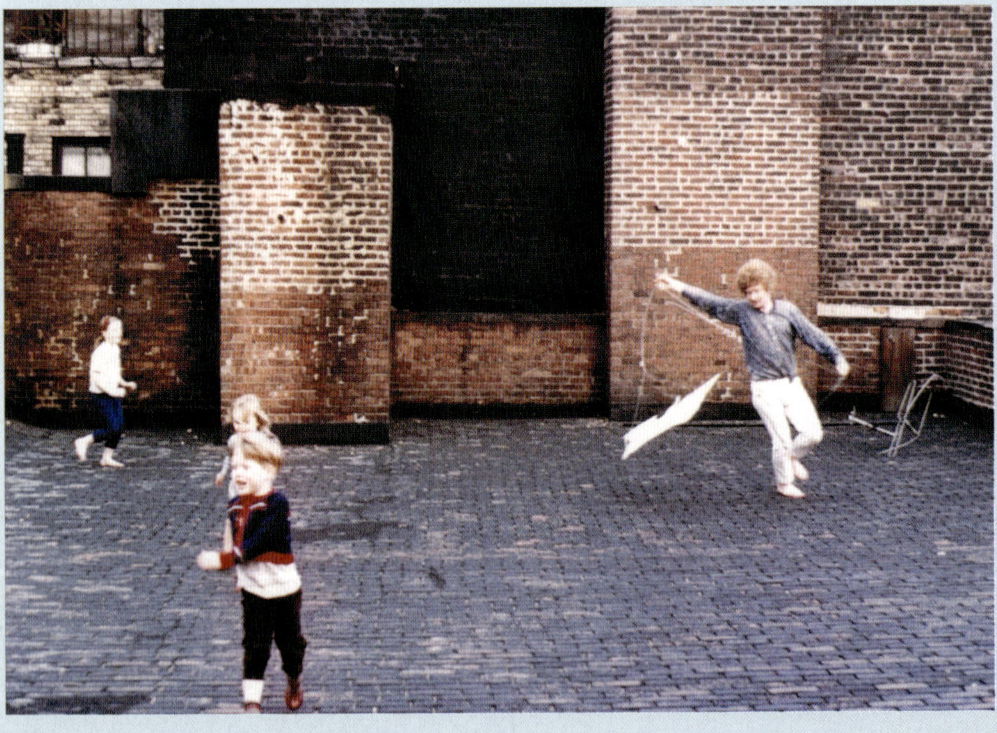

ROBYN CRICHTON, ARKIE WHITELEY, MATTHEW CRICHTON AND BRETT WHITELEY
Photo by Richard Crichton

'Here's a photo of the penthouse garden,' Flo says. 'The Whiteleys kept some ducks there for a time. It was an amazing place.'

Flo remembers that Stanley loved having their kids and Arkie because it gave the hotel the atmosphere he wanted. He was concerned it was becoming known too much as just 'the artists'' hotel.

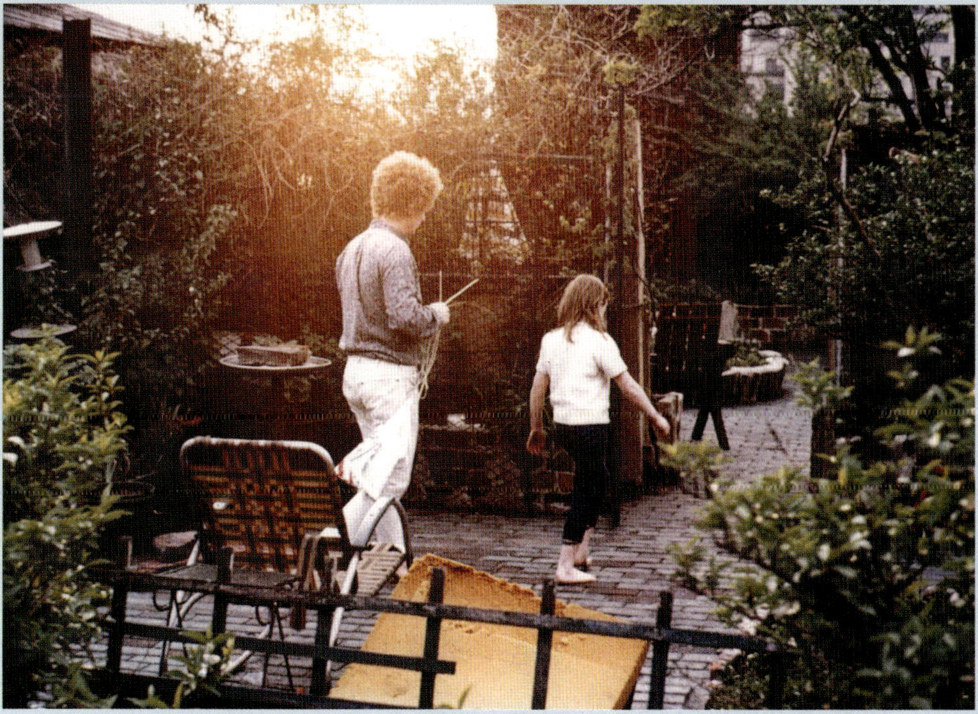

BRETT WHITELEY AND ROBYN CRICHTON WALKING THROUGH THE PENTHOUSE GARDEN OUTSIDE THE WHITELEYS' APARTMENT *Photo by Richard Crichton*

Flo picks up more photos of Barbara and Bert during their stay at the Chelsea.

She says, 'Here they are at the top of the Empire State Building. Look at Bert with his camera ready to take a photo. Typical!'

Flo laughs and continues, 'That was Bert: observing, framing. Often if you took a photo of Barbara and him, he would be taking a photo of you.'

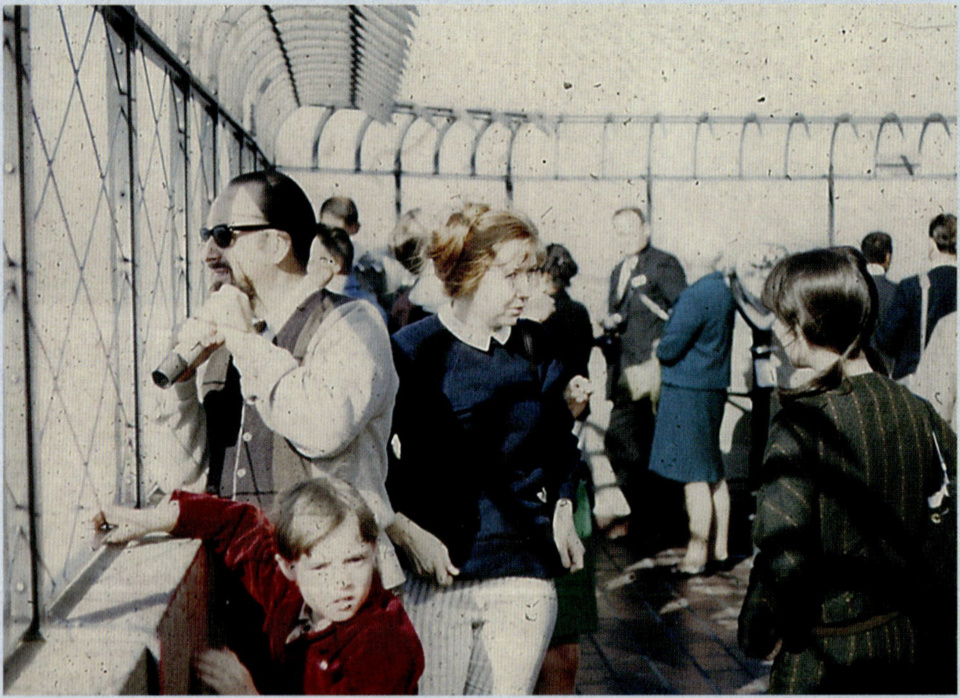

BERT AND BARBARA TUCKER WITH FLORENCE CRICHTON (BACK TURNED) ON THE VIEWING PLATFORM OF THE EMPIRE STATE BUILDING Photo by Richard Crichton

She moves to another photo saying, 'This one's taken down in Little Italy at the festival. Bert and Barbara were good with the children. We were all part of each other's lives, then.'

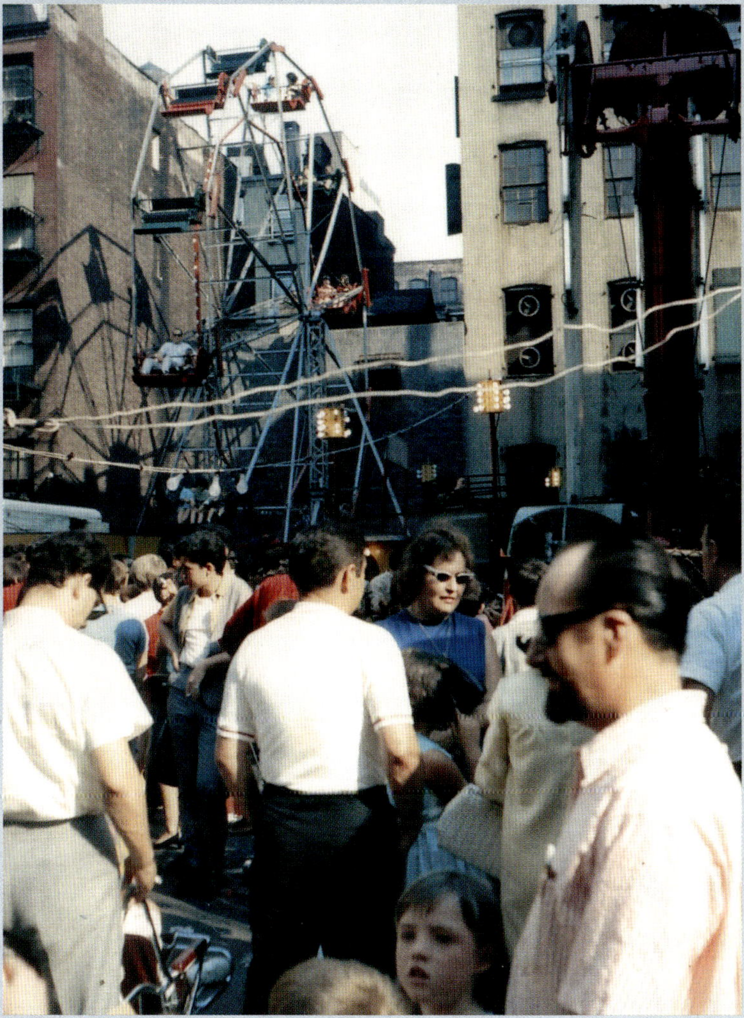

HEADS OF THE CRICHTON CHILDREN AND BERT TUCKER, FAR RIGHT, AT THE LITTLE ITALY FESTIVAL IN NEW YORK Photo by Richard Crichton

More photos are spread on the table. 'These were all taken in the very early days of us knowing Barbara and Bert,' Flo says. 'We went on this funny little camping trip together, near Port Campbell. Look how relaxed we all are.'

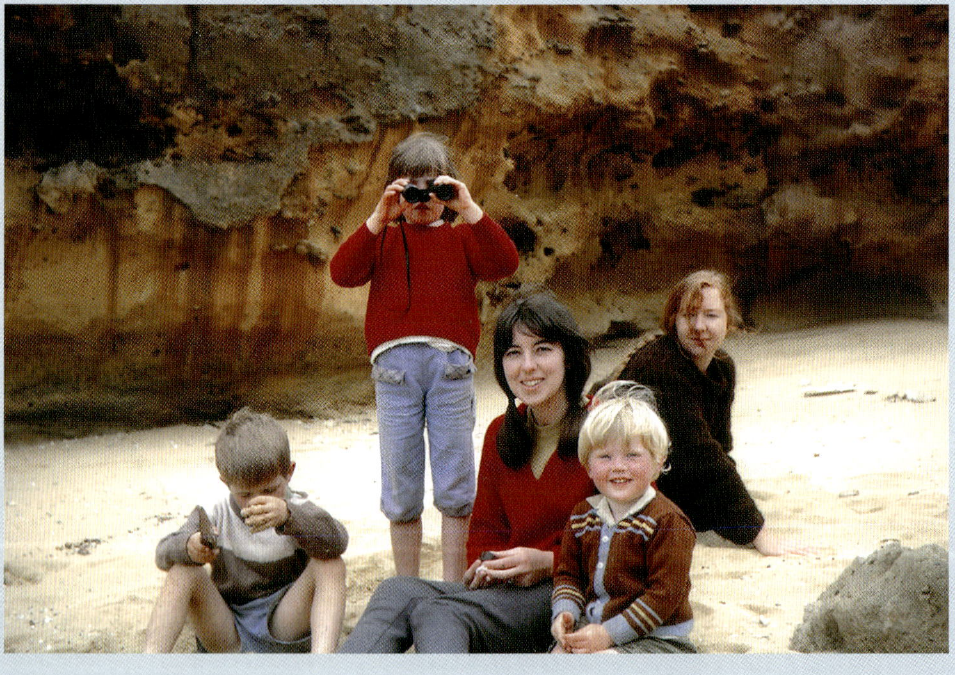

ANDREW, ROBYN, FLORENCE AND MATTHEW CRICHTON AND BARBARA AND ALBERT TUCKER ON A BEACH NEAR PORT CAMPBELL Photos by Richard Crichton

'Bert and Barbara had taken us camping in the Wyperfeld country,' Flo says, and to the Barmah Forest, so we said, 'Next time, let's go to the coast! And we went down the Great Ocean Road through the Otways and along that rugged west Victorian coast.'

'It was all very easygoing,' Dick remembers, 'but Bert always had his camera to hand. You had to get used to that.'

'Barbara and Bert enjoyed that trip,' Flo remembers. Dick says, 'We were all so young, then. Look at this photo I took of Bert at that time. He really wasn't a beach person, always preferred the bush, the open space, but Barbara loved the beach.'

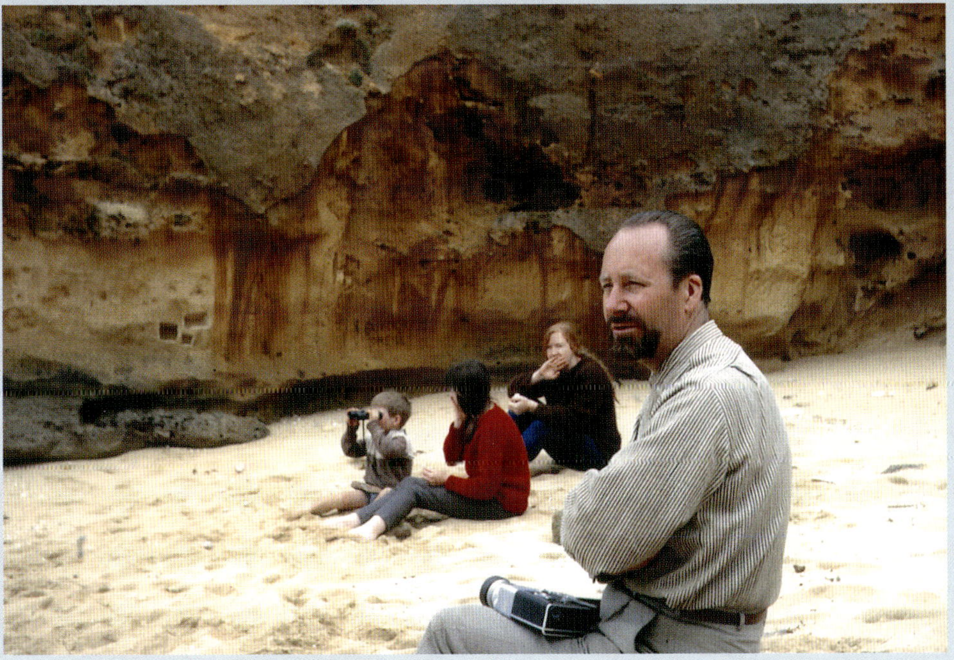

Flo smiles. 'Here's a photo of one of the picnics we went on at Springbrook with Barbara and Bert and Fred and Lyn Williams and their children.'

Dick says, 'There's Fred and Bert at the edges of this photo, and Flo, Barbara and Lyn in the centre. They were such happy, good times.'

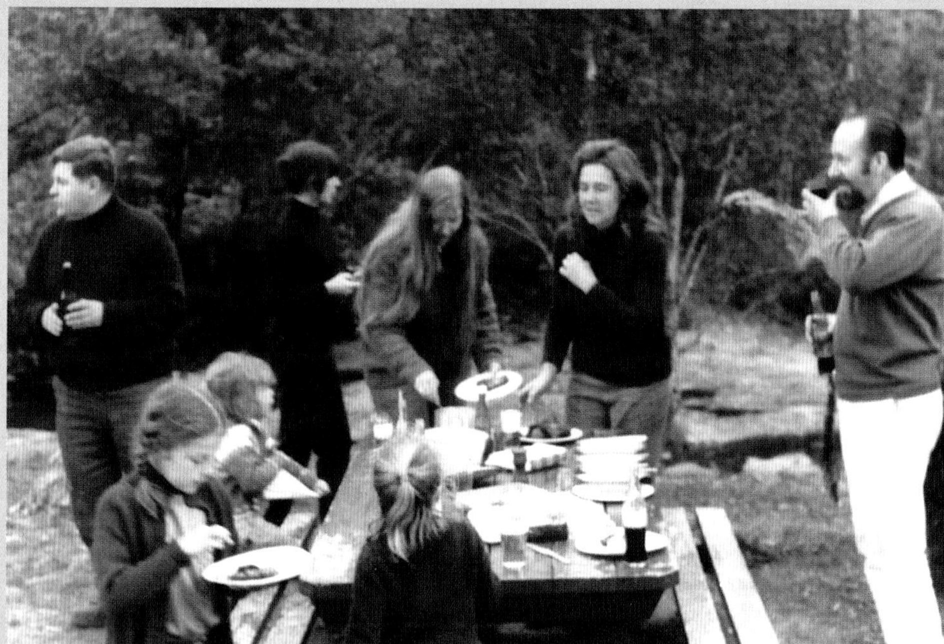

FRED WILLIAMS, FLORENCE CRICHTON, BARBARA TUCKER, LYN WILLIAMS, ALBERT TUCKER AND CHILDREN *Photo by Richard Crichton*

'We stayed a few times with Barbara and Bert at Noojee. Barbara's brother, David, had bought land there, and later Bert and Barbara did too. They bought an old railway carriage and placed it under a shed roof. It was another form of camping for them,' Flo says.

The photo shows them all in the railway carriage clearing up after dinner.

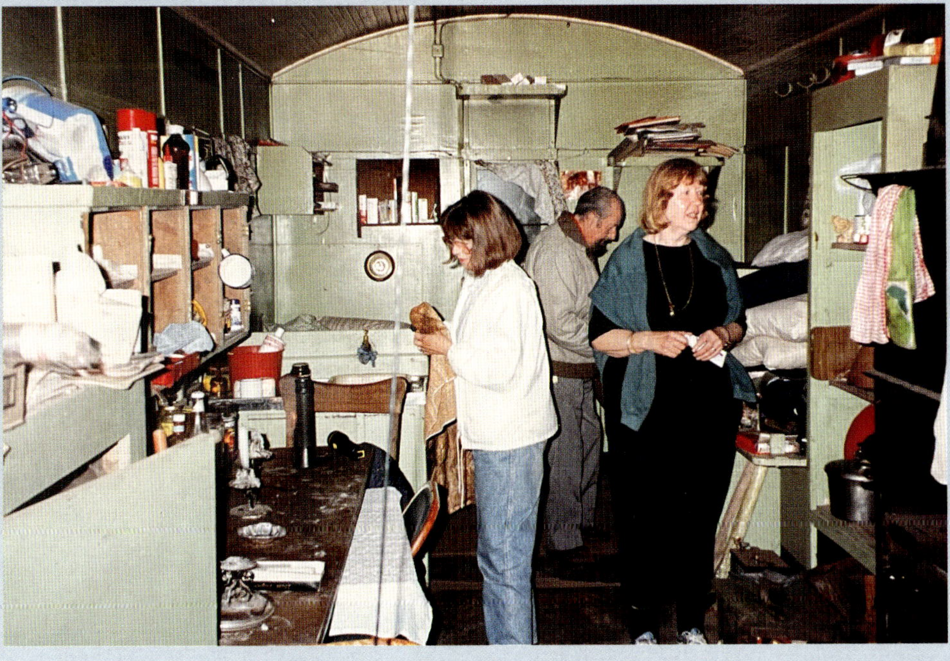

FLORENCE CRICHTON, ALBERT TUCKER AND BARBARA TUCKER INSIDE THE RAILWAY CARRIAGE AT NOOJEE Photo by Richard Crichton

‘And here’s one—not a great photo,’ says Flo, ‘but I like it because it shows Barbara walking the old wooden trestle bridge at Noojee. The bridge was closed. There were “DANGER” signs everywhere, but Barbara wanted to walk it anyway—and did! She was brave, intrepid, adventurous, determined, independent. That was Barbara.’

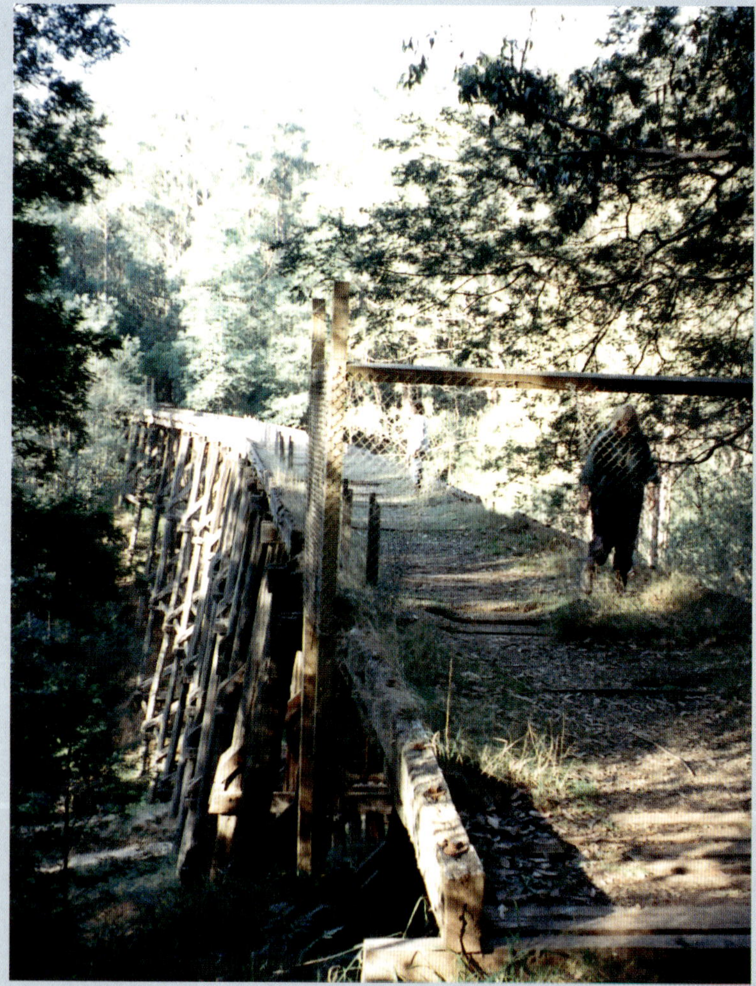

BARBARA TUCKER WALKING ALONG THE WOODEN TRESTLE BRIDGE AT NOOJEE   Photo by Richard Crichton

Flo says that she mentioned to Barbara the annual picnic of the Nepean Conservation Group at Point Nepean National Park, and asked if she'd like to come. She turned up with half of her family, her sister, Joan, and her brother, Peter. 'Look how Bert has his camera up—him taking a picture of the photographer taking a picture,' Flo says, laughing.

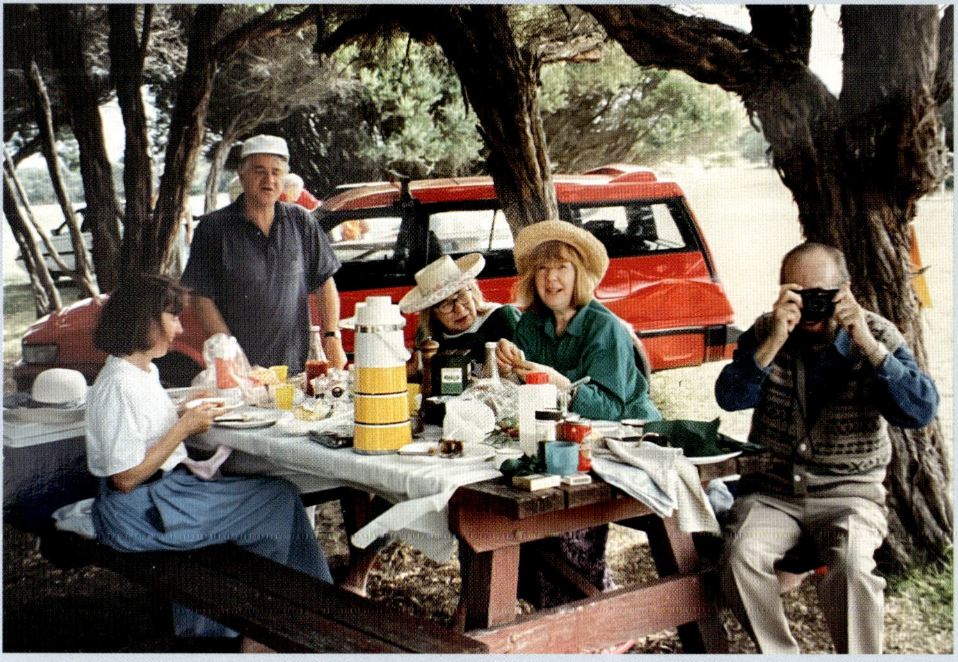

FLORENCE AND RICHARD CRICHTON, JOAN JONES, BARBARA TUCKER AND ALBERT TUCKER
Photo attributed to Peter Bilcock

Flo mentions that Barbara spent much more time at the Blairgowrie house than Bert did, and that she was very generous with the house. When Michael Keon was not well at one stage, Barbara let him stay there for a long period.

'Here we all are,' says Flo, 'gathered in the living room at Barbara's Blairgowrie house.'

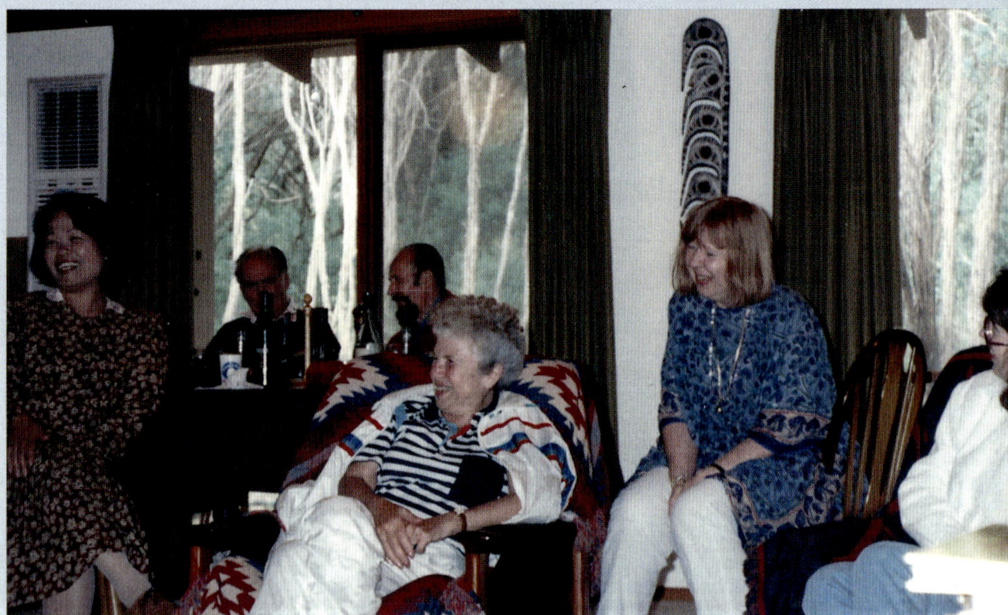

AURORA (WIFE OF MICHAEL KEON SENIOR), MICHAEL KEON, ALBERT TUCKER, LEISL SINGER, BARBARA TUCKER AND FLORENCE CRICHTON Photo by Richard Crichton

The next photo they share is taken in Bert's Middle Park studio.

'This is from the time when Irish artist Oliver Whelan was staying with us,' Flo says. 'We took him down to visit Bert in that studio. Bert had moved from using the stables at the St Kilda house in Blessington Street as his studio, preferring to work in the Middle Park studio. I think I took this photo from the little mezzanine area that held a kitchen. You can see Ollie with his children, and Bert and Dick.'

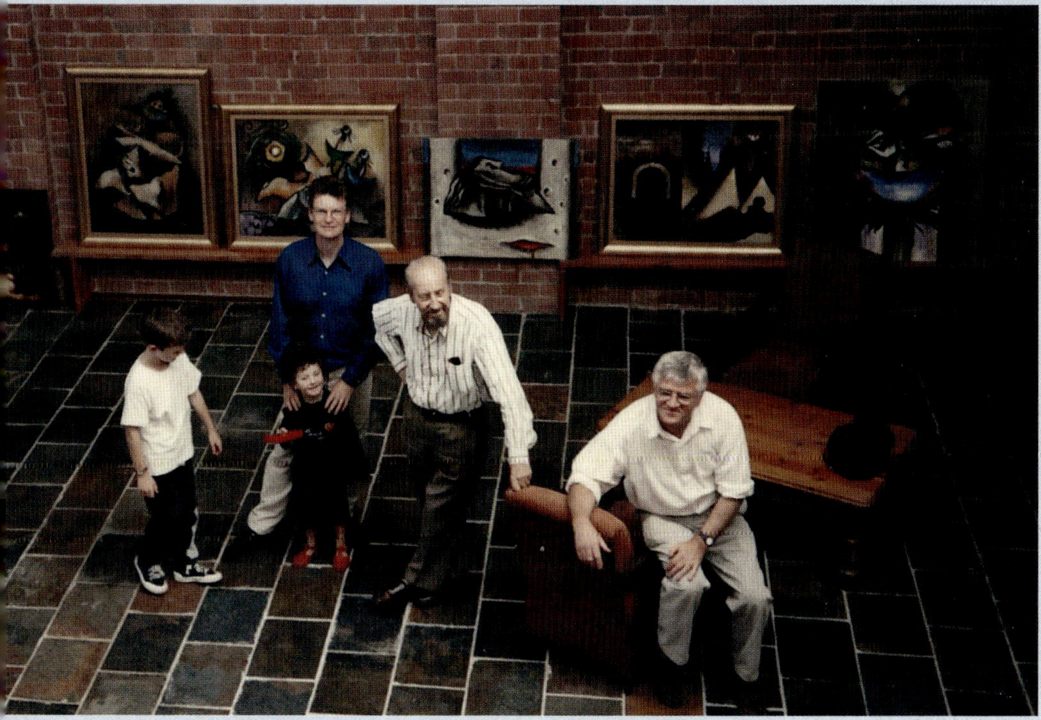

OLIVER WHELAN WITH CHILDREN, ALBERT TUCKER AND RICHARD CRICHTON INSIDE BERT'S MIDDLE PARK STUDIO Photo by Florence Crichton

'Here's a photo of Bert and Dick in front of a marvellous old gum in Eltham Park. It's a favourite one of mine,' Flo says.

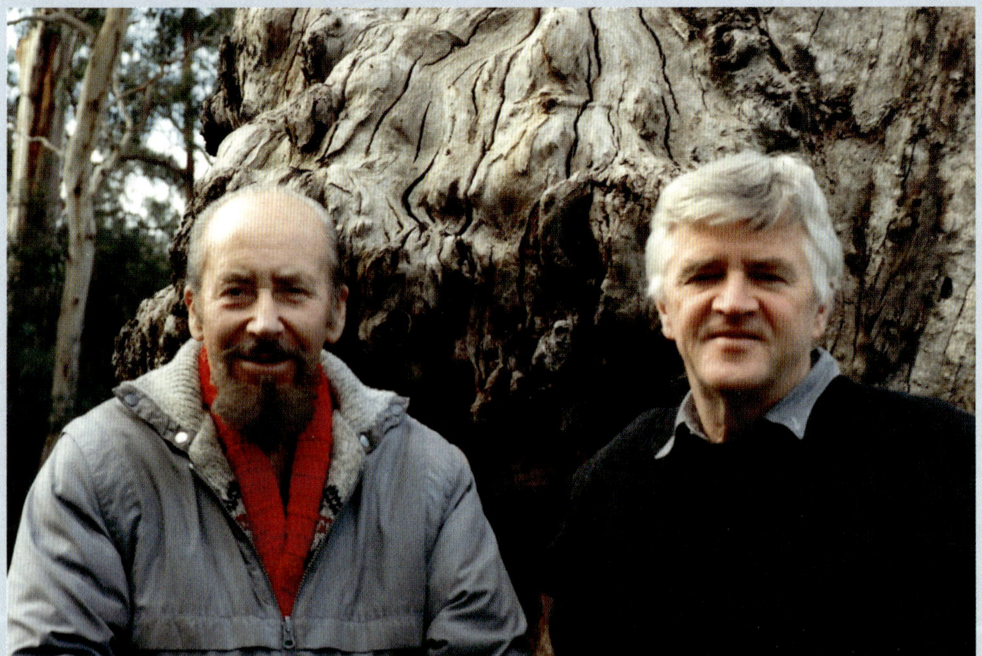

ALBERT TUCKER AND RICHARD CRICHTON
Photo by Florence Crichton

And then Flo chooses a photo that looks as if it could have been taken at Springbrook, except, she says, it's at Hoddles Creek, taken on a late visit when they walked down into the gully on the property.

'The trees were huge and the vegetation so lush. It was a wonderful walk, though none of us knew it was the last walk up there with all of us together.'

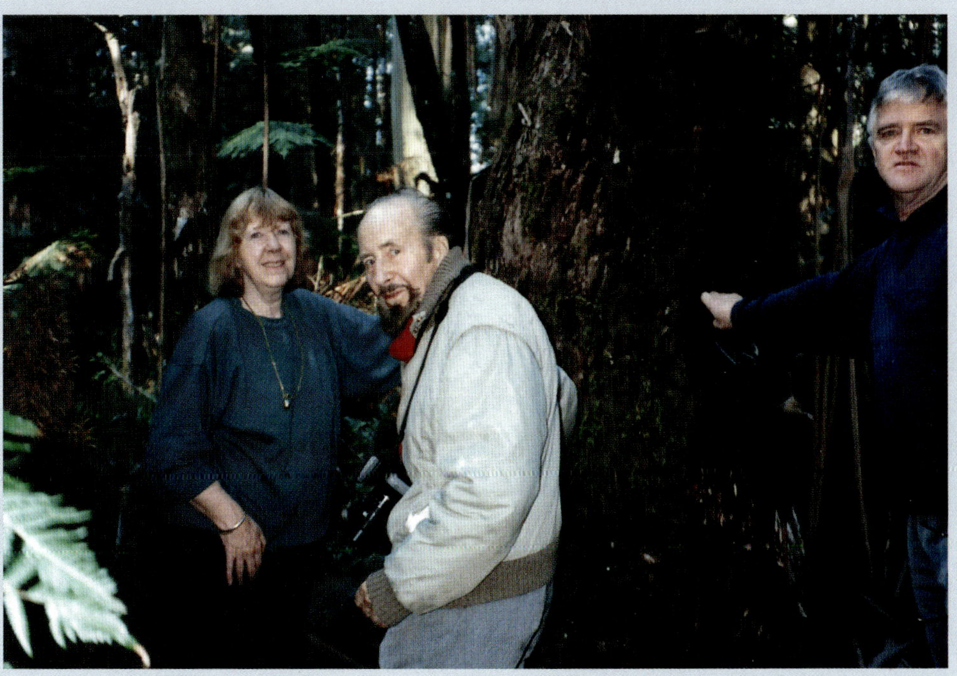

BARBARA TUCKER, ALBERT TUCKER AND RICHARD CRICHTON
Photo by Florence Crichton

Looking at the photo, Dick muses that he didn't appreciate at the time that Albert was getting frailer. He remembers the vigorous, younger Bert. He talks of Bert bringing Sidney Nolan to the Eltham house to look at Dick's work, him coming home to find Bert and Sid sitting at the dining table eating biscuits.

Flo remembers these visits vividly, and how interested in Dick's work they were. One conversation sticks in her mind about iconography, whether there was a 'Melbourne iconography' because Bert and Sid said they thought they saw something of this in their own work and could see it in Dick's work. There was a lot of discussion about a 'Melbourne iconography' between them.

'We had some memorable conversations about jazz,' he recalls, 'and folk music. She would talk about music with real knowledge and curiosity, and we'd all talk back. We had a similar love for crazy humour and jokes. Barbara's were a bit ruder and sharper than mine, at times.' Dick smiles at the memory. 'We'd talk about the dogs, about television, go on about films. And people. On the occasions Bert wasn't with us, Barbara was always just herself, very entertaining. They were different people,' he says, 'but it was a good union.'

Photos are strewn on the table. Flo selects one of Barbara at Christmas lunch at Hoddles Creek. She's with her sister Linda and brothers David and Peter. In this photo, Barbara looks firmly and astutely into the lens, calmly appraising the photographer: I'm still here, her look seems to say. And you are, too. And I'm glad.

Flo stirs and shifts the piles of photos. Near the centre, there's one on which Flo stops. It's the first photo we looked at, of the Crichtons and Bert and Barbara, taken at the big Hurstbridge house. Poised, composed, it is Barbara who draws the eye, the pale blue collar of her shirt throwing light on to and framing her young face, her halo of red hair, her elegant hand reaching for a book on the coffee table. Barbara looks out at us, confident and fearless. ¶

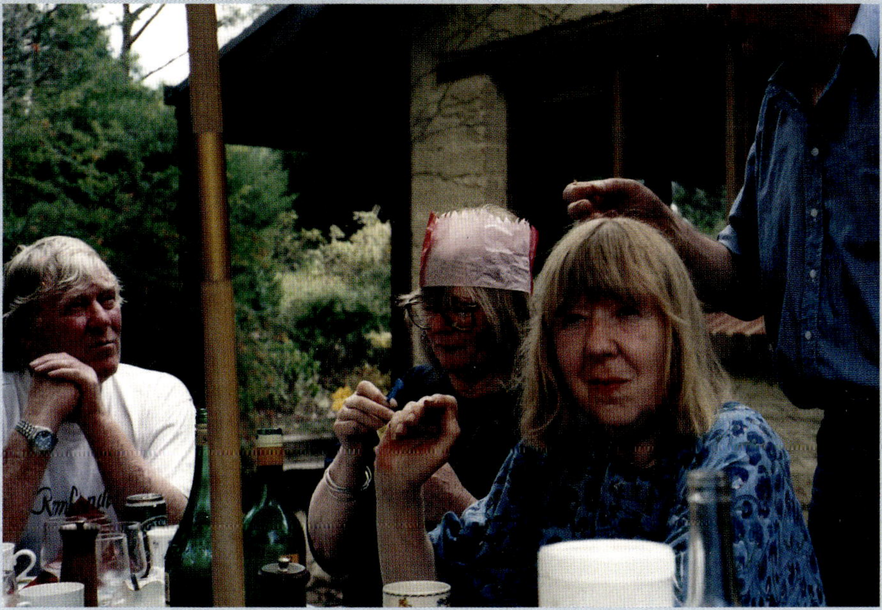

DAVID BILCOCK, LINDA BILCOCK, BARBARA TUCKER AND PETER BILCOCK AT CHRISTMAS LUNCH AT HODDLES CREEK *Photo by Richard Crichton*

FOUR LETTERS *FROM* BARBARA

POSTSCRIPTS *by* BERT

These four letters, reprinted with Flo and Dick Crichton's permission, were written to them by Barbara. Two have postscripts from Bert. They date from 1967–69, covering a period when the Tuckers travelled in Europe, London and America. For Barbara, it was her first visit to all these places. For Bert, it was a return.

The earlier letters convey Barbara's sense of discovery. Though Bert's comments are brief, their warmth to the recipients, his implicit happiness with Barbara, his preoccupation with his work and his wonder at revisiting the ruins of Rome can be felt intensely. Once in New York, the Tuckers settled at the Chelsea Hotel for an extended stay.

The Crichtons joined them there when Dick took up his Harkness Fellowship. They were hoping they might travel through Europe, like the Tuckers, prior to arriving in New York. Parts of Barbara's letters and Bert's additions are thoughtfully concerned with the practicalities of a young family affording such an additional trip on the grant. Both are concerned about the effect on children of the high levels of pollution that they experienced, in Rome particularly.

In the event, the Crichtons went directly to New York and joined the Tuckers in the Chelsea Hotel. Brett Whiteley had also been awarded a Harkness Fellowship and knocked on the Crichtons' door, perhaps looking for the company of Australian artists. Flo remembers Whiteley noticing people moving out of the apartment above their place and promptly organising with the desk to rent it. The Whiteleys moved in to the Chelsea the following day and the two families saw a lot of each other over the next year. The Tuckers were still in residence there as well, but left to return to Australia shortly after the Whiteleys moved in.

In their second year in America, Flo and Dick moved from the Chelsea to Bridgehampton, south of New York, to give their growing children more playing space. In letter 4, Barbara writes to them there, the Tuckers having returned, ten months earlier, to Australia. ¶

At sea,
Two days
from Singapore

[Early 1967]

Dear Dick and Flo,

Have just had my first experience of the exotic East! It is an incredible place ...

Chinatown was the most fascinating place in the whole of Singapore. Two long streets or at least these were the two we saw. Seething with people, mainly Chinese, food, clothes and all sorts of goods, they kill fowls on the spot then pluck them in a vat of hot water. I have never felt less safe in my life. There were about seven of us and we were the only Europeans amongst them. Any moment I felt I may be knocked off and put in the hot vat to be plucked ... This street was called Sago Lane and is not on the usual Tourist map. The next one down was the Street of the Coffin-makers ...

The climate in Singapore at the moment is as close to unbearable as I can imagine, not so much the heat but the intense humidity. Even on board the ship for the past week it takes a whole day to dry a cotton blouse. Once you leave the air-conditioned interior of the boat, one is assailed by hot, humid, sticky air that stops you in your tracks and sends you running for the cool air inside. I have never experienced such humidity before.

We are now regretting the fact that we did not allow more time for shopping in Singapore, however we did manage to buy a smaller tape recorder which was very cheap but very good, Bert bought himself a half frame camera and I bought myself a beautiful sari and blouse—heaven knows when I will wear it, but it's worth it just to look at it. There were many other things we could have bought that were so very cheap but because of the voltage differences they would not have been of much use until we arrived back in Australia and we would have to carry them around with us, so it becomes impractical.

The longer we are on the boat the more we enjoy it. For the first week I hovered between interest and boredom, but now the time seems to go much faster. I have an hour of Italian lessons in the morning, read, sleep, read and go to the pictures, eat and talk with a few people on board whom we enjoy being with.

Our next stop will be Suez where this letter will be sent from and where we will also get off the boat for a day and travel to Cairo by car, see the Pyramids, Sphinx, Mosques, bazaars etc. on the way have dinner in Cairo, then rejoin the ship and off again. I'm feeling rather excited about it.

Pardon me but I'm beginning to sound like a bloody Fitzpatrick travelogue. Australia is now appearing to be very far away indeed and the further we go, the more it disappears from mind. This is probably just a phase and I will start feeling homesick soon. Who knows?

Please write to us soon if you have the time and energy. If you haven't got our addresses then David and Noël can give them to you.

Bert sends his love to you and the kids, as do I.

Barbara

POSTSCRIPT BY BERT TUCKER

Having a marvellous time apart from a stretch of sea sickness—most unexpected—a heavy bloody cold, paralytic boredom with the horde of inevitable nit-wits on board. Singapore fascinating, looking forward to Egypt and Cairo. I've got a bit of work done, cold's over, sea—the Arabian sea—at the moment is calm, and I can occasionally talk to the writer David Martin who is a few cabins down.

Love to you all,

Bert

C/– American Express Co.
(Too late to write
to this address)
Piazza di Spagna
Roma Italia

[Franked 31 March 1967]

Dear Dick and Flo,

In Rome and what a wonderful city. We have spent over a week exploring it and have hardly scratched the surface. It's a strange feeling to walk past or enter buildings which are 2,000 years old. It's the first really big city I've been in and Bert says London is much larger. It's hard to believe. You can spend all morning walking and still cover only a minute fraction of it. It's rather overwhelming and difficult for me to take it all in in a short period.

One aspect which is rather hair-raising is the expense. I would say for both of you and the children just for eating in the cheapest way possible on stools in a cafeteria would cost $10 a day. Double that amount if you want to sit at a table. To sit down to have a bare cup of coffee or tea costs us $1 (Aus) for one slice of cake 45 cents. So I'm afraid you will have to rethink the Europe bit. Bert turned a pale shade of green when he noticed the prices.

Another thing that worries me is the amount of gas fumes in the air. The city is choked with traffic all belching out their vile fumes which makes it hard to breath at times. Oh, for a few whiffs of Hurstbridge air. However, I'm giving the horrific side of it. It is a beautiful city to be in and the buildings are magnificent, the Romans pleasant and courteous. Shops are filled with many things that I just never see in Melbourne.

We have had to send most of our luggage on to London because of the inconvenience and expense of handling it. Just getting the luggage from the ship to the hotel in Naples, a distance of 1 mile, cost us $A11, so you must travel light.

A few days ago we went to an exhibition of sculpture by the Italian artist Manzù. It was sheer delight and I have never been so impressed by sculpture before. We also went to St Peter's, the Vatican, and for all its grandeur, famous works of art including The Pietà, it left me rather cold. Manzù's work leaves a far greater impression on me.

If you haven't got a pencil or a bit of paper let me know and I will send you some. 'Dig!' Why don't you write?

POSTSCRIPT BY BERT TUCKER

Now that the first confusions are over Rome is marvelous, better even than I remember—apart from too many cars, people and petrol fumes.

Wander around in a dream now the bed/food nonsense is organised. The ruins are out of this world, places to dream in ad infinitum. Just organised free access to galleries, museums, etc. Wish you were with us—

Love to you both

Barbara and Bert x

Paris, 4th May [1967]

Dear Flo and Dick,

Thanks for your letter. We received it when we arrived in Paris yesterday. We miss seeing you all so a letter is the next best thing. However, it shouldn't be long before we see you again.

We left Rome just over two weeks ago and since then have been to Siena, Florence, Venice, Cremona, Padua, Italian and French Rivieras and now Paris. The car we bought proved to be very good and we only had one puncture on the way over. No other troubles. We've seen so much that it is difficult to tell you all about it. That can wait until we see you.

Venice is the place that I have the fondest memories of. The beautiful old narrow streets and squares and no traffic. It really is a fairy-tale city. There we saw Peggy Guggenheim's collection of modern art. Impressive! Florence is very beautiful but the flood damage is quite extensive, whole streets were dug up trying to repair the damage. We also got caught in the midst of floods in Venice.

We are finding France more agreeable as far as people and traffic are concerned ... The French, although also prosperous, wear and do as they wish and don't give a damn what you're up to either. The difference in character is apparent immediately you cross the border.

It would be easy to spend months around the French Riviera. There we saw a new museum called the Museum Maeght. A very impressive modern structure devoted to modern art with many pieces of Giacometti's sculpture and Miro's sculpture all through the garden. I found the building more interesting than most of the painting inside. We also visited the cell where Van Gogh was kept in the Asylum at St Remy. The building is still functioning as an Asylum and there are Van Gogh landscapes everywhere you look.

Another thing that endears us to France is that we find it a lot cheaper than Italy. This came as a surprise as we had been expecting the opposite. Hotel accommodation is cheaper and the food is better and cheaper. Most important if you are here for some time ...

Although I am enjoying myself I still get waves of homesickness for the peace and comfort of Hurstbridge. You had better prepare yourselves for the same twinges although I think it is much worse when you can't speak the language of the country you're in. It's a great barrier between you and the rest of the population.

We will be leaving for London in about two weeks so this should ease the situation. My Italian is abysmal and my French non-existent. If it wasn't for Bert, I would be lost.

Hope you find someone for your house soon. Give our love to the kids and tell them we'll see them soon. Write again with the latest news.

Love to you all,

Barbara and Bert

Haleys Gully Road
Hurstbridge,
Victoria 3099
Australia

January 10th [1969]

Dear Flo and Dick,

Sorry to take so long replying to your letter but we have had one hell of a year. One week after our return from overseas last year [1968], David and Noël separated and we have been looking after Neil [their son] ever since ... It has been very hard on the kids ... All this seems to have happened one hundred years ago instead of less than a year ...

We also went through a couple of months of having builders walking in and out of the place. We have had two large rooms added to our house at the back. A big bedroom with another bathroom adjacent and a walk-in-wardrobe and a new large studio for Bert on top of that. We seem to have staircases going in all directions but actually it comes together rather well and we are very happy with the results.

The garden is really looking marvellous and we were thrilled to see how much the trees had grown in our absence, although after the last couple of days we were lucky to have any garden or house left. I mean the bushfires which you may or may not have read about. They didn't come near our place but the wind was ferocious, they probably would have if it had lasted long enough. The worst area around here was Diamond Creek–Research–Warrandyte. The electricity was off here all day so we didn't have a radio to hear where they were. All we saw were clouds of black smoke with an eerie orange light of the sun shining through. 101 degrees with a 60 mile an hour wind. It sounded like an express train coming over the hill. Your area was also ok, it was more towards Research. Another dangerous fire day is expected tomorrow with high temperatures and winds—but at least they know it's coming and everyone is on the alert. Forty houses burnt in Diamond Creek alone and many areas are just charcoal.

I drove past your place a few months ago to see if all was well—everything seemed in order except that the weeds were a bit high. This was probably due to the tremendous amount of growth we have had everywhere after much rain last year which must have been by way of compensation after the drought. It's probably all lawn by now; I will try to have another look before we leave.

Your place in Bridgehampton sounds great. Do you prefer it to living in New York? I'm sure it's much better for the kids as they have much more room to play.

Thanks very much for the Village Voices. We enjoyed reading them and realized how much I had forgotten of the crazy, mad world of New York after living in the seclusion of Hurstbridge for the last ten months.

We are leaving Australia once again in ten days time and should be in New York some time in March and I really don't know how I will react to it again. We will be in Mexico for a while and we hope to see a lot more of it this time. The ten days we spent there last year was just an appetizer.

Hope you are all well and we will write to you when we arrive in New York.

Love to all,

Barbara and Bert

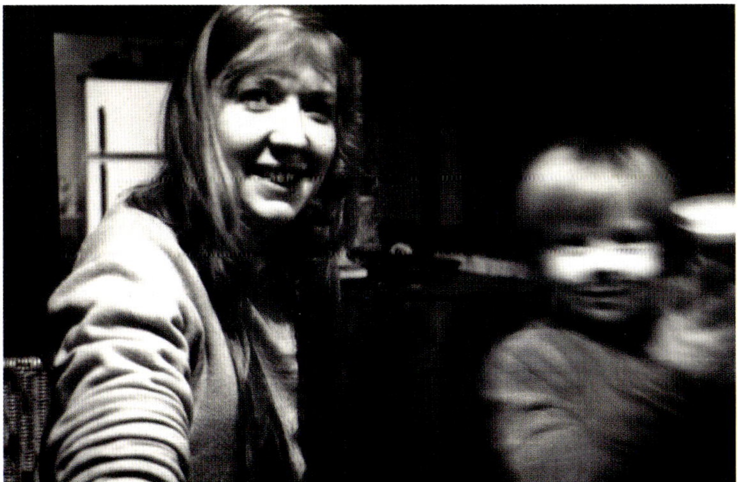

BARBARA TUCKER WITH NEIL BILCOCK C. 1964
Photo attributed to Albert Tucker

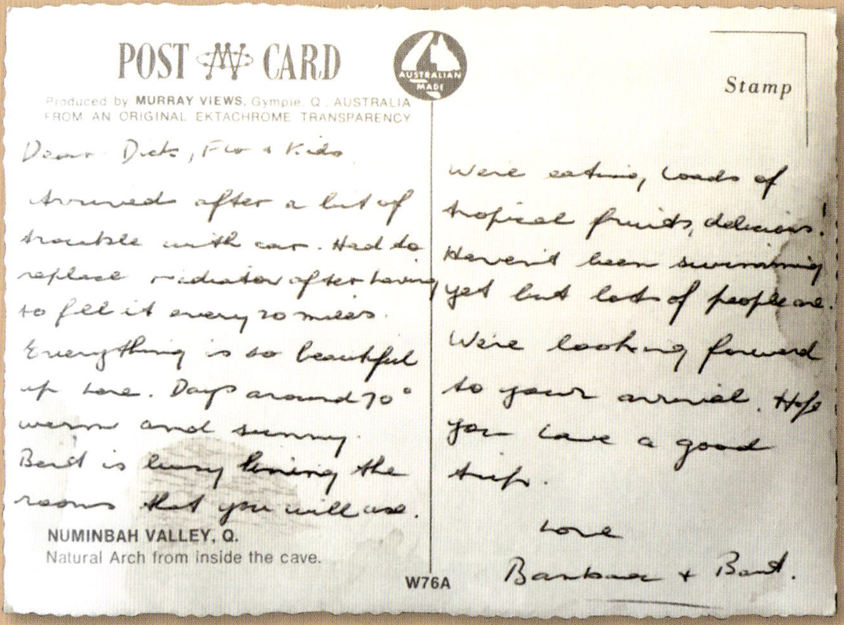
POST CARD

Produced by MURRAY VIEWS, Gympie, Q., AUSTRALIA
FROM AN ORIGINAL EKTACHROME TRANSPARENCY

AUSTRALIAN MADE

Stamp

Dear Dick, Flo & Kids

Arrived after a lot of trouble with car. Had to replace radiator after having to fill it every 20 miles. Everything is so beautiful up here. Days around 70° warm and sunny. Bert is busy fixing the rooms that you will use.

We're eating loads of tropical fruits, delicious! Haven't been swimming yet but lots of people are. We're looking forward to your arrival. Hope you have a good trip.

Love

Barbara & Bert.

NUMINBAH VALLEY, Q.
Natural Arch from inside the cave.

W76A

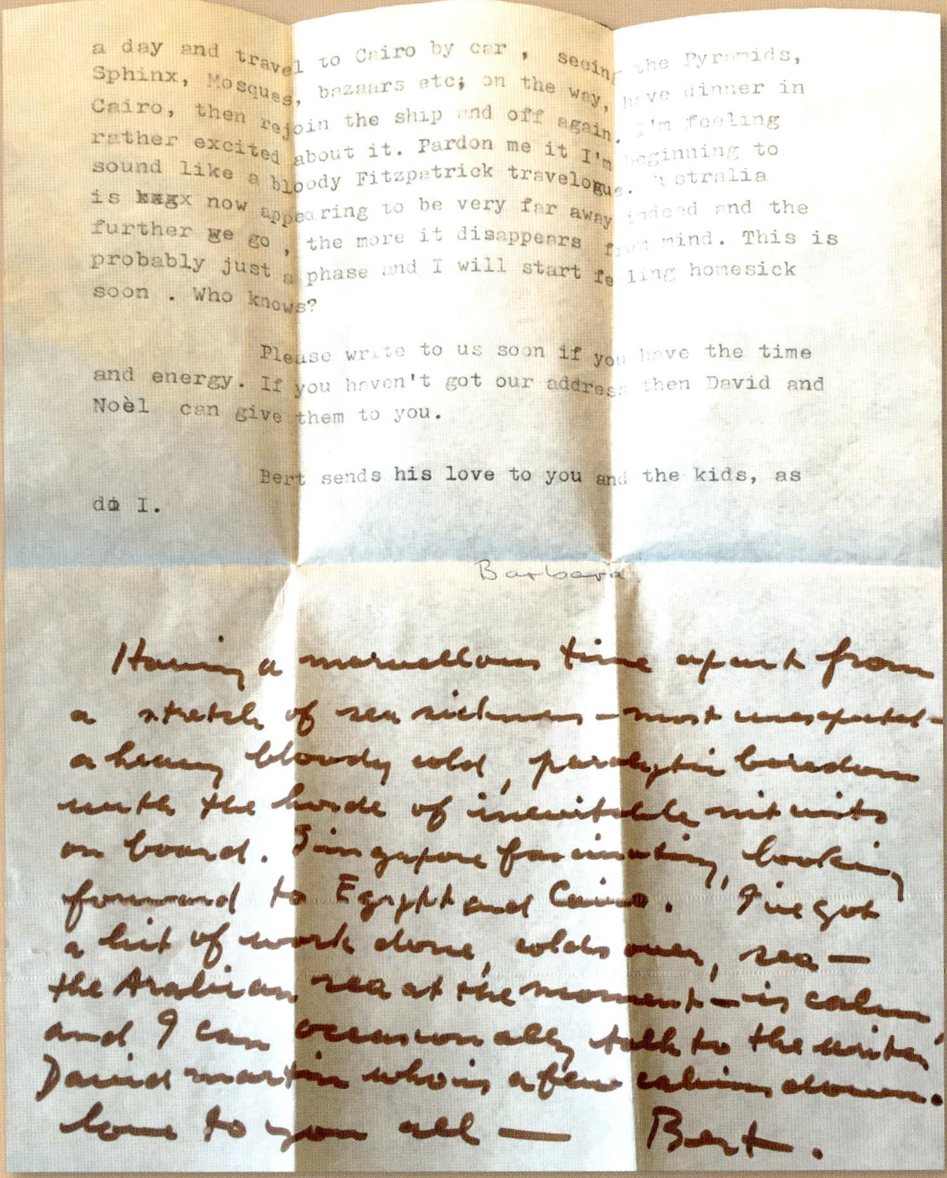

a day and travel to Cairo by car , seeing the Pyramids, Sphinx, Mosques, bazaars etc; on the way, have dinner in Cairo, then rejoin the ship and off again. I'm feeling rather excited about it. Pardon me it I'm beginning to sound like a bloody Fitzpatrick travelogue. Australia is ~~kagx~~ now appearing to be very far away indeed and the further ~~g~~we go , the more it disappears from mind. This is probably just a phase and I will start feeling homesick soon . Who knows?

Please write to us soon if you have the time and energy. If you haven't got our address then David and Noèl can give them to you.

Bert sends his love to you and the kids, as do I.

Barbara.

Having a marvellous time apart from
a stretch of sea sickness – most unexpected –
a heavy bloody cold, paralytic boredom
with the horde of inevitable nit wits
on board. Singapore fascinating, looking
forward to Egypt and Cairo. I've got
a bit of work done, which over, sea –
the Arabian sea at the moment – is calm
and I can occasionally talk to the writer
David Martin who is a few cabins down.
Love to you all — Bert.

III

THE ART OF FAMILY

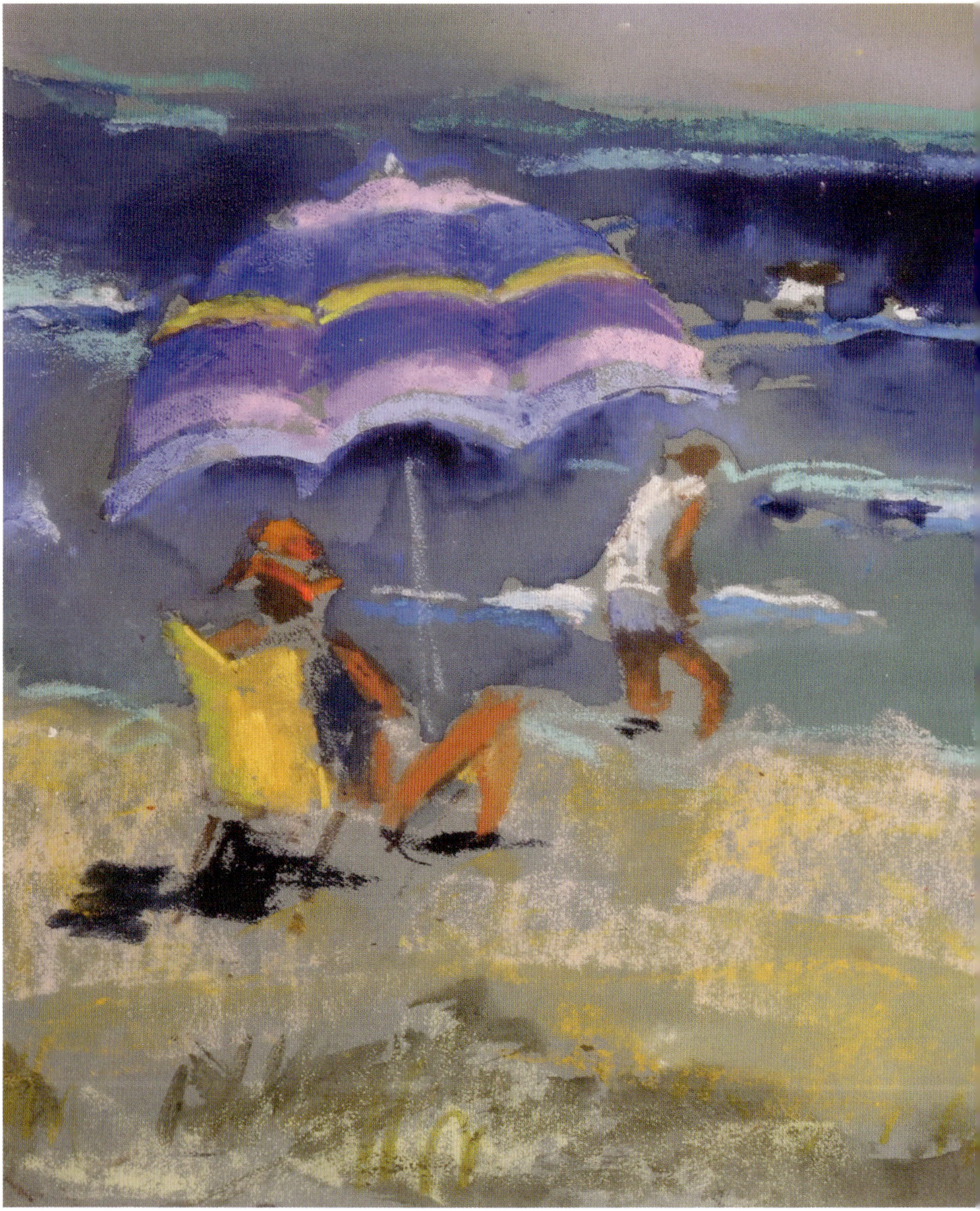

ALBERT TUCKER
ASPENDALE *1984*
WATERCOLOUR AND CRAYON ON PAPER
33 × 55.5 CM
PRIVATE COLLECTION

COURTESY SMITH & SINGER FINE ART

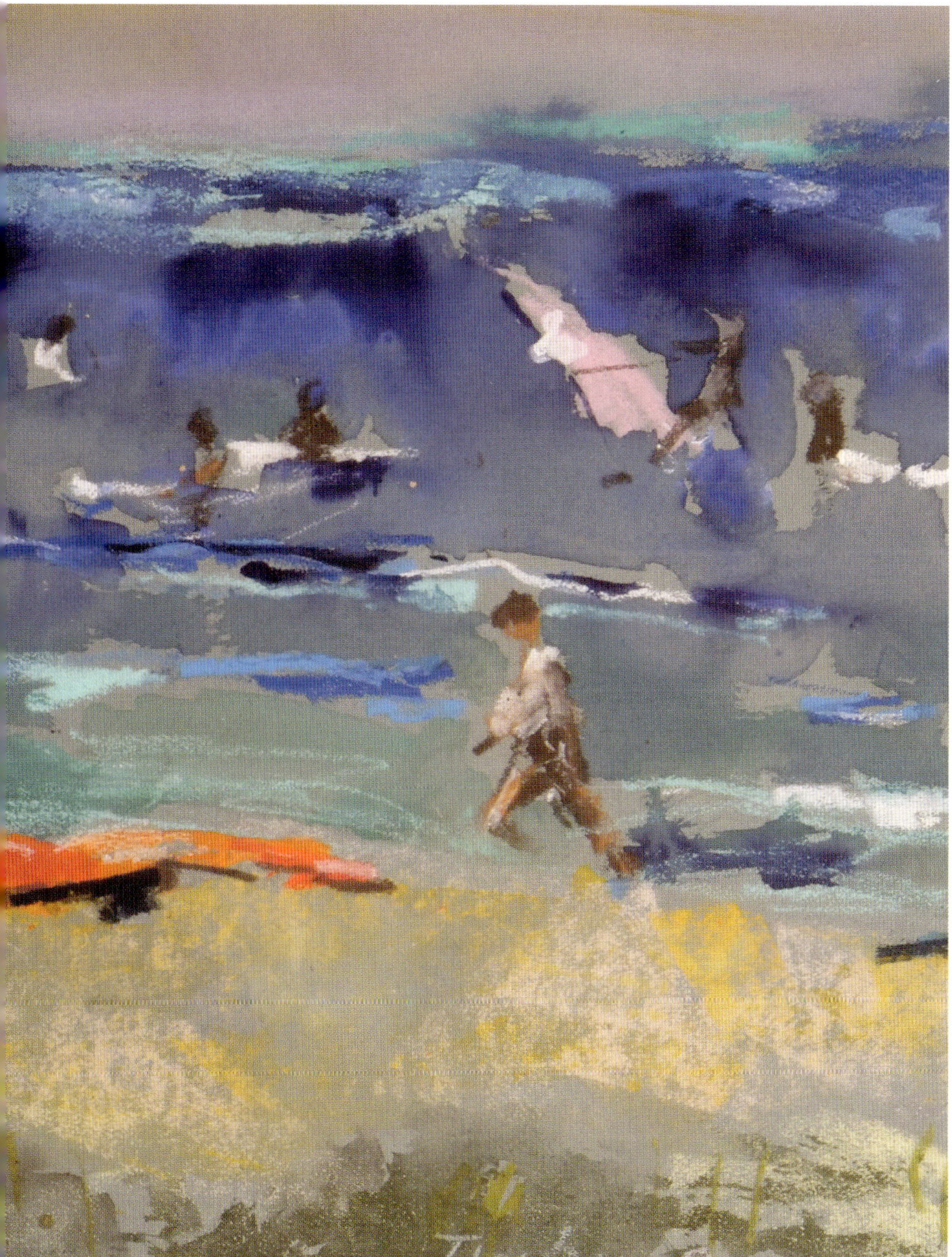

MY AUNT BARBARA

DARREN JONES

When I was twelve years old, my aunt Barbara—always Babs to me—gave me a birthday gift of three-dimensional noughts and crosses. There were three levels of clear Perspex with nine holes on each level and coloured marbles to replace the noughts and crosses. Babs had one herself. I think she treasured it almost as much as I did. I know this because she never lost any marbles, not a single one ... and they're easy to lose. The magic of this game, Babs told me, was that it taught you to look at problems from all angles, something that I later learned was her special area of expertise. It remains for me a most potent symbol of my aunt's ability to separate the wheat from the chaff. She had a special knack for cutting through the layers of a problem to its absolute core.

Like her sister, my mother Joan, Barbara was a stunning beauty, but a bit younger—and in my mind so much wilder—than Mum. She was the bohemian, wild, daring, red-head hippy auntie that liked to push the boundaries and take risks—like bathing topless at family Christmas parties. Very impressive in the eyes of a twelve-year-old boy!

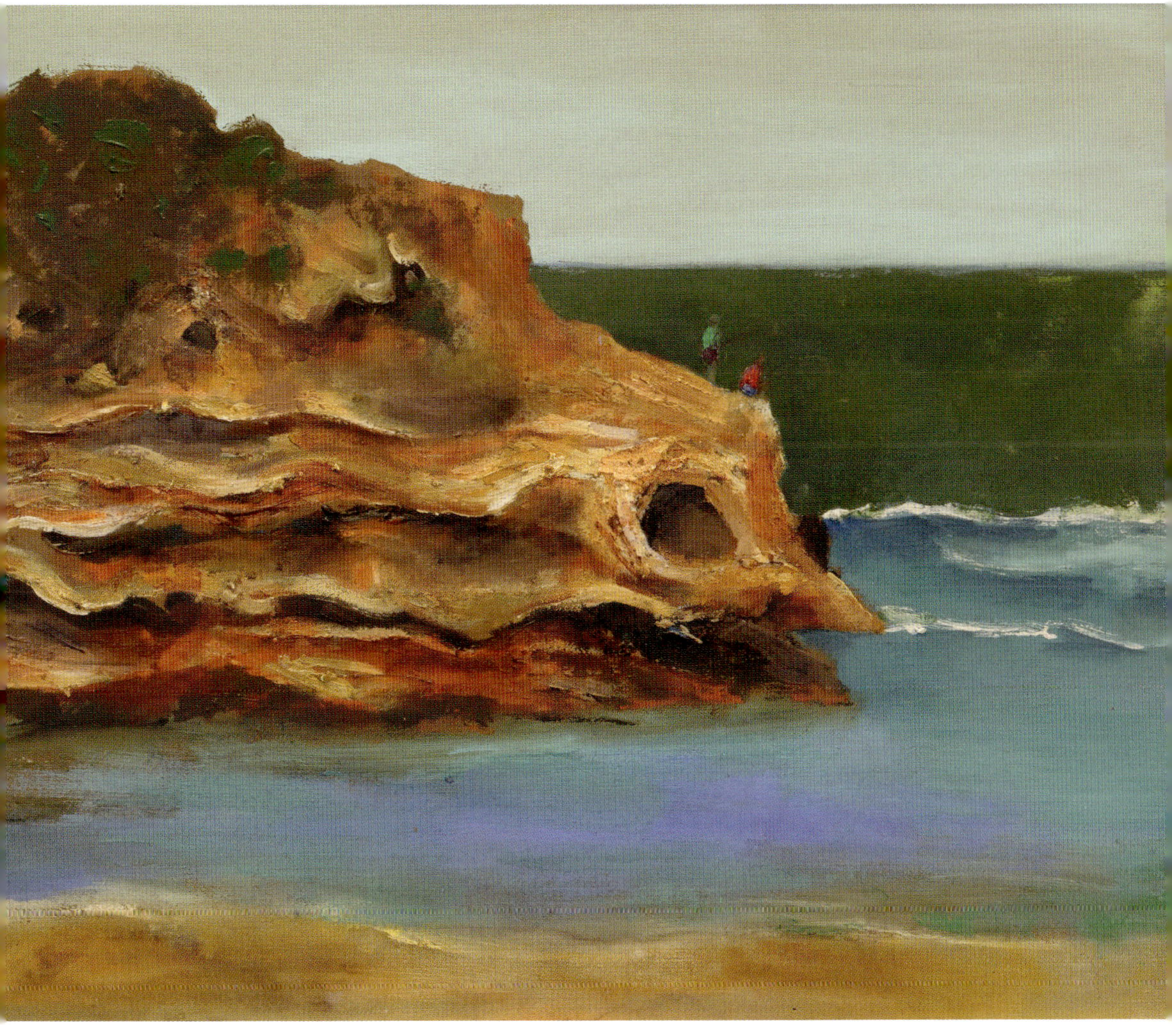

ALBERT TUCKER
BLAIRGOWRIE HEADLAND *1982*
SYNTHETIC POLYMER PAINT
AND WATERCOLOUR ON CARDBOARD
38.7 × 49.8 CM
PRIVATE COLLECTION
© ALBERT & BARBARA TUCKER FOUNDATION
COURTESY SMITH & SINGER FINE ART

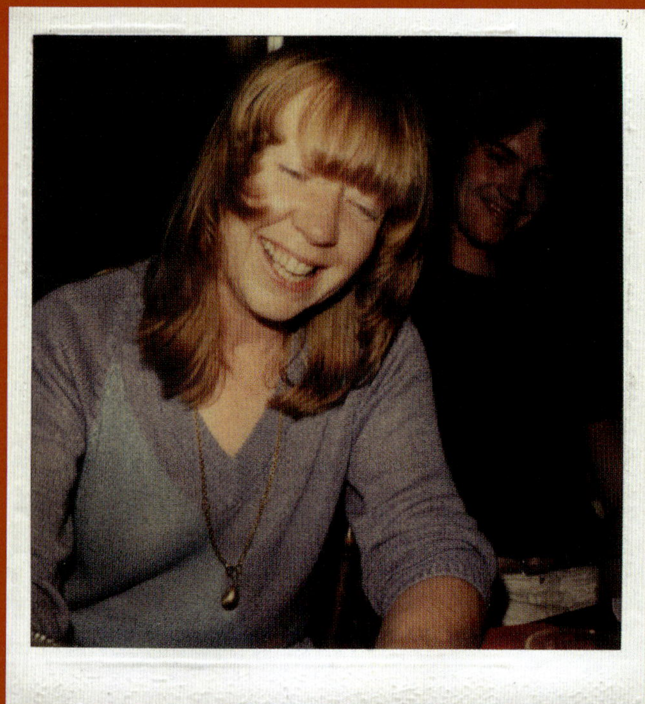

BARBARA TUCKER AND DARREN JONES 1982
Photo by Albert Tucker

Through my formative years Barbara and Bert made a huge impression on me. For a while, they were the coolest people I'd ever met. Maybe they still are. Barbara never chose to act the way she was expected to. In fact, I think she prided herself on doing quite the opposite. She possessed a flexible and astute mind coupled with a bubbly and relaxed demeanor—but, of course, she also possessed the legendary Bilcock intuition. Passionate about the written word and knowledge of all sorts, she never stopped learning and never stopped teaching, often in the most unexpected, remarkable and, dare I say, even mystical ways.

Late in 2014, Barbara said to me: 'If anything should happen to me, Darren—if I die for instance, please don't worry. I'll be all right. I've had a wonderful life.' Two years earlier, she had asked me if I would help manage affairs with the estate. I accepted the invitation as an absolute privilege and an honour. Looking back, I really had no idea what I was getting into. As Lesley Harding pointed out, I'd been fast tracked into the art world.

It didn't take long for me to comprehend just how much effort Barbara had been contributing to managing Bert's affairs since his passing in 1999. She remained totally committed to their joint vision for the future while carefully maintaining the integrity and legacy of one of our greatest artists.

Managing the myriad of relationships and governance issues required to do this is no easy task. It requires constant surveillance and diligence. In the face of frequent adversity Barbara handled herself with grace, dignity and charm. Problems were always faced head on with zealous enthusiasm.

I hope my presence and support managed to lift some of the pressure from her during the past couple of years. We had a lot of laughs and a lot of fun. Beyond all, I feel it was a great opportunity for us to spend time together. She taught me so much for which I am eternally grateful. We were not only aunt and nephew, but good friends. My dear sister Caitlin was also a critical support during this period for Barbara, myself and for the management of the estate.

Barbara's death on 16 May 2015 was the end of an era for our family. About that there is no doubt. But of course, this also heralded a time for new beginnings. Caitlin and I have been bestowed with the most incredible privilege of directing the Tucker estate into the future. We are committed to remaining faithful to Barbara and Bert's visions for that future. This vision includes exciting opportunities to help support many worthwhile charitable organisations.

We would like to acknowledge all Barbara's close friends who offered her and our family such wonderful big-hearted support during the difficult time of Barbara's illness and death. I'd like to mention in particular Margaret Johnston, Harry and Jill Redner, Hazel Anderson, Patricia Walker and Justin O'Brien.

While we stand here at Heide on the occasion of the memorial service for Barbara, we would like to acknowledge that recognition should go to Heide for the great work they have done over the years supporting Barbara and the estate. In particular, we want to express our appreciation of the work of Lesley Alway, Lesley Harding, Kendra Morgan, Warwick Reeder, Ted Gott, Katarina Paseta, Jason Smith and, more recently, Kirsty Grant.

Sotheby's Australia should also be mentioned. Gary Singer and Geoffrey Smith have given wonderful support to Barbara over the years and their contribution to the ongoing welfare of the Tucker estate today is valued.

Last, but not least, we would like to acknowledge Dr Gerard Vaughn and Dr Deborah Hart from the National Gallery of Australia, for their past and present engagement with Barbara Tucker and the important, wonderful and intriguing work of Albert Tucker. We sincerely look forward to continuing and further developing the important relationships that Barbara and Bert built around themselves and the estate.

The gallery we are standing in here at Heide, and the work we see all around us, bears testament to the forward vision of Bert and Barbara, their sense of community and the spirit of giving. These are all qualities that we as directors of their legacy will honour and embrace. ¶

This tribute was offered at Barbara Tucker's Memorial Service at Heidi.

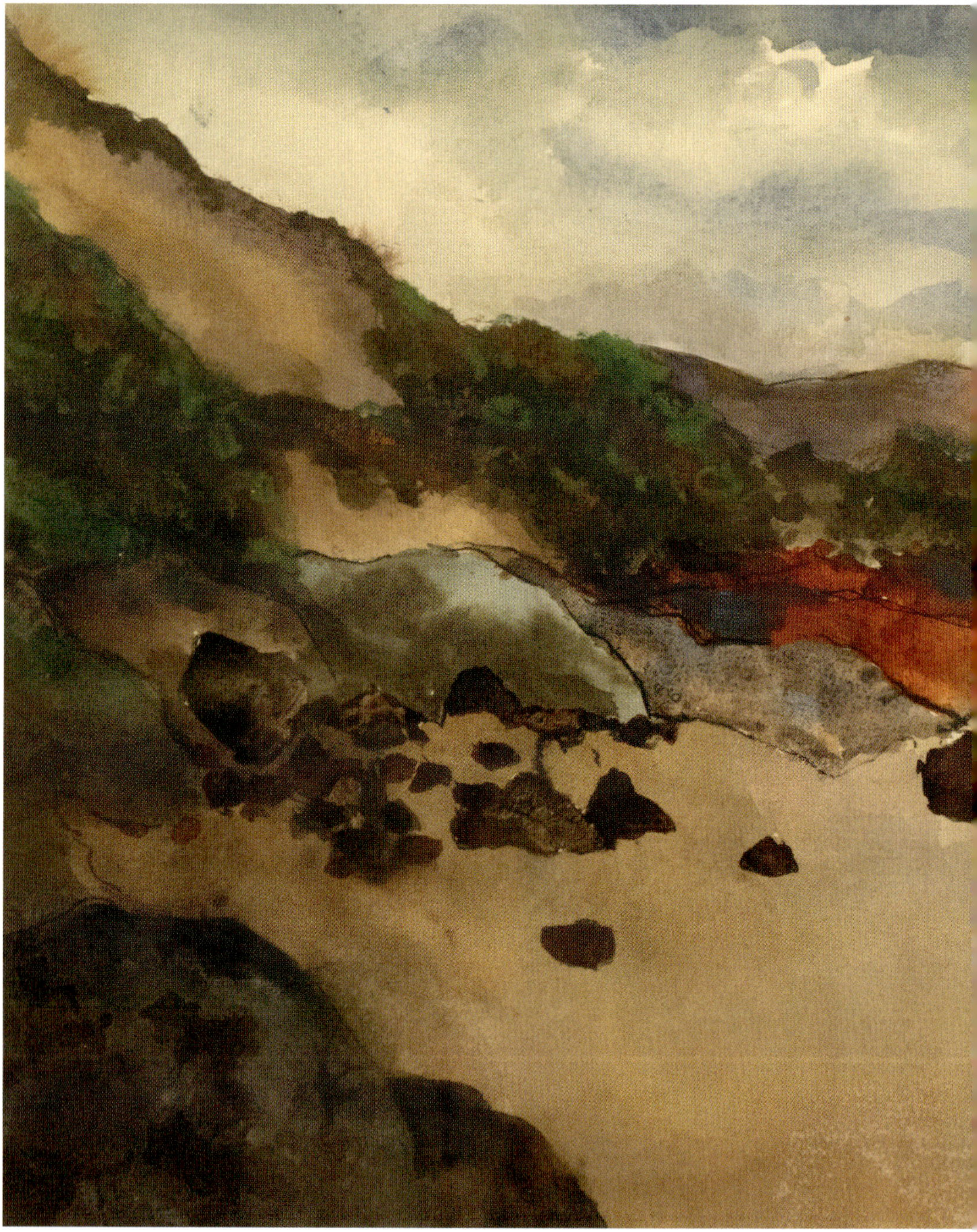

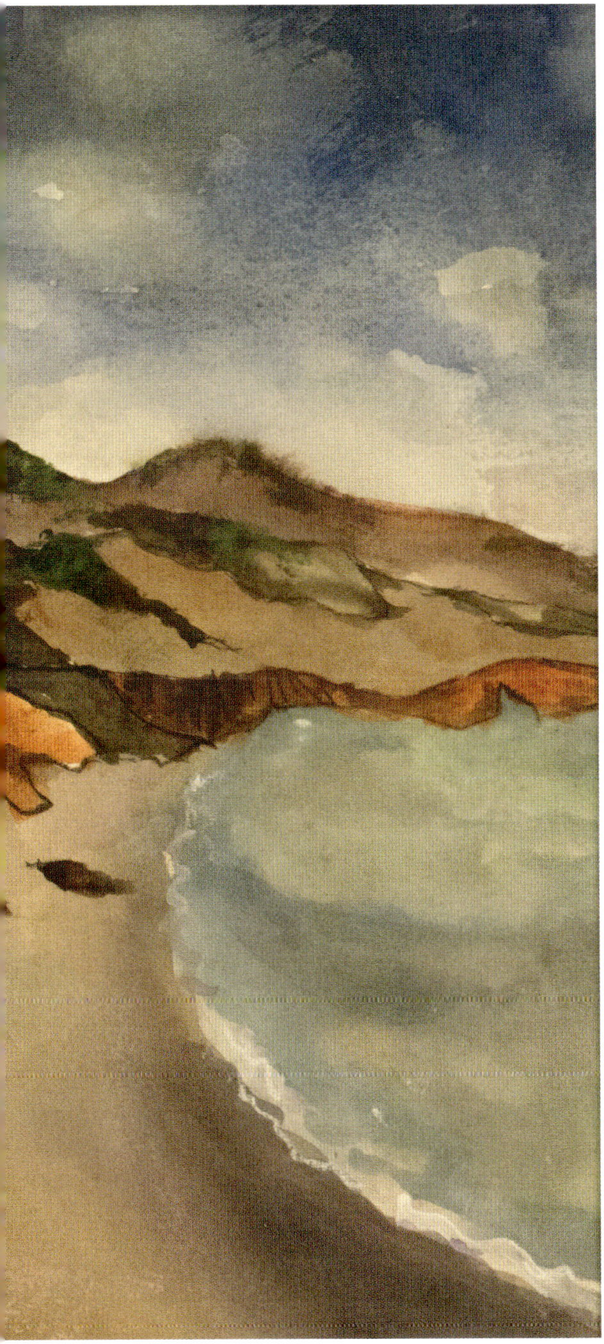

ALBERT TUCKER
BLAIRGOWRIE *1974*
WATERCOLOUR ON PAPER
28.7 × 37.6 CM
PRIVATE COLLECTION
© ALBERT & BARBARA TUCKER FOUNDATION
COURTESY SMITH & SINGER FINE ART

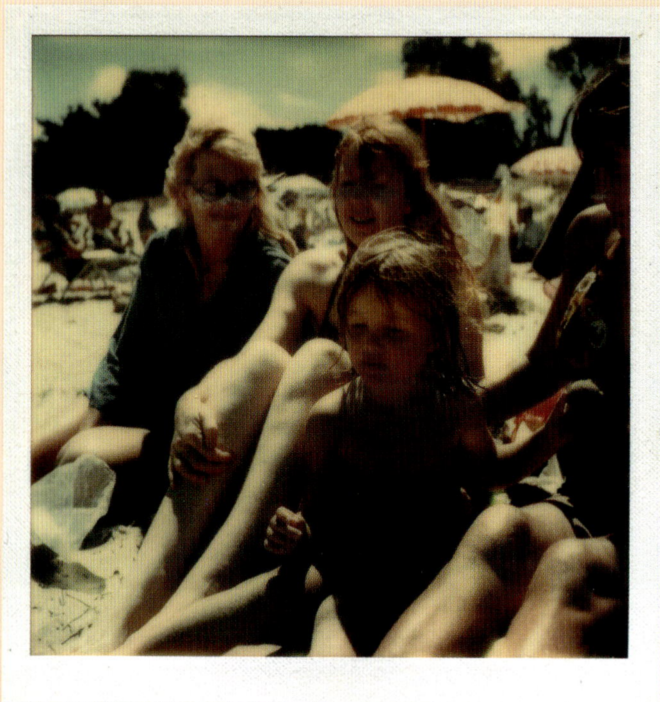

LINDA BILCOCK, BARBARA TUCKER, CAITLIN JONES AND JOAN JONES 1973
Photo by Albert Tucker

MY SIREN AUNT

CAITLIN GRAHAM-JONES

When I think of Barbara, I do not see her as older, or frail, or at the end of life.

I see her long red hair, charged with life. She is wearing a batik sarong, pink thongs, and we are walking towards her favourite rockpool at the back beach at Blairgowrie. None of the majesty of the environment goes unappreciated as she exclaims and drinks in the calm turquoise blue of the pool, the crashing wildness of the distant breakers.

Once in the water Barbara swims slow. She is immersed in the water element and to my young eyes she is my 'siren aunt'. It would not be such a stretch to imagine an aquamarine tail trailing behind her. I too swim slow. I follow her and gaze down at our white shimmering legs treading water beneath us. It feels good to swim slow, to take in this life, the moment, the elements.

Swim slow, take in life, experience the elements. Barbara embodied these qualities.

Not long before she died, I took Barbara to her favourite cafe in Balaclava. They make really beautiful pastries and when we sat down, Barbara asked if I would mind if she did not use a knife and fork. 'Not at all,' I replied, wondering if there was some unseen physical issue that was making holding utensils difficult. 'I just love the feel of food in my hands,' she said. So while I prudishly used my metal knife and fork, Barbara experienced her pie in an altogether different manner, making a wonderful crumby mess and covering her clothes in buttery heaven.

Like Barbara, I married an artist. I know that I have an incredible internal reference in Barbara for how to live with and support artistic endeavour. From her (and my mother) I have also learnt the importance of having a fiercely independent streak—that we can be strong, adventurous, wild women who are unafraid to put the kettle on for the men we love—being me, and loving you.

Somehow, Barbara managed to keep this hold on her freedom and also to have amazing stewardship over Bert's legacy after he died. She never did this in an ego-based way, to be seen as 'the artist's wife', but rather with a kind of love-based loyalty that never faltered. I can only imagine that at times this was a difficult role for my aunt, who may well have preferred to be swimming in a rockpool than facing up to formal events. But she did it always with the right touch: not too tight, not too loose. ¶

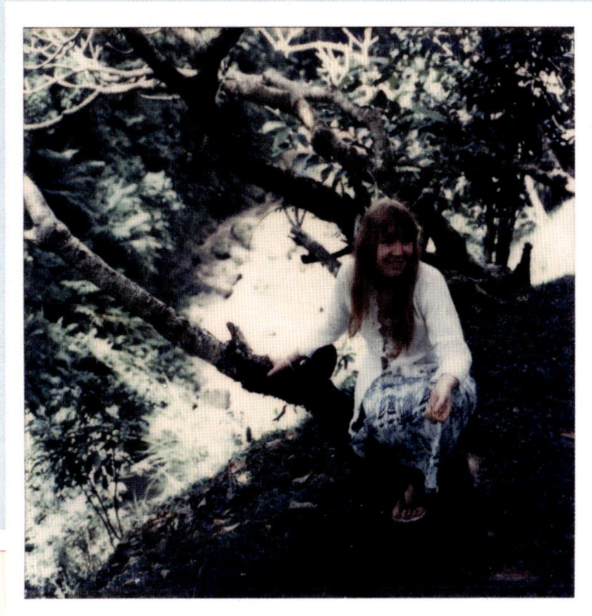

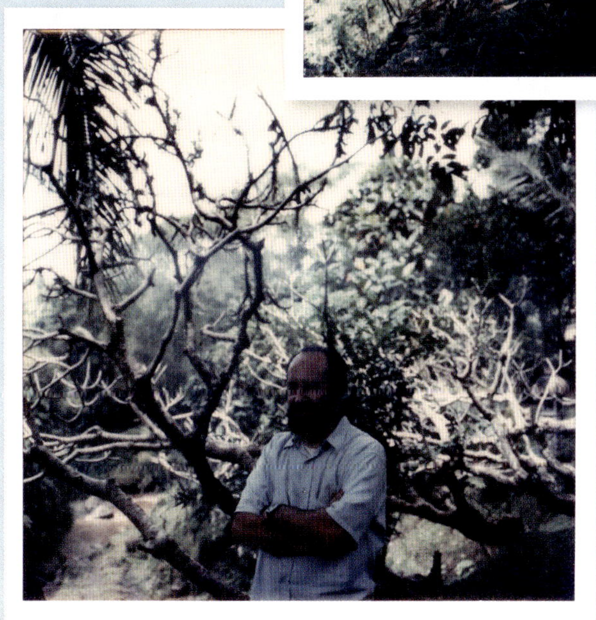

BARBARA AND ALBERT TUCKER AT BLAIRGOWRIE 1979
Photos by Albert Tucker and Barbara Tucker

FRAGMENTS *OF* BARBARA

A BROTHER REMEMBERS

PETER BILCOCK

My first memory of Barbara is of her riding her bike to church—well, actually of the girls, my sisters—to the Catholic church in Croydon, a country town, very much just country on the outskirts of Melbourne at that time. My father eventually put me in the Catholic school there. He left home when I was about ten. He was a non-religious man, didn't come from a religious background, but he put me in that school. It was a strange choice. I resented it, resent it still, because Catholic schools in the 1950s—the nuns—the things they did then would be highly illegal, unheard of, now. Barbara was probably in her late teens when my father left.

My first memory of Barbara apart from her riding her bike was her first job, which was a receptionist at a real estate agent. You walked in off the street and you were in her office. That was the only conventional Barbara I remember, because it was going in another direction from then on.

Barbara was always her own person. Even though we were a family unit, quite close, really, it was my other two sisters Joan and Linda who were together a lot, whereas Barbara in a strange way was a separate entity, which is what she turned out to be anyway. She always had separateness about her. There was part of her that was somewhere else, in her thinking.

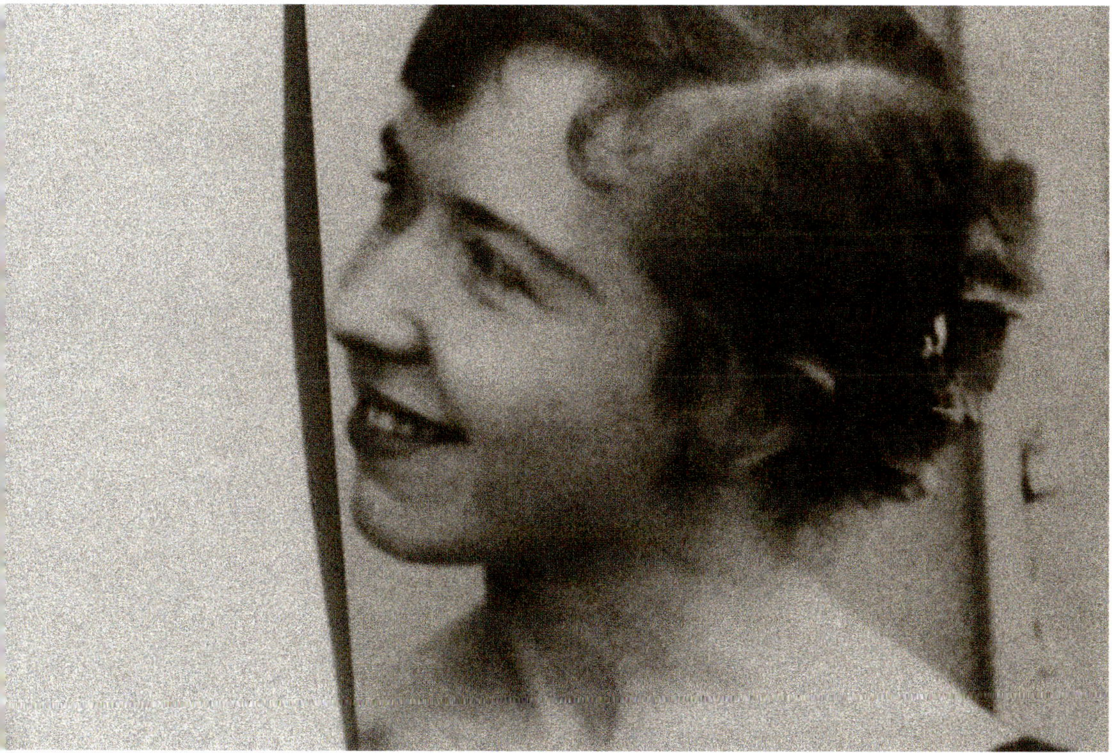

THE YOUNG BARBARA TUCKER Photo by David Bilcock Snr

I think the 1950s have been described as a kind of 'Laminex prison', which they were. I remember Barbara bringing the man who became her first husband home to meet the family. He was a very good-looking devil-may-care type. He had an irreverent, cynical amusement about convention and the mundane. And he fascinated me. He was the most exciting person I'd met—because someone like that, in the 50s—it was like meeting an alien.

I think he appealed to Barbara because she found in him something that was in her. She shunned convention and the 'proper' life of the 50s. Her bloke was a breath of fresh air to me. But the rest of the family did not approve at all, of him or of the marriage. They found him very 'improper', if you know what I mean. The only thing I knew he did was put up tents for the army for a living, which was a strange sort of job. He didn't have a 'proper job' as I recall. Very flighty, in a way, certainly not an office type content with regularity and routine. I don't know how Barbara met him, perhaps through friends. I remember Barbara leaving home around that time, I think. She spent a great deal of time living at the Boyds' place in Murrumbeena, 'Open Country'. Whether that was before or after the marriage, I'm not sure. The marriage didn't last all that long.

I remember an episode that Barbara told me. She and her husband were coming back from a fishing trip down at Foster, Fish Creek, in Gippsland. He drove this old Delage, which is a French luxury six-cylinder car. But it was an old bomb of a thing, really. I remember her saying that they broke down somewhere—well, actually, they ran out of petrol in some country town. They had no money for food or petrol and Barbara remembers that quite vividly. I remember Barbara telling me that, in a kind of 'Scarlett O'Hara moment', she made a pledge to herself that she would never go without cash again, that she would never be broke again.

I think that had a big effect on her because she was very determined to 'make a go' of it. You see this in people who have been through the Depression. They're very conscious of the value of a dollar, even today. I think that episode really affected Barbara. That bohemian lifestyle was exciting but she saw you still needed comforts and cash.
I don't remember her breaking up with that first husband, but this moment was part of it, I think.

You've got to take care of the practical to be able to take care of the creative. To have no cash—that's one of the worst things we've all been through. But there was one good thing about that first husband. He introduced her to classical music, which she had a love of ever since, and Barbara passed it on to me. So something good came out of that.

Not long before that marriage, Barbara had started bringing home all these people—bohemians, I suppose you'd call them—painters, sculptors. I remember a couple of them were shabbily dressed and they had big bushy beards, unkempt, quite extraordinary in the clean-cut 1950s. I'd never seen men quite like this and they were pretty unwashed. I remember sitting there and thinking how they smelled! But Barbara was looking for that world, introducing herself to the bohemian world. She brought home quite a few men and women like that, but they were all of the same mould—anti-establishment, anti-conventional.

All of my three sisters were determined and strong in character, but Barbara was strong in very particular ways.
I remember a time that the three girls went camping down at Anglesea. They arrived there late and they only managed to put up this army hammock, an enclosed, jungle-type hammock. Anyway, it was a rainy night. Guess who slept in the hammock and the other two girls, including the oldest sister, had to sit underneath it—Barbara slept in it, of course.

Joan was the oldest in our family; Barbara and Linda next, then David. I was the youngest. There was another girl, another daughter, but she died at a few months old, I think. It was before my time.

There's a photo of Barbara I love, one of her in a loose, Indian-print dress. She's in a garden with dappled light falling on her face, her dress and her long hair.

Barbara had a rare combination of spirituality and practicality that you feel even in this photo. It's the photo I have on my wall in a row with pictures of the family: Joan when young, Linda when she was older, one of David not so long before his death, and an old grainy photo of my mother and father when they were young. It's a good row of photos to look at each day as I drink my tea at the table.

My sisters thought I made a good cup of tea. I remember when I was quite young walking down the hall in the family house in bare feet with the sound of the family still sleeping. I remember the sound of my sisters' voices, Barbara's voice, floating out into the hallway, 'Peter makes such a good cup of tea. He makes the best tea.' So of course, I made tea for my sisters and took it to them still sleepy in their beds. It makes me smile to think of that. That was my first awareness of 'feminine wiles', I think.

Bert just appeared one day. He had a beard and he was smoking at that stage. He was quite charming, and I found him fascinating. You know, I always did. I remember Bert said he fell in love with Barbara's hair. It was the first thing he noticed about her. And this was very soon after the end of her first marriage. How soon after I don't know, but quite soon. Whether they met through mutual friends or at the Boyds' house—it might have been there.

But Bert was just suddenly there—in Barbara's life. I think she found with Bert what meant most to her—

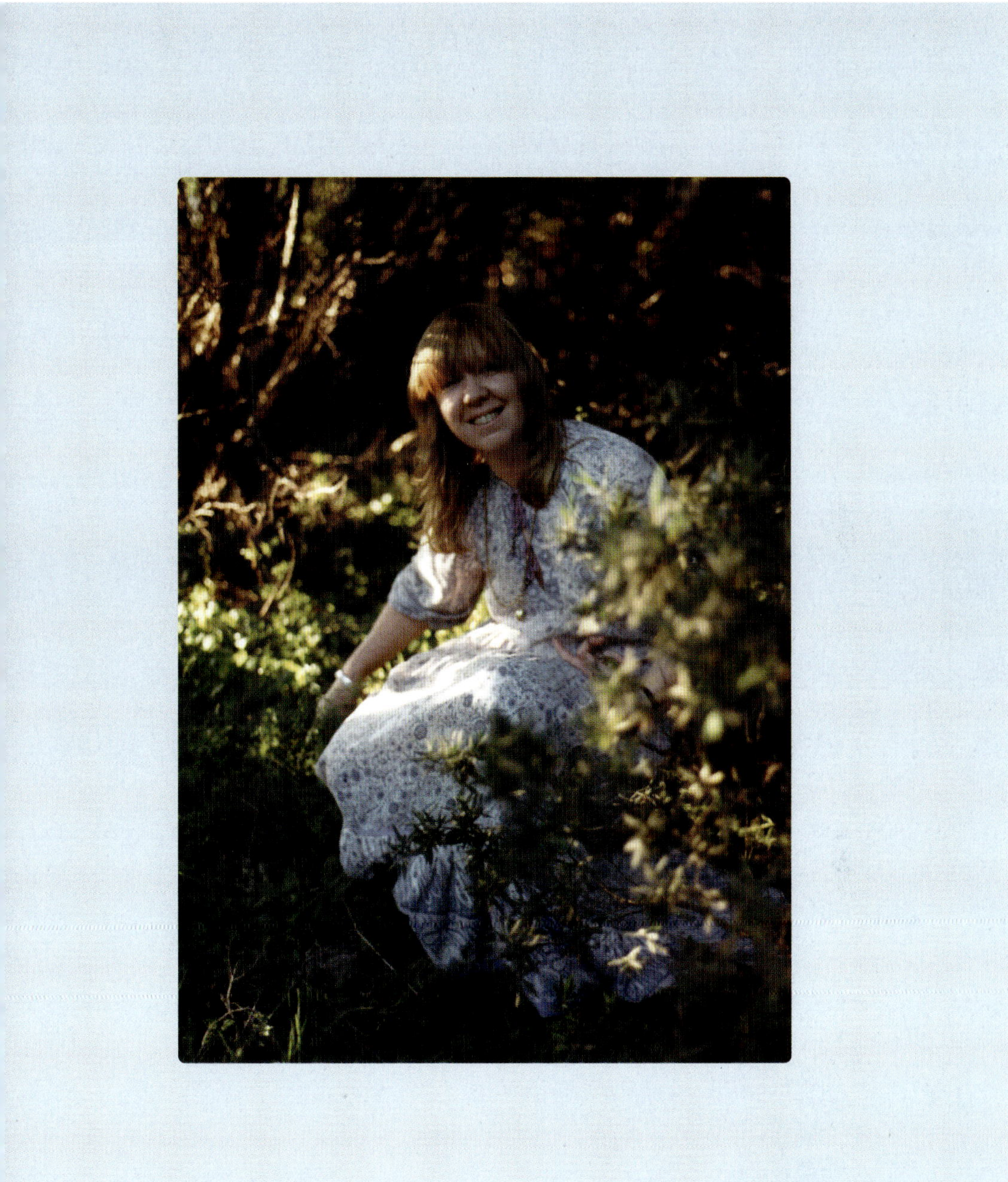

BARBARA TUCKER C. 1979
Photo by Albert Tucker

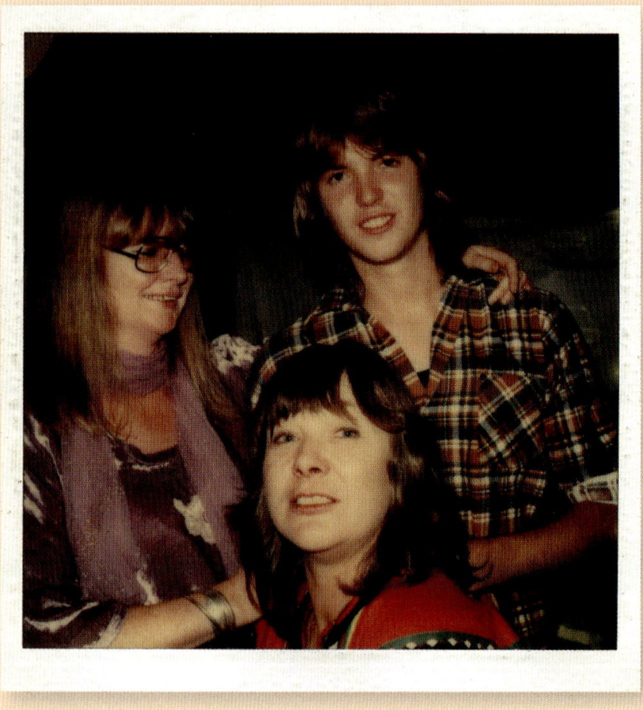

DARREN JONES WITH BARBARA'S SISTERS JOAN AND LINDA
Photo by Albert Tucker

artistic freedom with security, the two worlds together. But everything else that went before that was a very valuable learning curve for her.

Of the three girls, Barbara was the most volatile. Later she was capable of being serene, she was mainly serene—but I'm going back earlier. I took Barbara's bike for a ride once and it had flat tyres—I think I ruined her tyres. I got found out and I got the biggest hiding of my life. I remember this red blur of fury, hair going everywhere. It was very frightening. My father was very similar. He had an explosive temper and gave me a few to go on with in my life—hidings, that is. Joan and Linda were much the opposite in that they were very calm. I only found out later that St Barbara is the patron saint of explosions, and I thought yes, that fits well. But even to this day she could still have a temper but it was very rare—it was mainly her calmness and the spirituality side that you saw. The explosions—she always said that she felt guilty—that she'd broken her own beliefs by losing her temper.

She had the most infectious laugh and a very quirky sense of humour. Barbara and I both shared it. She had this high-pitched sound—not a scream—when she was telling a funny story. It was very infectious. And such a warm voice. Her 'hello' was so welcoming, she was pleased to see you and gave a very soft, gentle welcome.

She was also the most generous person I've ever met—very, very generous to people. It was remarkable, how generous. Going back to the earlier days, being without money, without cash—we all experienced that because we were a poor family, very poor. It affected us all. Even in later years when she had plenty of money and the bookshop and everything, Barbara would still look for a bargain. She'd learned the value of money, knew its value, especially because she knew what it was like to be without it. But though she could be careful because of those early years, she was also so capable of enormous generosity—and generous to many people. I used to water her garden for her down here at Blairgowrie and she had the cheapest nastiest little hose fittings and I said to her, 'Barbara, you've got all this money and you still buy these cheap fittings. It's false economy. What are you doing? The quality remains long after the price is forgotten.' But I don't know—why did she do it? I think those early years affected us all.

The Blairgowrie house at Munro Street was a little three-bedroom place tucked away amongst the ti-trees. Barbara loved being near the ocean and to be able to get away—to get away to that solitude, cut off from her normal activities. It was an escape, in a way, a sanctuary. She loved her own company, but she was generous with invitations for family and friends to stay, too. And Bert went down, too. He took wonderful photos of her.

I quite often went there to stay for a couple of days. I know friends stayed with her there, too. Later she had a place built on the next block—a similar design and everything, but just a bit bigger. She lent the Munro Street place to a Melbourne writer, Micheal Keon. Barbara used the larger one, often just herself but sometimes with friends.

Barbara spent a lot of time down the back beach, exploring those Sorrento rockpools. She had a windsurfer—she could stand on it for about five seconds before she fell off. It made me laugh. But she kept trying it and trying it, you know. There's a photo of her standing up on it—it was a very quick photo, I think. I tried the thing—and I lasted less time. It was important for Barbara to get down there.

She had another place at Christmas Hills for a while as a holiday place, which might have been a big part of why they

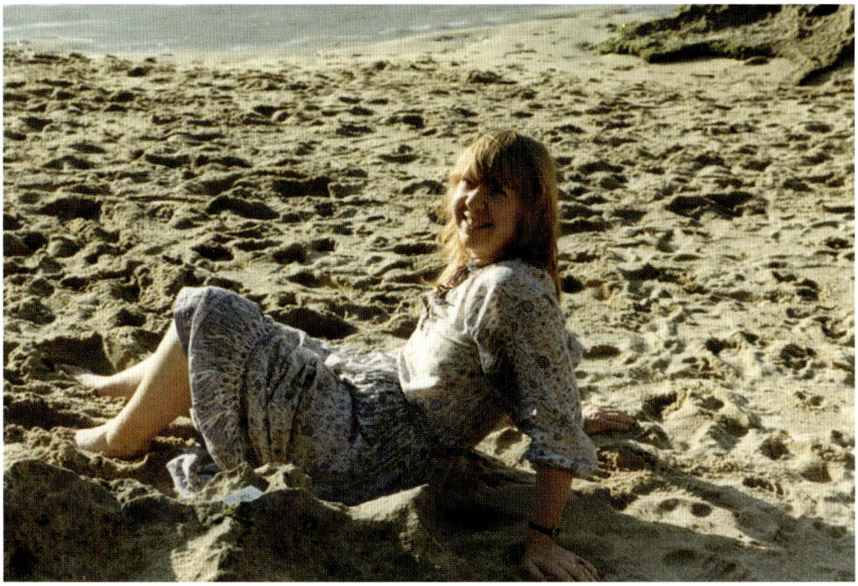

BARBARA TUCKER, BLAIRGOWRIE C. 1979
Photo by Albert Tucker

went to Hoddles Creek after the episode of the theft of Bert's art—that was an episode. I got caught up in that. I remember Barbara telling me that it appeared that the defence lawyers were going to try and hang the theft on us—Barbara and me. I had to go to court and was put through all these questions about how often I'd been in Bert's studio and I said just a couple of times, not often. They had nothing to go on. But I had the police and everything. Two detectives came down to Tootgarook. They were distressing times and a complete betrayal of Bert and Barbara's trust.

Bert's studio and the paintings were off-limits. Barbara was very aware of his creative process. Barbara warned all our relations, 'Don't talk to Bert about his painting.' She warned everyone early on not to, so you had to think before you spoke to Bert. Barbara was very protective of him and the art. I never discussed or asked Bert about his painting, never. Mind you, I wouldn't have known what to ask him anyway. But now and again I'd go and help physically move things if he asked, but that's all it was, you know, very distant manual everyday things. Nothing to interrupt his thought processes.

But I got on very well with Bert. I spent quite a bit of time with him. I'd visit them quite often up in Hurstbridge. They seemed very settled there in the 60s and 70s. He was doing the *Explorer* series round the time I was frequently there.

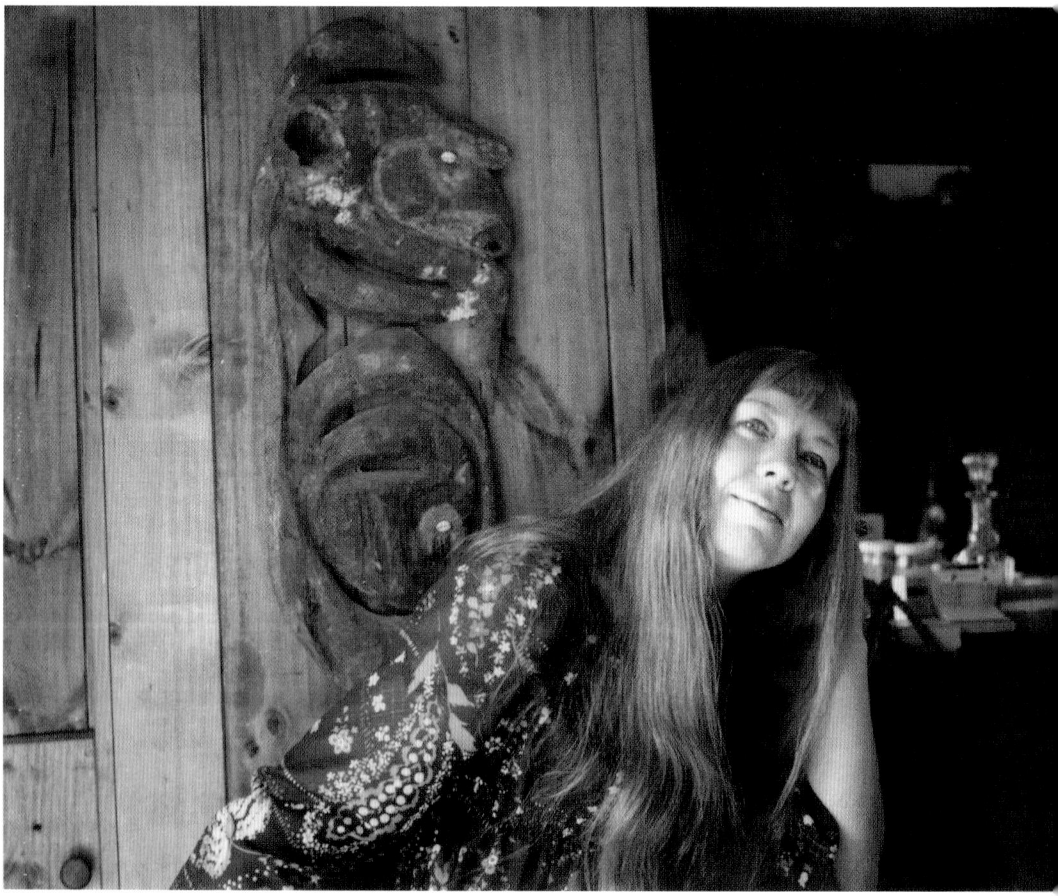

BARBARA TUCKER OUTSIDE BERT'S STUDIO C. 1962
Photo by Albert Tucker

We were downstairs one night when it started raining inside the house, raining, water coming down everywhere. It was a two-storey house, the living area downstairs and Bert's studio upstairs. Apparently the guttering or something of Bert's studio couldn't cope and the whole place was soaked—it was amazing.

Very odd things happened in that house. I won't say that it was haunted, but we all had experiences of strange things happening up there. I remember one night in the bedroom someone was running their fingers down the louvre doors on a wardrobe right next to the bed. I think it was Barbara who saw a figure there. My brother and his second wife lived in the little cottage next to the house and apparently something struck her one night. I got the impression it was just a presence trying to attract attention.

Bert and Barbara were very happy there, but Bert hated progress—it started to get built out so they sold up. It was a very odd move to Blessington Street, St Kilda, going back to the city. But Bert did the place up in the way he wanted it, with a lot of wood, wood panelling everywhere. Bert liked the natural things, and yet he hated trees being cut down. So it was a paradoxical thing.

He was very happy up at Hoddles Creek. As he said, 'Here I've found Paradise.' But really it was too late because he didn't have much time left. He knew that, I suppose. But it was just right for him then.

I found it very odd that Barbara had that last house in Toorak. It was very unlike her. She actually admitted it herself. Maybe it was a comfort thing, a convenience thing. She liked to have solitude, but also to be able to be in contact. And it was close to lots of things, and friends. She liked to talk things over, needed to discuss things with people. And there was the swimming pool, which she'd never had. Perhaps it was—well, what about a touch of luxury after all these years? And it was a beaut place to hang paintings in, with all the walls and no sun on them. But the Toorak house wasn't a cosy place for her. And so different from the Springbrook place and the other places where she and Bert had been happy.

Bert bought Springbrook because he wanted to preserve a part of this very lush rainforest in its pristine state. There was a humble little cottage on it and I drove up there with Bert one time. It took us about two and a half days to get there and we stopped two nights on the way and didn't talk about painting. But we always seemed to manage something. I don't remember thinking 'what do I talk about next, what do I say next'—it was always very easy with Bert. And Barbara I think flew up just before or after we arrived to join us there.

Springbrook was a fascinating place. The cottage was very simple in this landscape of hills and gullies and a lot of undergrowth and huge trees and water. There was a waterfall there called Pearlingbrook Falls, I think, which we drove to though it wasn't all that far. But the place was alive with snakes—an incredible amount of snakes. I saw a huge python crossing the road one day. I stood and watched it and its head had disappeared into the undergrowth and its tail hadn't even emerged. It was enormous, perhaps thirty-five feet I'd say and a huge body. I remember having a shower out the back near the outside toilet—just walls put together—and in the dim light curled up right next to me on a kerosene tin was a snake. I don't know what I did.

Wherever you went there were snakes and wildlife and Barbara and Bert were unfazed by that. Barbara went to stay the night with a friend who had a property with a ramshackle house very close by and a snake come up through a hole in the floor of her bedroom. Barbara found some pressing excuse to leave and booked in at Holiday Inn for the next evening.

She had her limits. Snakes in the house weren't the go. Bert and Barbara's place might have been a humble little cottage, but she made sure the snake holes were plugged. I remember Springbrook as teeming with life and just amazingly lush. It's still preserved, that place, I think. I've got a vague memory that they gave it to the state government with conditions that it be preserved.

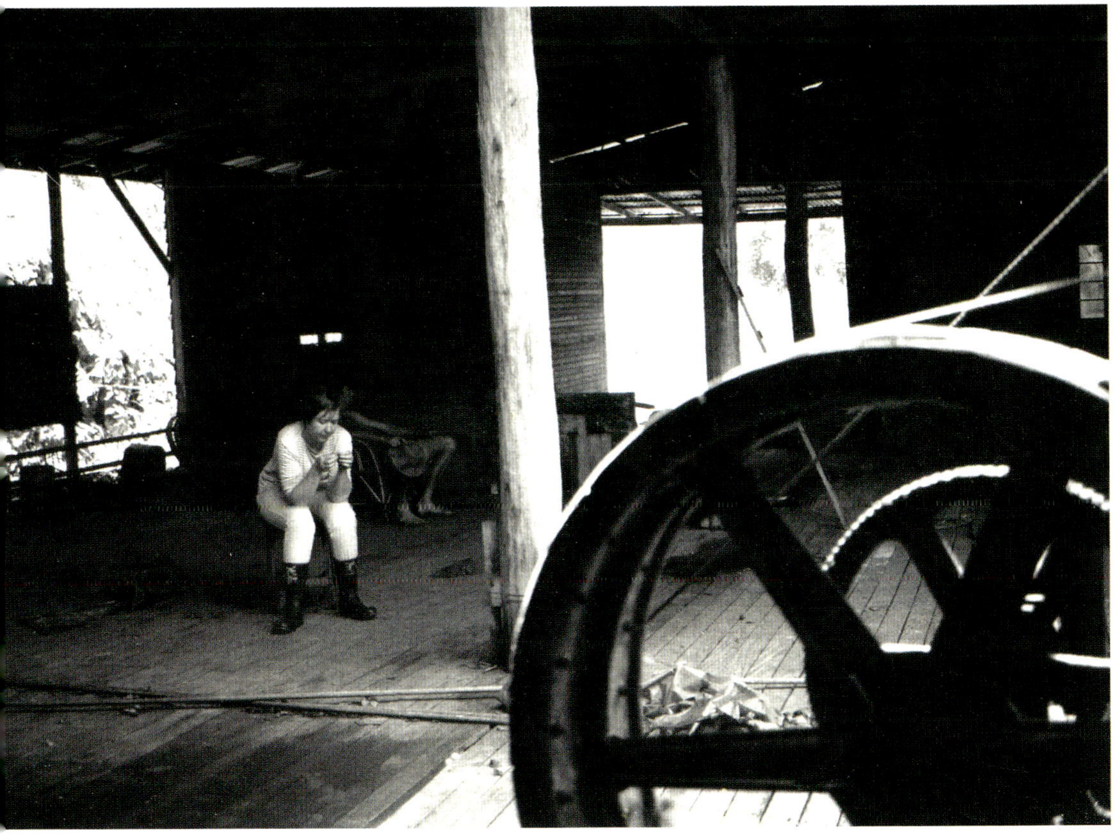

BARBARA TUCKER IN THE BANANA SHED AT SPRINGBROOK
Photo by Albert Tucker

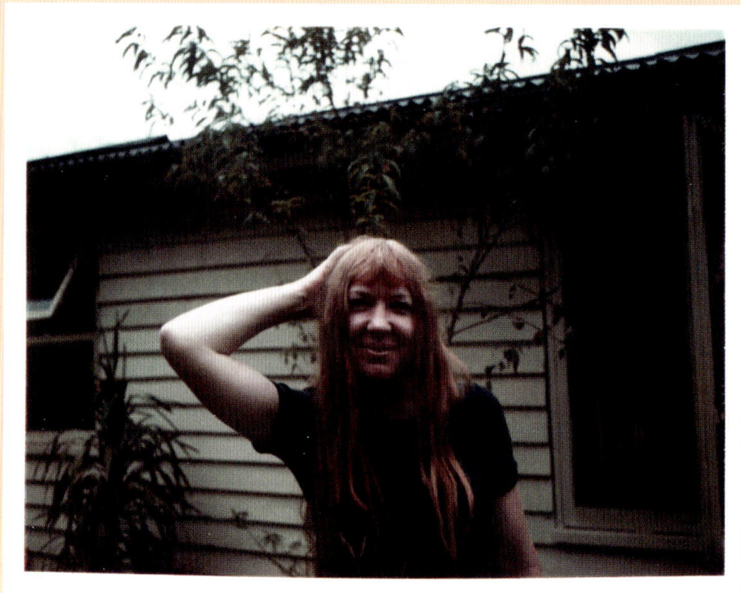

BARBARA TUCKER AT SPRINGBROOK
Photo by Albert Tucker

Barbara as a sister was generous to me—there were many kindnesses, and very real affection. For instance, she bought me a car at a point I really needed one and didn't have the money for it. She also gave me one of Bert's paintings—a painting of a little thing at Sorrento at the back of Barbara's place—rock formations and the little rockpool. Bert did a couple of similar paintings—not really a series. I think they were just paintings he wanted to do. I chose one because of the solitary figure in it. There's one with a group of figures but I liked this one—it felt like me in it. When I first came down I'd quite often walk along the cliff tops by myself. When it's off season there's no one about and I'd have such a sense of the power of the place—this old power, I put it down to, which Bert gets into the painting.

Everyone's got a different version of one person, haven't they? They see them in this light or that light. But what you want is people who were there. I witnessed Barbara as a sister, Barbara with Bert, and then later the pressure Barbara had—with the custodianship of Bert's art, which was an enormous amount of work—and other things. I admired Barbara, admired her so much. And I loved her company. I miss her very much. We were very close. I think we had only one dispute in later years and I don't know what it was over—you know how it is. We were all pretty close.

That's the problem with being the last—everyone goes before you. Suddenly they're not there. Barbara's not there, and I miss her company. I can't look at the family video with all the kids—everybody moving as if alive. You have to find out for yourself how to deal with these things. ¶

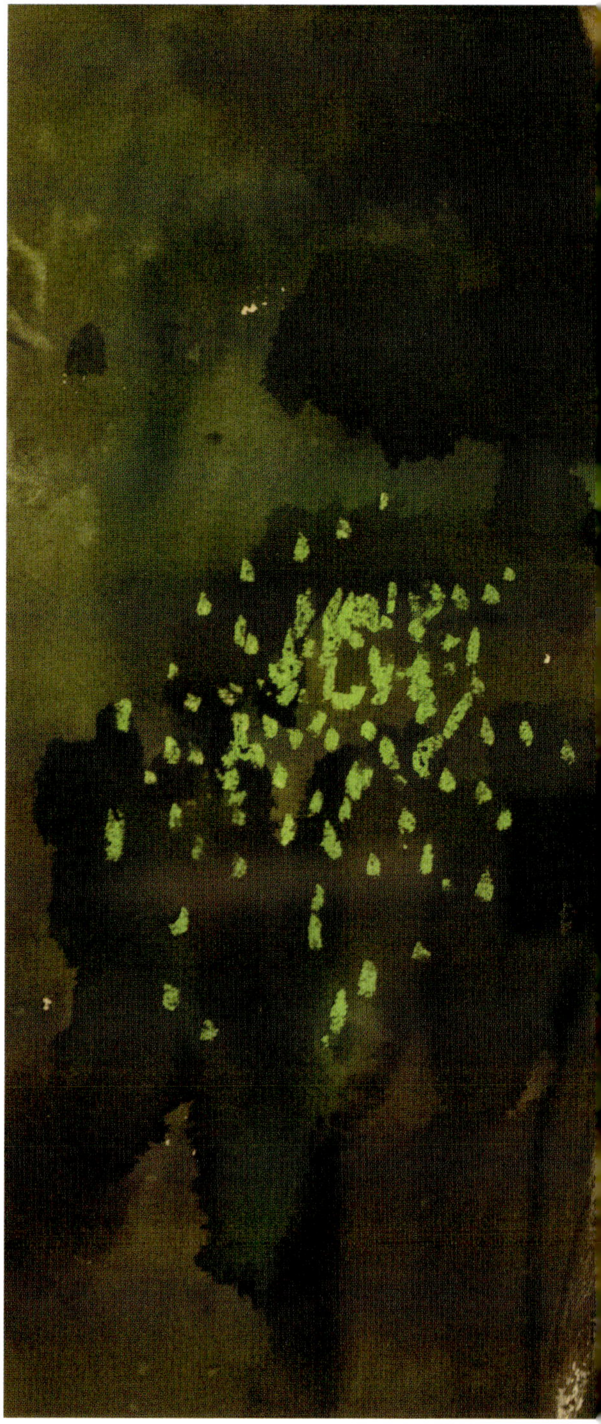

ALBERT TUCKER
SPRINGBROOK *1973*
SYNTHETIC POLYMER PAINT AND WATERCOLOUR ON PAPER
29.5 × 38.5 CM
PRIVATE COLLECTION

COURTESY SMITH & SINGER FINE ART

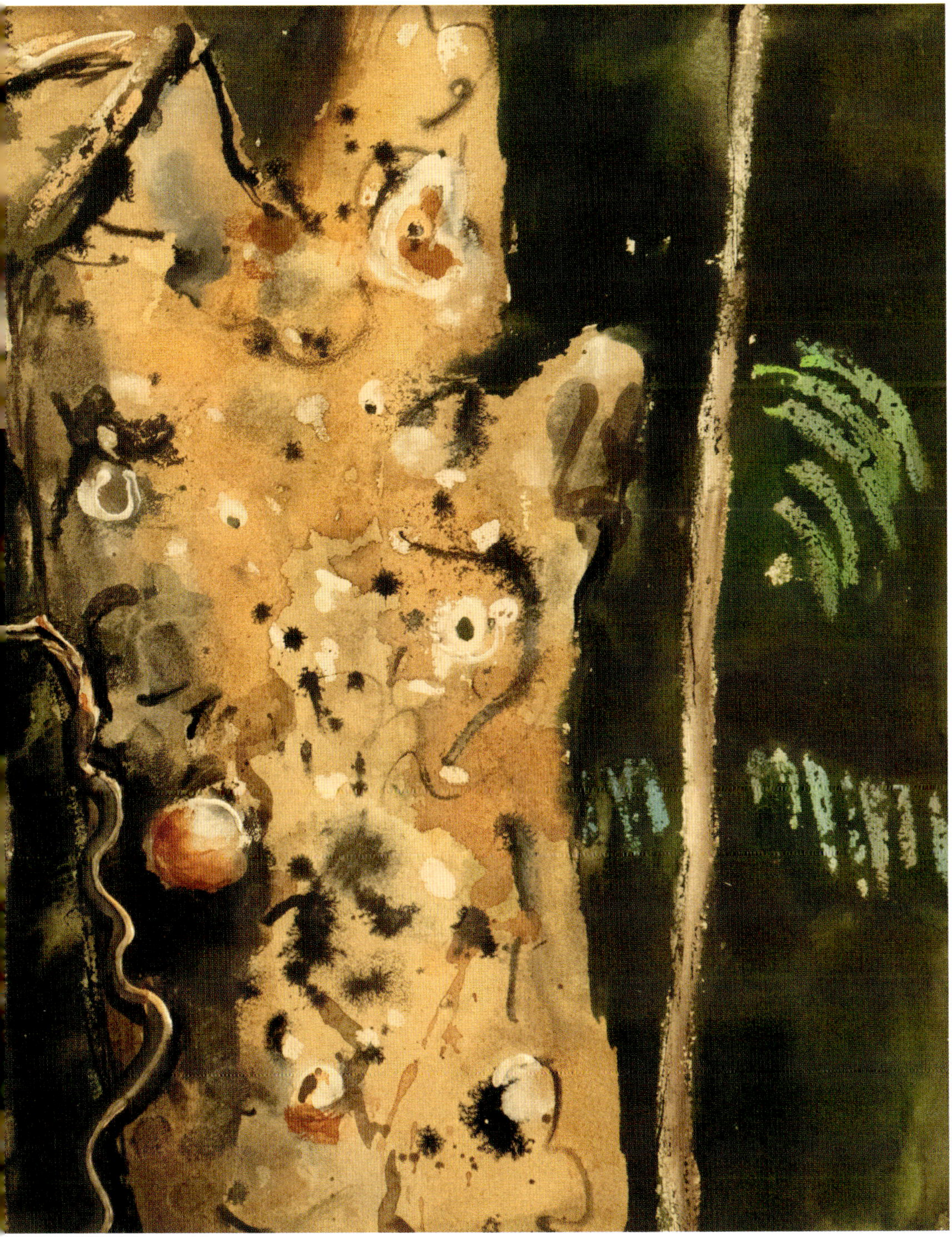

BARBARA: *ALL THE* DIFFERENCE

JUSTIN O'BRIEN

I shall be telling this with a sigh
Somewhere ages and ages hence:
Two roads diverged in a wood, and I—
I took the one less travelled by,
And that has made all the difference.
ROBERT FROST, THE ROAD NOT TAKEN *1916*

Barbara Bilcock was born on 23 November in 1934 in southeast Melbourne. Thirty-four years later I was born on the same day, in the same area. She was my mother's best friend in those early Croydon years, my godmother and, as it turned out, a great friend to me and my new family with my wife Eva in Kakadu, where she twice visited us.

Barbara married Albert Tucker in 1964 and was devoted to him for the thirty-five years of their marriage and, following Bert's death in 1999, to his legacy and the management of his estate. She was not just the wife and widow of the artist, however. For my family and me it was always Barbara first, then Bert. For my siblings and me, Barbara was an inspiration: a comfort and affirmation of the value of the road less travelled.

She was a beautiful and gifted soul, a capable business-woman and a great supporter and promoter of the arts. Barbara's generosity is too significant to capture in its detail here, but a quick summary will at least give an outline.

Barbara was a founding member of the Redmond Barry Society at State Library Victoria. Recognising both the importance of the library to Bert and his earlier gift of a Barrett Reid portrait, Barbara made a major donation to the library in 2004, followed by many other significant donations, including paintings, papers, photographs and some of Bert's memorabilia, including Ned Kelly's rifle.

Barbara also gave generously to the National Gallery of Australia, National Portrait Gallery, Art Gallery of New South Wales, National Gallery of Victoria, Monash Gallery of Art and Benalla Art Gallery. Then, of course, there were significant donations, worth many millions, to Heide, here all around us. Barbara was keenly conscious of the significance of these donations to Heide, that they, completed a circle of sorts, in a real, substantive way put right things set in motion a long time ago, helping to bring healing and transformation.

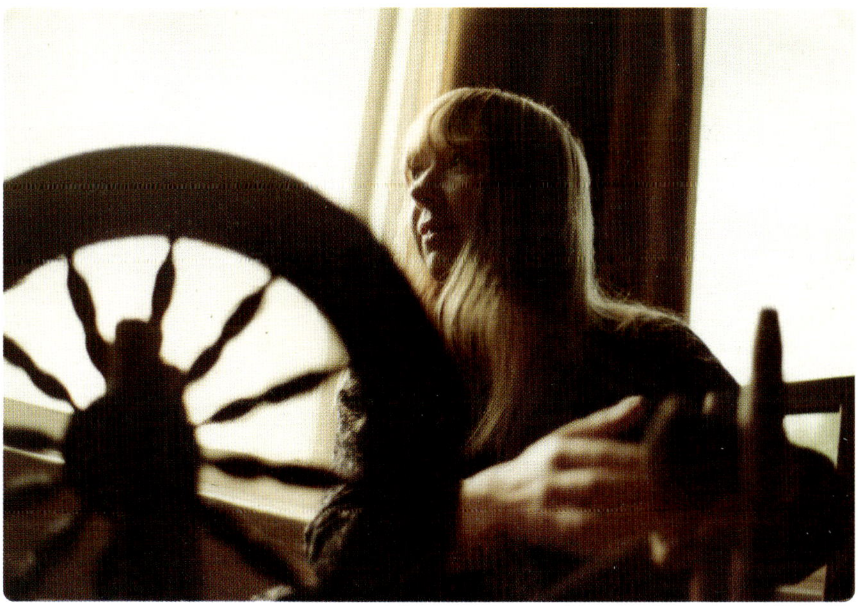

BARBARA TUCKER AT HURSTBRIDGE C. 1970
Photo by Albert Tucker

Barbara Tucker was no 'Penelope', no handmaiden behind the great man. She was more the soulmate and rock, the catalyst, the enabler whose great vigour, whose love of life and profound, subdued richness of spirit, would support Tucker throughout their life together.

Barbara enabled some of his bravest work—I believe his most personally courageous work—his crescent-shaped antipodean heads, where he plunged mercilessly into the subterranean depths of Australia's violent colonial past, into our heart of darkness. This feat was undertaken at great personal expense and would not, simply would not, have been possible without Barbara tethering him to reality, whatever that is, as best she could.

I am reminded of Carl Jung's ultimately fruitful plunge into the unconscious following his traumatic break with Sigmund Freud, which rendered him incapable of work, riddled with doubt and despair. From his experience during this period of anxiety, visions and troubled vivid dreams Jung discovered his Elijah, whom he termed Philemon, and ultimately developed his theory of the collective unconscious and the archetypes. He later stressed this was all possible, in large part, because of the support of his family. As he wrote, 'It was most essential for me to have a normal life in the real world as a counterpoise to that strange inner world.' Barbara provided Bert with just such a counterpoise throughout their long marriage.

What, however, of herself? What enabled this agent of change? Barbara was buoyed by a deep sense of quiet purpose, allowing her to be determinedly focused in a disarming way, encouraging others. She elicited from us all our better selves. She was subtlety itself and nuanced in a delightful and liberal way. She had such certainty, such knowledge—I don't think it was belief—in the surety of the cosmos; that there is enough of the spirit, the Holy Spirit writ a billion times told lovely across space and time, for all of us to be comfortable, here and now. Her knowledge and experience in this domain of the spirit were exceptional and drew the attention of none other than Colin Wilson, who once described her as 'a remarkable Australian mystic'.

Barbara made her own life, make no mistake, but she did so in such a merit-worthy way that her personal agency, her sheer will, was lost on a good many passers-by. She remained undimmed despite this.

What buoyed Barbara was the constant affirmation of the rightness of her view, in the way beautiful and fortunate things would come her way, and which she would incorporate into her being. I like to think her signal message to me, captured during our last meeting at Cabrini Hospital, was the interconnection of all souls, or 'interbeing' as Thich Nhat Hanh has termed it. Some of you will know that during those days she drifted in and out of 'our world'. I felt a great peace awaiting her as I sat with her.

At one point she gazed intently upon two of our children who were with me that day, Patrick and Ella and said, 'Justin, we are all *so* connected, so interconnected, all souls ...'

I knew Barbara marvelled at this reality, this too-often difficult wisdom, because she recognised and accepted it utterly. That day, as before, she felt and *saw* that interconnection.

I want to end with some poetry, from Rumi: *Every forest branch moves differently in the breeze, but as they sway they connect at the roots.* ¶

This tribute was offered at Barbara Tucker's Memorial Service at Heidi.

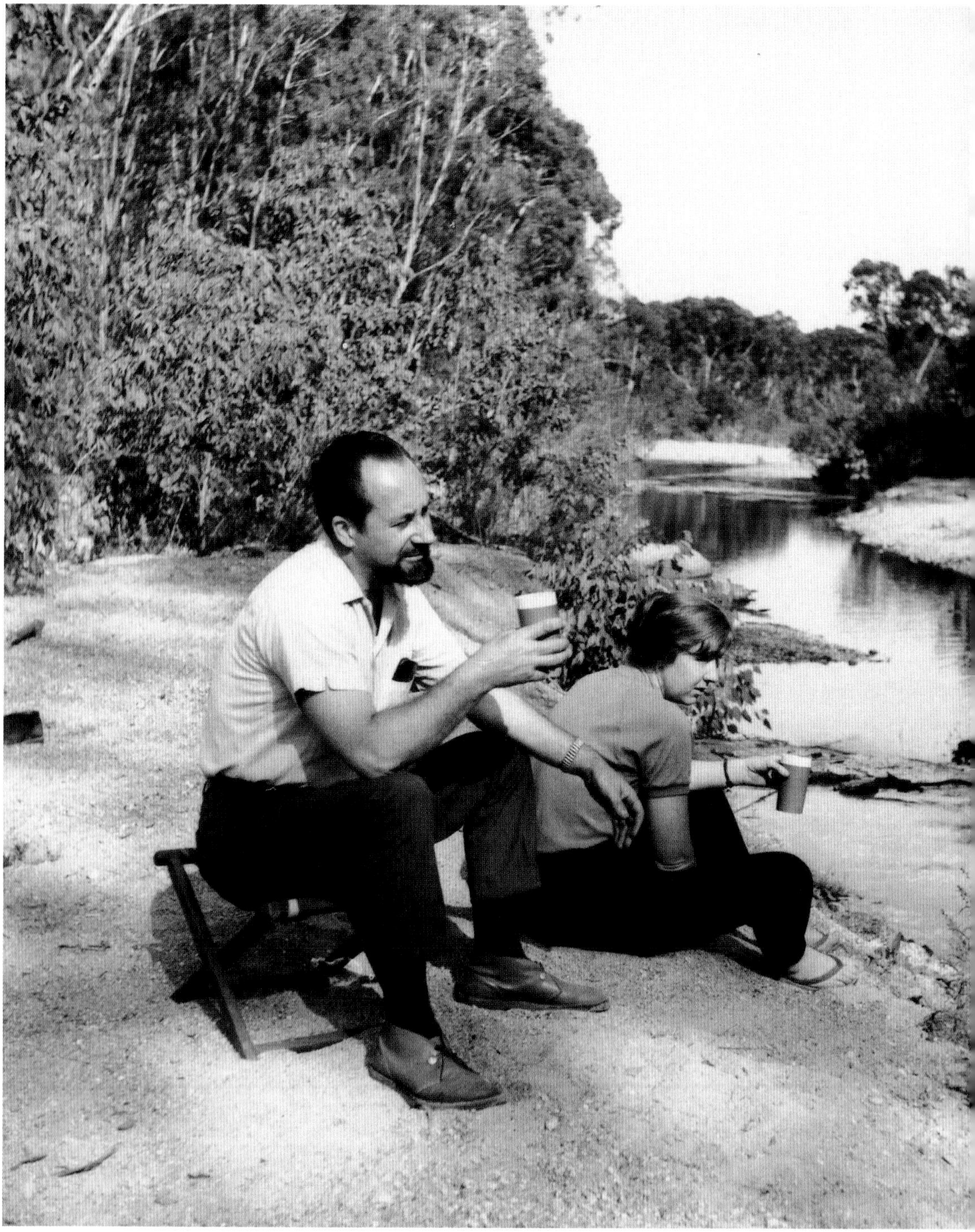

ALBERT AND BARBARA TUCKER ON THE BANKS OF REEDY CREEK 1964 Photo by Ian Jones

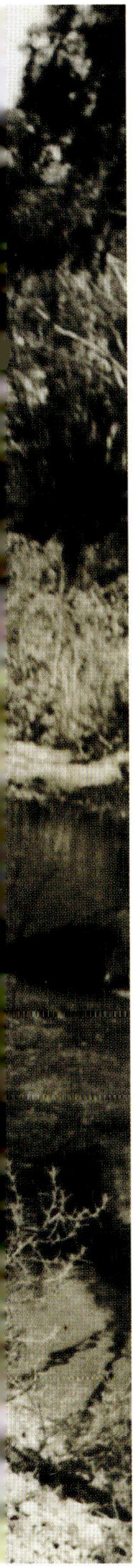

TALKING *WITH* BARBARA LONG *INTO THE* NIGHT

IAN JONES

I met Barbara quite early in the piece, in my 20s. I was on the scene when Barbara married her first husband Sam. I liked him. I had met Bert earlier in the piece when he was interviewed at Channel 7 on his return to Australia. It must have been very late 50s or early 60s. I'd never heard of Bert at the time, though I'd heard of Nolan and Boyd and some of the others. But I was fascinated by Bert's pictures that were shown when he was interviewed—some of what later became known as the *Images of Modern Evil* and the *Antipodean Heads*.

I was quite surprised when I heard Barbara and Bert were seeing each other, after Barbara divorced Sam. Then they were married. We didn't see a lot of each until then.

I came to know Barbara and Bert more closely in 1969. At this stage, they were visiting Mexico. My most striking memory of Barbara is from Mexico City. We did everything together on that trip. It was the most time I had ever spent with them. We shared in what was, for me, an amazing and exotic experience. It was intense. There was a shift in our relationship.

In Barbara's marriage with Bert, her life was as the artist's wife. That's just how it was in those days. When we got together, so often it was the men talking with the men, and the women talking with the women; still is today, as often as not. It was what happened in those years, with my generation, a set of expectations that men did this and women did that and the twain met elsewhere.

When Bert and I got together, we often became engrossed in conversations. We would sit and talk by the hour. He took me into his studio once, and I was fascinated to see the amount of material he kept. I remember so much work of other painters, a terrific Boyd etching, some Crichtons, though no Nolans that I recall. I learnt it was rare for even a family member to be allowed in the studio. I'd have loved to see Bert working, but I never dared even ask. I realised that I was privileged to have seen his working studio.

In Mexico what struck me was that Barbara was equally in the conversations. We saw quite a bit of the consular people, and I was amazed by how assured she was with them, and at the numerous functions to which they were invited. When I went with them I noticed her confidence, and how at ease they were as a couple. I got a new understanding of Barbara and her capacities during my stay with them in Mexico, and of Bert and Barbara together.

We had a fabulous week together, in Mexico City and travelling around. We went to Teotihuacán to see the Pyramid of the Sun and the Moon. We went on a couple of trips through the countryside, which looked like Australia, with pepper trees instead of gum trees. I did not expect that.

It was a memorable time, including one night in Mexico City when we went out together to the street where the mariachi bands play and where they sell chilli dishes. I suspect Bert whispered to them to give me the absolute hottest, thinking it would knock me flat. I thought it was delicious, which spoilt the joke. Bert liked chilli, but I don't think as much as I did.

What I remember most is the vivid conversations. Barbara talked a lot with Bert and me about pre-Columbian civilisation and art. They were fascinated by it. Bert bought a couple of pieces by local Indians saying they were 'in the Mayan style'. He said to me, 'These are not forgeries or fakes. They are an ongoing artistic tradition, using the same materials, the same methods. They have a value of their own.'

I first met Barbara when I started going out with her sister Joan in the 50s. She was one of the stars of *Hit Parade* at Channel 7, where I was a young program director. Joan was a well-known jazz singer, a very good one. She had a group called Joan Bilceaux and Her Quintet, for a bit. The Basin Street Blues was really a trademark vehicle for her. When she sang the opening words the audience just exploded. She could belt it out and really sell a number. She was tall and graceful. She had won a Mannequin of the Year Award, been runner-up in Miss Victoria 1952. She could dance well and deftly learned all the moves for *Hit Parade*. She had starred in A.R. Harwood's 1952 film musical *Night Club* as the singer Nina Fleming. So when Joan and I started going out and got engaged we drew quite a bit of attention.

That is the background to my relationship with Joan. I think we were victims of the television glamour-machine in a way, which I don't think did us any good. It gave me a taste of what it was like to be in the public eye, which I did not like at all and made me understand some of the pressures in Barbara and Bert's life.

Behind all this, Joan's family life at Croydon was a spectacular contrast. She lived in a very modest house opposite the market with her mother, a lovely woman, who had to do all the housework herself, which was a bit of a battle for her, obviously. But she was the soul of the house.

She was really terribly deaf. It meant all the girls spoke very clearly. They were used to projecting and spoke with beautiful enunciation. This is the context in which I first came to know Barbara, and Linda and I also briefly met their younger brother Peter. Barbara was just Joan's sister to me in those early days.

I left Channel 7 in 1963, feeling that I'd gone as far as I could go. I let it be known that I was leaving and hoped to get job offers. The Crawford's offer was far and away the best, not necessarily in terms of money, but because they offered a breadth of opportunities for working in television drama not available elsewhere. They let me go to England to work with Tony Richardson on the script of his Ned Kelly film that of course, inevitably, became known as the Mick Jagger Kelly film.

The plan was that on the way back to Australia from England, I'd stop in at Los Angeles to study budgeting techniques of American films. Because I knew that Barbara and Bert were in Mexico at this time, I decided that I would go back to Melbourne via Mexico City. That's how I came to stay with them (and got a new understanding of Barbara and Bert).

Apart from Mexico, it's the Hurstbridge years that are most vivid to me. During the 70s we used to go often of a weekend morning and stay for lunch. It was there that Bert and I talked very briefly about his war years, but mainly about his post-war European adventures in a Kübelwagen, which belonged to his American girlfriend and partner, Mary Dickson. He was travelling around Europe and people sometimes assumed he was a former German soldier. He had a mechanical break-down at one stage and took it to a garage, where they found a shell-fragment in the engine.

During those Hurstbridge years, Bert and Barbara often camped with us in the Beechworth area. That is Kelly country, of course. Bert and Barbara had a life-long interest in the Kellys. I'd first gone to Beechworth with Joan in the winter of 1959.

It was bitterly cold. We spent that first night at the Hibernian Hotel, freezing. But it didn't deter me and we returned to camp often in the Woolshed Valley, later with Barbara and Bert. I took a photo of them on the banks of Reedy Creek, where we used to camp. It was reproduced in *The Age*, once.

Bert and I used to walk around the ranges together. An author interviewing me suggested that the reason was to get away from the women. It wasn't that. It was just that the ranges there were terribly rugged and it was not the walk for everyone. Back then, it wasn't really deemed suitable for a woman. It is terribly, terribly rough going.

Bert and I went up Byrnes Gully, which is a unique area because the bottom of the gully is very peaceful, just a leaf carpet, young pines and gums, no undergrowth at all and a little creek running down from the ranges over pink granite rocks with amazing opalescent water. It is an idyllic place. But as you go up the gully the sides become steeper and rocks and trees start to tumble down and eventually you've got a complete shamble of rocks and fallen trees that you have to scramble through until a waterfall, usually dry, blocks the gully, and you climb up that and get a stunning view back down the gully towards the Woolshed Valley, a gold rush valley that once had ten thousand people in it. Now it looks like virgin bush or grazing land. But there's the odd thing—a patch of iris, cherry plums, a weeping willow or a fireplace revealed after a bushfire's been through.

Byrnes Gully was a magical place. Bert loved it. He took a lot of photos, and was going to paint it. Foolishly, I said at camp one day, 'Bert's going to do some paintings of Byrnes Gully.' As soon as I said it, I knew it was a mistake. I don't know that he ever did paint it. I don't think so. You never talked about a project before it was done. 'You're discharging the energy,' Bert said. And Barbara shared that view. She talked to me about the creative process being precarious, too easily disrupted or abandoned.

Barbara and Joan knocked around the camp. Reedy Creek in those days was white alluvial gravel, a river's width, with two channels of the creek running through it. I got a very clear picture of it as it was in the Kelly period from a marvellous old man called Bill Knowles who was the grandson of a man involved in the Kelly story. Back in the 60s it was very much the way it was in the Kelly period. Now it's choked with scrub, but back then it was extraordinarily beautiful. Barbara loved it. She loved being in amongst the gums and the quiet, just the sound of the creek running.

Though I knew of Bert and Barbara's interest in the Kellys, I hardly knew about Bert's Kelly pictures at that stage. I knew about the Nolan pictures. I naively imagined that Nolan heard childhood stories about the Kelly gang and had been prompted to paint because of them. But as I understand it, it was actually Bert who introduced him to the Kellys. He'd given Nolan a book about the Kelly gang which I'm pretty sure from Nolan's titles and approach was *The Inner History of the Kelly Gang and their Pursuers*, by J.J. Kenneally. Kenneally, who was a very talented journalist, claimed that it was the 'first unpartisan account'. He was ten during the Kelly outbreak and had childhood memories of it all. He became a founding member of the Australian Labor Party. Bert said that Nolan's first pictures of the Kellys had handkerchiefs over their faces like bandits, and Nolan was very interested in a series of Bert's paintings, especially one called *The Watcher on the Balcony* (*Image of Modern Evil 24* 1945) Bert thought it was his own recurring iconography that prompted Nolan to create the Kelly icon.

Barbara and Bert camped many times with us up at Reedy Creek. There was one particular expedition that I did with Bert to an area called the Police Caves, which was where the police surveillance party was camped, with Aaron Sherritt, to watch the Byrne homestead, a couple of kilometres away—which underlines the farcical nature of the police tactics and the degree to which they were conned by Sherritt. They were sleeping in this pile of boulders half way up the range, directly above the major Woolshed Valley township, which had about four thousand people in it. There was one real cave formed by the boulders where Superintendent Hare used to sleep. I took a photograph of Bert in this cave. I'd been looking for ages for the place that Aaron Sherritt slept, being described by an officer as 'a hollow below a large boulder in the lowest part of the clearing'. Every likely spot seemed too shallow and too steep—he would have just rolled down the hill.

One day I was there with Bert and noticed a huge boulder as big as a room, concave underneath, with a hollow below it, a kind of double saucer shape, and we thought this could be it. So forgetting everything, snakes and so on, I crawled into it, and there were leaves all round the edges where the floor met the concave roof. Stupidly, I ran my fingers through it and there was an old sardine tin, more like a herring tin today, no key on it. There were two of these in remarkably good condition and we found a couple of beef tins which I knew were very early because the lid had a dab of solder in the middle which is the way they used to preserve meat, cooking it in the sealed tin. They'd put the meat in the tin, then cook the whole thing with a hole in the lid, and then after put a dab of solder on it. There were a couple of bits of broken bottle. Bert got me to stick them all on a boulder and to sit down behind it. Then he took a photograph of me with my prizes, with me slightly out of focus, looking even more dazed with excitement at what we'd found.

We looked around for more artifacts. Bert, who had a terrific sense of archeology, said: 'Look, you've got a bunch of young guys here, for weeks on end. I reckon that when they broke camp they'd just throw everything down the hill.' So we investigated down the slope, and for about thirty metres down the slope we found bits of broken bottles of various descriptions. I filled a backpack with them, which I've got to this day. We were able to reconstruct the range of grog that this party was consuming. It was extraordinary. 'They lived fat and cut it thick,' said the grocer who supplied them.

When we got back to camp we showed Barbara and Joan our collection of broken bottles and bits and pieces. I think Joan thought our level of excitement was a bit crazy, and was probably worried about more 'stuff' because I was an inveterate clutterer, a hoarder, really. But Barbara was very interested in the relics connected to the Kelly story and we talked long into the night by our campfire about the finds. It was an exhausting but memorable day for all of us.

Then there's the episode of the Kelly rifle. I was out filming something when I got an emergency call to contact Joel's auction house, for whom I'd done a bit of work. I was told they had a rifle that had come from a friend of Kate Kelly's. They asked me to authenticate it. But I was immediately suspicious. Genuine friends always called her Kitty Kelly. In the family, they were Kitty, Neddy, Jem and Danny. When they said it had 'N.K. son of Red' on it I was very dubious because Ned was always E.K. So I told them I couldn't comment. A dealer in Sydney, Stern, I think, bought it. But Bert was so interested in the rifle that he persuaded the man to swap it for a painting. I groaned when I heard this and thought—a fake for a Tucker painting! Oh Bert, you've been had!

However, when I saw the weapon at Barbara and Bert's, the N.K. was remarkably like the way Ned did his brand, which was E.K. reversed and conjoined. The N.K. had that quality about it, with the K coming off the second down stroke of the N. What they hadn't told me about was that it also had a pictogram on it: a deer's head, a K and an 8 and a heart with a 'u' and an r', which reads as 'Dear Kate, you are in my heart'. The auction house didn't know it at the time but Ned's sweetheart was Kate Lloyd.

Further, examining the rifle I found the word 'Moses' scratched into the wood. This was the pattern of rifle used by the Aboriginal troopers from Queensland. One of them was called Moses, and though I can't document it precisely, it's likely one of them had gone missing being liberated by a sympathiser and had found its way to Ned. He would have been delighted because he had great respect for them. They were the only police who worried him in any way. Ned may have had contact with and knowledge of Aboriginal ways through Esau Shelton, whose son Dick Ned had saved from drowning in Hughes Creek at Avenel. Esau presented him with a green silk sash, which he was wearing when he was gunned down at Glenrowan. Esau got to know Aboriginals at Echuca. When he saw the tribe at Avenel he encouraged them to make little baskets and trinkets and sell them outside his pub. He could have taken Ned to them. I've often wondered how Ned developed, in an amazingly short time, an incredibly intimate knowledge of an enormous area of land.

We found endless interest in the Reedy Creek history. These were the kind of things Barbara and Bert talked about with me long into the evenings by the tents under the stars. We talked about politics and art, history, friendships, family. Those trips to the Woolshed Valley were marvellous. Those were years in which strong bonds were formed.

Barbara and I shared a wry sense of humour. After Bert's death, she invited me to an exhibition of Tucker paintings

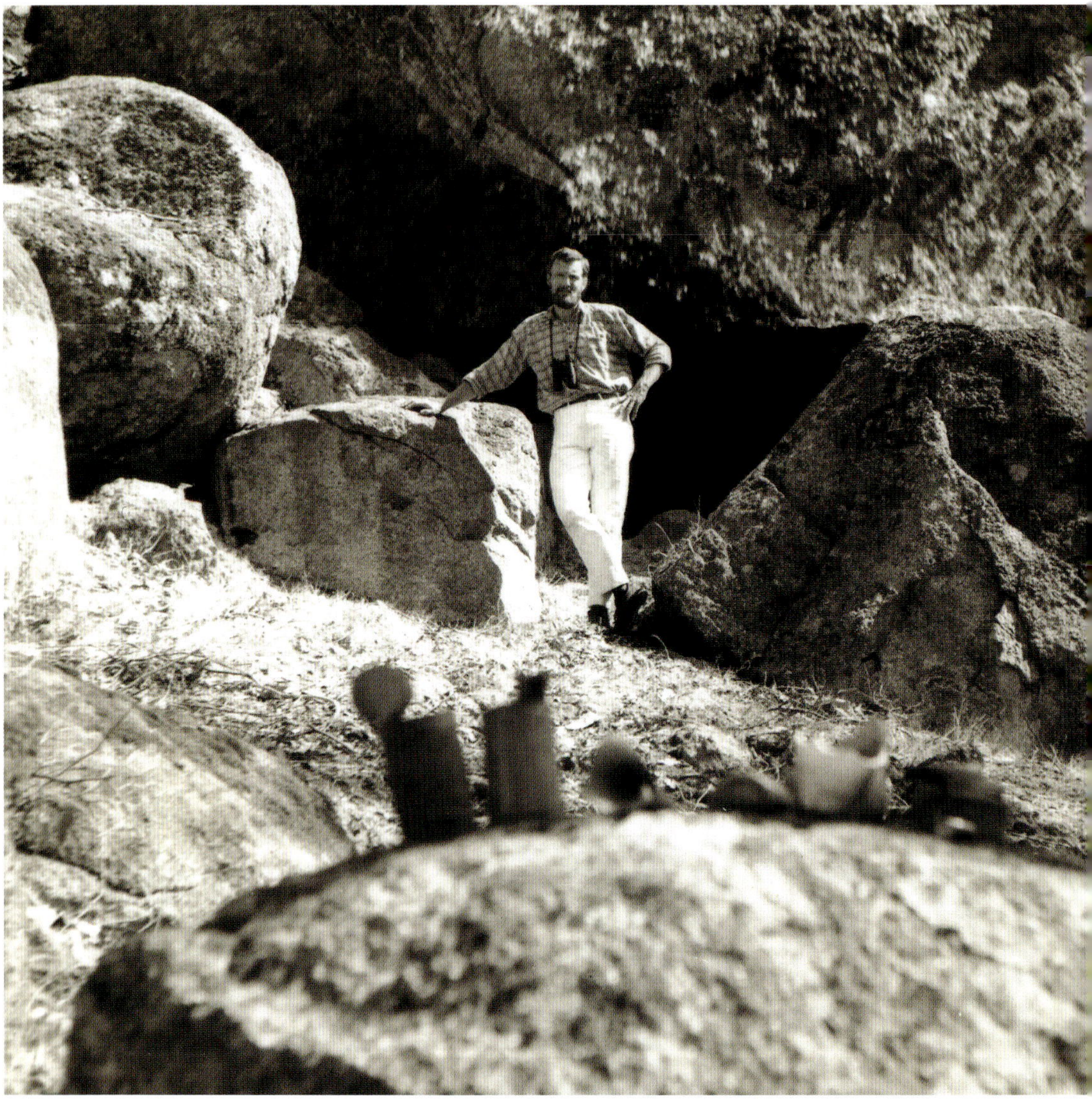

IAN JONES AT THE POLICE CAVES 1964
Photo by Albert Tucker

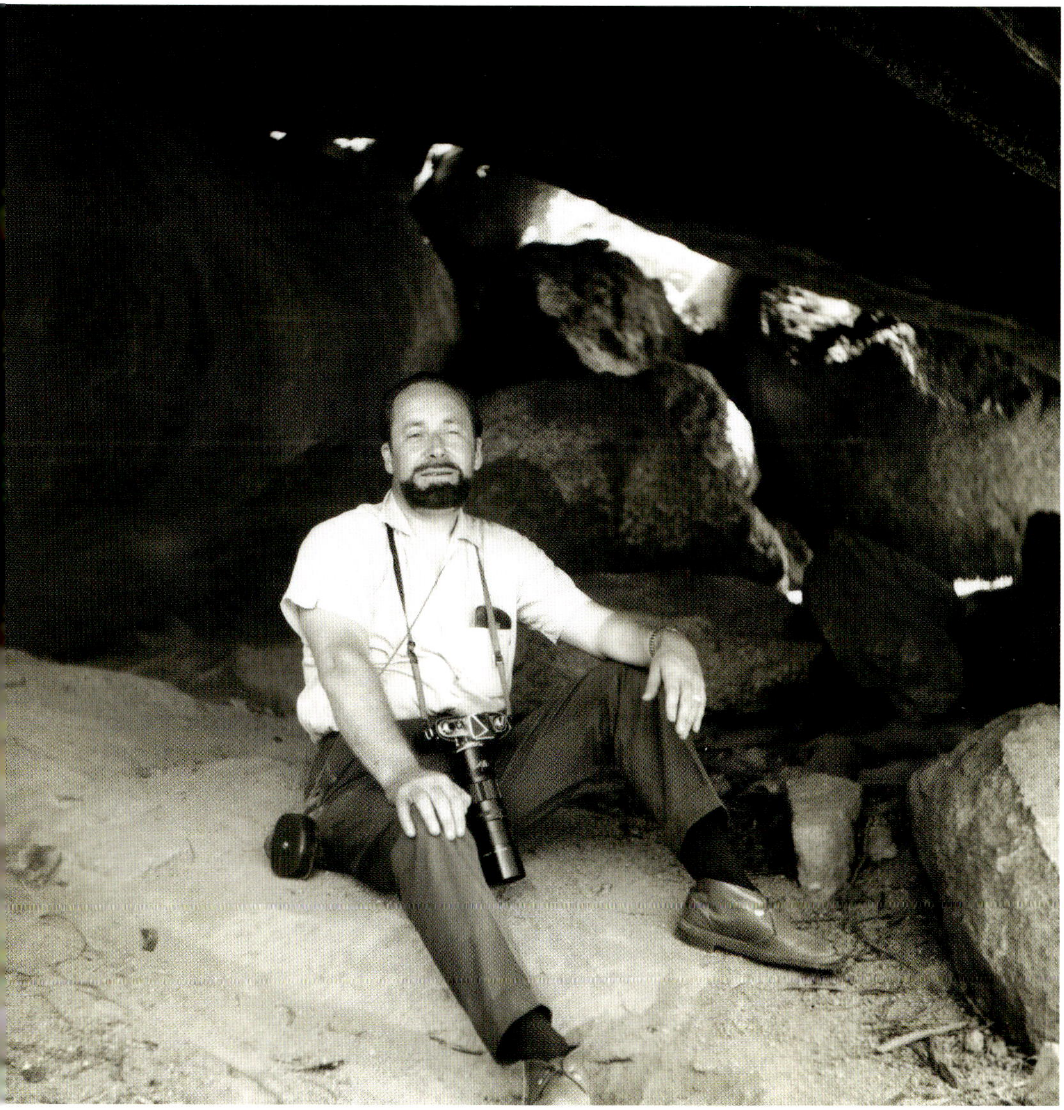

ALBERT TUCKER IN THE POLICE CAVES 1964
Photo by Ian Jones

curated by Ivan Durant at the Benalla Art Gallery, which was exclusively antipodean heads and parrots. I was slightly irritated but I kept getting this image of an antipodean head cut out of corrugated iron. Back at Beechworth, I thought, 'Why not?' So I got the catalogue and copied an antipodean head on to corrugated cardboard, stuck it on a canvas. I did an acrylic sketch of the armored bushranger with parrot flying overhead, a tree and a wisp of smoke. Presumably I meant it to be Stringy Bark Creek. I scrunched up toilet paper as collage to create veins on the neck, and the burl on the gum tree in papier-mâché. The thing that pleased me most was the roundness of the trunk and the light on the shoulders. A painter friend was intrigued by it and thought the boldly veined neck was the best thing, and the parrot. Making a Tucker parrot look friendly, the challenge—that was enormous. I think the painting came out of a feeling of closeness to Bert, my affection for him. It's only the second painting I've done in my life. Having done it, I was a bit hesitant and felt I had to confess to Barbara. So I brought her over and asked, 'Do you think it's too cheeky?' She laughed and said, 'Actually, I love it. I think it's better than some of the fake Berts I've seen!'

I had a closer relationship with Barbara after the trip to Mexico. We'd talked so much about art and culture and, well, life, really. We shared many interests and some odd interests, too. Sport fascinated Bert, but also what he and Barbara called 'erratics', the out-of-place artifacts—finds in archeology where an item appears too advanced for its context, like a piece of turned metal turning up in a coal scam, or a bearded, apparently European man carved in wood turning up deep in a gold mine at Ballarat. They knew most of it could be explained away—but the ones that couldn't, yet? Things like that caught Bert and Barbara's imaginations, and mine.

Barbara had a marvellous relationship with my older children Darren and Caitlin. Darren used to call her Auntie Bat when he was very young, and I did too, on occasions. There was wonderful family warmth around Barbara and Bert with them. Darren's relationship with Bert was very strong. I remember one day Bert said, 'Darren, now look, you're trying to wear me down. It's not going to work, because I was a child one day and I can remember trying to wear adults down. You're just trying to drive us mad. But it won't work.' And Darren said, 'Don't say nose things.' In later years, Darren was a very, very handy man, having worked at one stage with a builder. He had my father's ability, which skipped a generation. My father could build a house from the ground up, and would have done the plumbing and electrical work as well. Darren is like that. As a tiny child, he marched into our bedroom one morning, having taken the side off his cot. When he was a boy, he took a tape recorder to pieces. He couldn't put it back together, of course. When Bert and Barbara were down at St Kilda, Darren did a lot of work for Bert and became very close to him.

Barbara had a tumour, a dreadful thing. I found her warmer to me after that illness, whether it was some physical effect, or because you have a different perspective about life after a physical confrontation with death. I think, mainly, it was that we started not to take our friendship for granted. Our relationship grew warmer and deeper.

Barbara had always had very close relationships with her sisters. They formed a rowing team at one stage, which struck me as exquisitely unlikely. There's a photo of them all in a sculls-type boat. It characterised their closeness, sisters as a team. I think Joan organised it. When we camped at Anglesea one time, I got bogged in the sand. Joan said, 'Some of us had better get out!' Everybody got out except Joan!

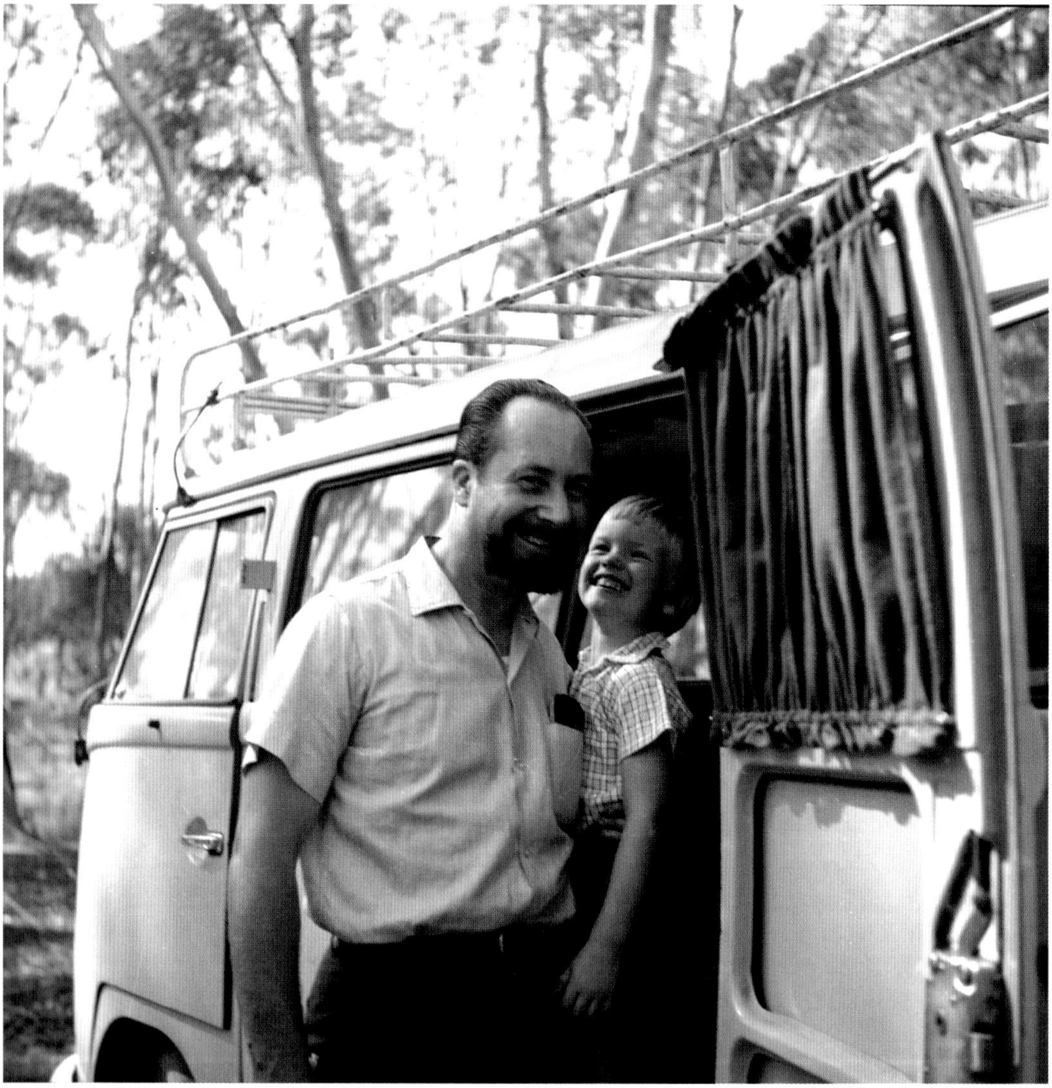

BERT AND DARREN JONES CAMPING 1963
Photo by Ian Jones

She was a great organiser, and very good camper. She started me off camping, in fact. I'd never been camping until we went up to Reedy Creek. And learning to camp brought all those years afterwards, of pitching tents with Barbara and Bert, in the Woolshed Valley. I used to go up on my own at times, up there, in a two-man tent, sleeping with my head outside the tent so the bush would wake you up in the foredawn. I never worried about snakes, for instance, though I'd hear a kangaroo or two bounding past.

I remember seeing the stars blinking in that wide black night sky, I remember listening to the sound that early morning kangaroos make. It makes me think about the way Joan and Barbara, the Bilcock sisters, had the capacity for striking out in the world, taking you with them, supporting you.

Barbara brought me into Bert's world, the art world, and she brought me, with Joan, into feeling completely at home with the natural world, camping out by a little creek running down from the ranges over white alluvial gravel shining with water. Barbara had incredible respect for the bush, for nature if you like, and for its connection to the making of art. I watched Bert listen to it differently with her. You responded to it differently. She had a capacity for fully entering into experiences, a bravery that brought greater enjoyment. ¶

BARBARAGANOUSH

GARY SINGER

Barbara loved food in all its aspects: selecting the produce as well as the preparation, the cooking and the eating.

One of my earliest memories of Barbara is her making and bringing a delicious babaganoush to my parent's place at Sorrento. She made it in large quantities because we all loved to eat it. It was so much part of her visits that I renamed the dip Barbaraganoush as hers was so exceptional. I renamed Barbara *'Ganoush'* and called her by that name for many years.

A few years ago, Barbara said to me, 'I loved it when you used to call me Ganoush and you don't do it anymore.' I replied, 'Well, you are not making Barbaraganoush for me anymore so you have lost the title.' To which she immediately quipped, 'Ah, I will have to do something about that!'

A few days later, Barbara telephoned me to say that she had made a special batch of Barbaraganoush. Geoffrey and I immediately arranged to visit and consumed on-site the Barbaraganoush with her and were presented with some to take home. I then reinstated her title as 'Ganoush'.

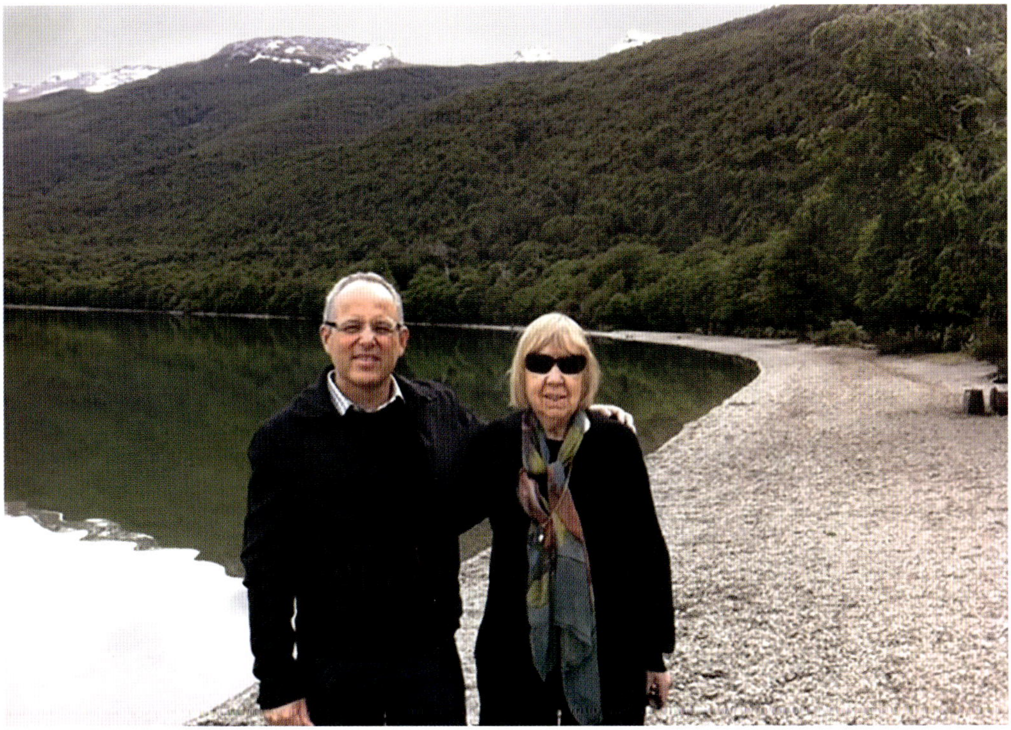

GARY SINGER AND BARBARA TUCKER, USHUAIA
SOUTH AMERICA, 27 DECEMBER 2012
Photo by Geoffrey Smith

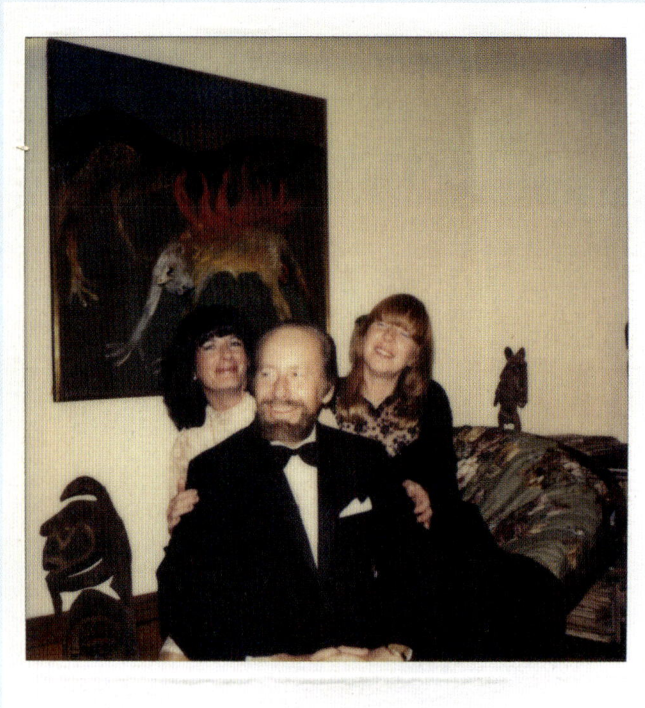

ALBERT AND BARBARA TUCKER WITH FLORENCE CRICHTON C. 1970S
Photo by Richard Crichton

Whenever you visited Ganoush she always provided you with something delicious to eat from her wonderful soups to her legendary shortbread biscuits made to her mother's recipe, to her scones with her homemade raspberry jam or orange and almond cake or whatever else she felt like cooking, including Barbaraganoush.

Of course, no visit to Barbara was ever complete without sharing the obligatory cup of tea!

On Geoffrey and my last visit to Kew Gardens, Barbara was talking about how much better she was feeling and was contemplating returning to her own house as she was not enjoying the aged care home. I immediately said that was great, and if she went home she could make her delicious borscht for us. Barbara gave us one of her mischievous looks and, after a short pause said, 'Maybe I would be better off staying here!'

One of my very favourite Barbara stories was when she was going through her wardrobe in desperation to find something to wear for a forthcoming function—it was the opening of the National Gallery of Australia in Canberra where she was to meet and dine with Her Majesty Queen Elizabeth the Second and Prince Philip. As she trawled through the coat-hangers of various brightly coloured garments, she flicked past an item of clothing that she had acquired at great expense and loved very dearly. She had never worn it, because it was so beautiful and exquisite and it made her feel very special. She said to herself, 'I won't wear that. I am saving it for best!' All of a sudden Barbara had an epiphany—with great clarity she said to herself, 'If this event is not "best", I don't know what is!'

The reason I love this story is that it beautifully captures Barbara's sense of modesty, humility and, above all, her great sense of humour. She was a wonderful friend and support and she is much missed. ¶

IV

THE ART OF FRIEND-SHIP

CARROTS, ORANGES, BEES *AND* BOOKS

FLORENCE CRICHTON

The five children in the Bilcock family grew up just across from the market in Croydon, Victoria, which was a colourful and much more rural place than it is today. For Barbara Tucker (nee Bilcock), the place evoked fond memories. When living in Hurstbridge many years later, she liked to drive across to shop at the market and visit her mother. On a few occasions in the 1960s she took me with her. Her mum usually greeted her with a pot of hot tea and scones just out of the oven—a habit Barbara inherited, much to the later delight of her many visitors! (Her flourless orange cake was even better than her scones—she was a great natural cook.)

From the stories I heard across the years, those five kids—Joan, Barbara, Linda, David and Peter, all of whom I later got to know—were almost a gang of their own, looking out for each other and sticking together against all odds (Croydon's Famous Five!) The close relationship between siblings continued right throughout their lives. When Barbara and Bert married, he suddenly became part of a large family—just a small cog in a big wheel.

Barbara's father, David senior, was a friendly, jovial man who worked with film and newsreels, enjoyed a joke and told excellent 'shaggy dog' stories, a trait that was passed on to his children, particularly David junior.

As an adult, Barbara still insisted on hearing—and learning—all the latest jokes and tall stories from David and she'd try them out, firstly on Bert and then on her friends. Her sense of fun and mischief endeared her to many people including my three children, who considered her as their adopted auntie.

Auntie Barbara always had something interesting on the go—from the latest board games to the unexpected surprise of a just-hidden 'whoopee cushion' placed strategically where she would then invite one of them to sit, always with hilarious results. The dogs, Ella and Gretel, were playful companions, and the big Hurstbridge garden had vegetables to pick for dinner, Barbara's stacked and productive beehive boxes to be careful of, and water bowls to be filled for the many kinds of birds and parrots that visited. Also, if you were lucky, a pair of tawny frogmouths could be seen huddling close together on a low branch of one of the many big manna gum trees. Bert's binoculars were always kept handy in order to spot the birds. On occasions Barbara could be seen clomping around the bush garden in her big boots and overalls or tending the bees in her all-white apiarist outfit, complete with helmet—a sight to behold!

Her experiments with food were interesting. Bert had a sweet tooth and the honey from Barbara's beehives was used generously—he later blamed his dental problems on this indulgence. There was also the carrot phase, when Barbara would visit the market and bring home big bags of carrots which were juiced for health reasons (according to Bert's numerous books on 'good health'). They both turned a strange golden-brown colour for a while! Bert liked what he called 'old fashioned food'—roasts, soups, stews, puddings—which Barbara provided generously for him and for their many visitors. I remain eternally grateful for Barbara's lessons on 'how to use a pressure-cooker', then a terrifying device that I learned to master under her instructions.

Barbara maintained friendships from her early days in Croydon, particularly with the O'Briens, whose eldest son Justin became her godson. He and her adored nieces and nephews and their families were an important and treasured part of Barbara's life. Though having no children of her own, she communicated naturally and easily with young people. She worked with Colin Badger at the Council of Adult Education, and later at La Trobe University Bookshop where she was the academic liaison person. These jobs served her well when the opportunity later arose to start up her own bookshop in North Carlton.

Our family's relationship with the Tuckers was most frequent and closest when they lived at Hurstbridge and we at Eltham, not far away. A lot of time was spent together just visiting, holidaying or on three- or four-day camping trips. Barbara was a much better camper than Bert, who was such a creature of habit that we all found ourselves falling in to his maddening routine of lunch around 12.30 and dinner around 6.30—whether hungry or not! Barbara was adaptable, spontaneous and adventurous and liked to swim and explore with us while Bert often stayed back drawing or taking photographs of the landscape.

In the US we all travelled together (four adults and three kids!) in a large station-wagon from New York to the historic civil war battlegrounds in the south, then north to Bar Harbor, Maine, to stay with friends. At such close quarters it was a real test of friendship, and we not only survived, but had a lot of fun along the way. Barbara, like us, had fond memories of her time in the States during the later 1960s.

Mary Dickson, an American woman who had been Bert's companion for a number of years when he lived in Europe, was then living back in New York's Greenwich Village. We had known Mary before we went to New York in 1967. A year or so earlier, Bert had received a letter from her to say that she had cancer and her time was running out. Barbara was the first to suggest that she come and spend some time with them in Hurstbridge and she and Bert financed her trip.

During her stay of a couple of months, Mary came on a camping trip with all of us (the Crichtons and the Tuckers) and shared other times, including a three-day boating expedition with Barbara, Bert and Dick. The holiday was an important and precious time for Mary and was a typical and admirable example of Barbara's generosity of spirit. In 1969, at her insistence, our family stayed with Mary for a short time before leaving to return to Australia after two years away. Mary passed away in 1972.

Friends and family would remember that, when staying with Bert and Barbara at their Queensland property in Springbrook, Barbara would supply everyone with hats and scarves—she kept a large supply—to prevent the local bloodsuckers (there were ticks and leeches in abundance) from getting a free feed.

After those memorable bush walks to see the waterfalls or the unique and beautiful Antarctic beech trees, Barbara would appoint herself as 'tick inspector'. There was always a handy supply of metho, salt and tweezers. Similarly, at her Blairgowrie beach house, which was a place of escape and replenishment (reading, swimming, beach walks) she was the one to deal with the mozzies, march flies and the occasional snake, but conversely she not only tolerated, but became quite fond of the tiny marsupial mice (*Antechinus*) that sometimes found their way into her kitchen.

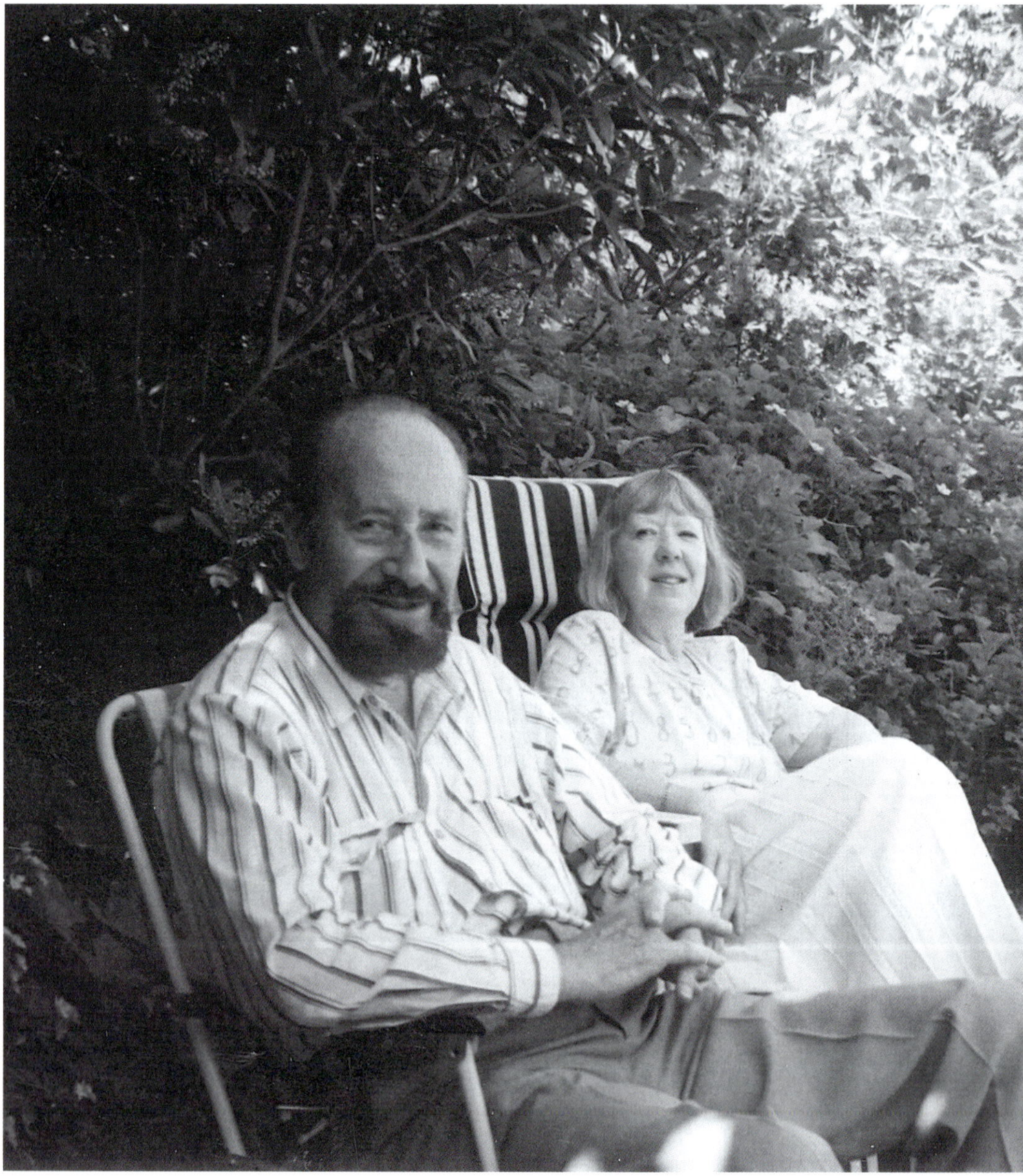

ALBERT TUCKER, BARBARA TUCKER AND FLORENCE CRICHTON
Photo by Richard Crichton

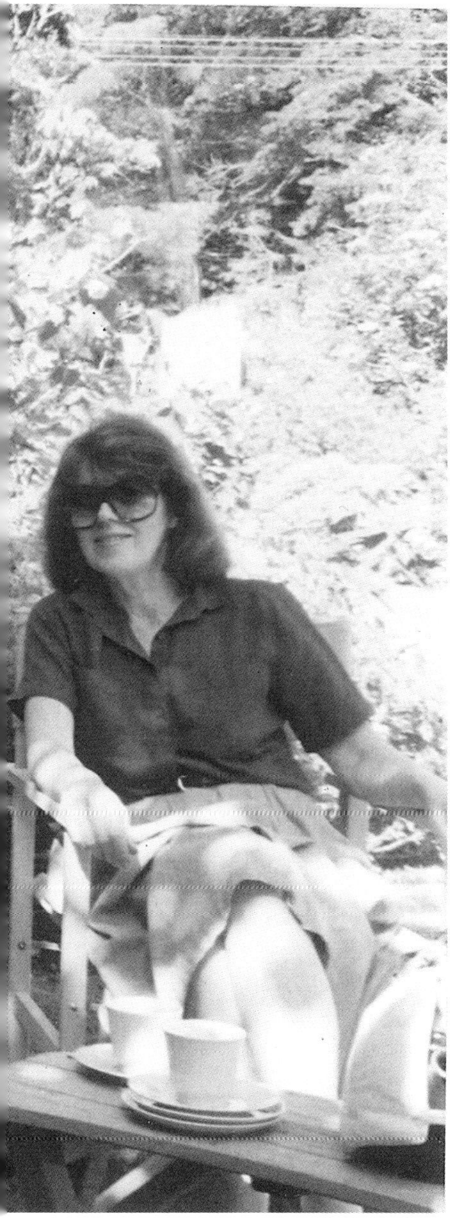

Visual art was not one of Barbara's main interests until later in life. The so-called art world held no real attraction for her and she grew into the role of 'artist's wife' almost reluctantly. She was an active person, both physically and intellectually. She read philosophy and practised meditation, but literature and music were her passions and she was very knowledgeable about both. Her familiarity with books and writing was a bonus for Bert who, as an avid reader, was the grateful beneficiary of her choices, for him, of recent publications. But Bert had a 'tin ear' and no musical interests, so Barbara enjoyed her love of classical music alone, sometimes when driving, or at concerts with friends, or at home wearing an enormous pair of headphones, often while Bert was watching TV.

Barbara enjoyed the company of family, close friends and overseas visitors and there was always the offer of a spare bed at Hurstbridge, St Kilda or Hoddles Creek. Of her later move to Toorak, she noted that she was probably the only person in the district who mowed their own lawn. She did enjoy the pool and the easy access the location afforded to the people and places she needed to visit.

The differences between Barbara and Bert, who were married for over thirty years, made for a rich life pattern for both—each constantly learning from the other. Bert, whose bark was worse than his bite, modified and softened many of his attitudes and opinions due to Barbara's influence, while Barbara absorbed and respected Bert's wisdom and experience, at the same time retaining her own view on things that she was not reluctant to express. He became more reliant on her as he aged—there was a more than twenty-year age difference—and of necessity, Barbara took on a heavier role assisting him with the day-to-day demands and challenges of a prominent artist—almost acting as his PA and entering a steep learning curve about the art world and its peculiarities, a role that she handled with tact and great aplomb, and one that continued after Bert passed away in 1999.

Their involvement with the court case following the theft of Bert's paintings was harrowing for both of them. Their joint decision to create a foundation to make donations to public art collections and environmental causes left a path for Barbara to follow, but it was also a huge responsibility. She handled it well, as those who knew her knew she would. Their legacy lives on, especially at Heide Museum of Modern Art. Our family is glad we had Barbara Tucker as such a good friend for such a long time—over fifty years. We miss her. ¶

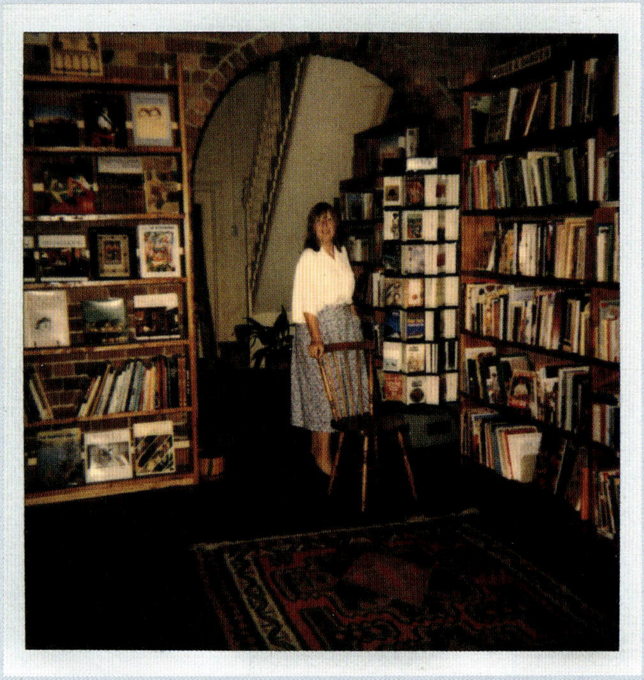

BARBARA TUCKER IN HER RATHDOWNE STREET BOOKSHOP
Photo by Albert Tucker

BARBARA TUCKER *AND THE* GIFT *OF* FRIENDSHIP

JILL REDNER

I first caught sight of Barbara across a crowded room. It was December 1996 and we were at Owen White's home in Kew, celebrating the publication of Michael Keon's autobiography *Glad Morning Again*. Michael had been a regular visitor at Heide in the early days, where he formed a friendship with Albert Tucker that survived despite their very different lives and widespread travels. Michael was an accomplished writer and journalist; he had been foreign correspondent for the Melbourne *Herald* during the tumultuous lead-up to the Chinese civil war in 1946–49. Later, he worked for the UN in The Philippines and married the sister of Ferdinand Marcos. He is a relatively unknown figure locally, however, except to the many friends he gathered during his remarkable life. There was thus much joy at this publication, the last before Michael's death in 2006, as many of the people present had discovered each other in his circle.

I realised Barbara was watching me; she saw that I saw and with a quick grin she disappeared. I surmised that she was curious, because a few weeks earlier my husband Harry and I had enjoyed lunch with Bert at the home of Michael and Aurora

Keon, but Barbara had not been present. Shortly after the book launch we left for eighteen months overseas. When we returned, lunches with Bert became a regular occurrence. Barbara, however, remained elusive. Years later, when we had become good friends, I asked her why she never came. 'I'm more comfortable in the background,' she said. I was puzzled. Barbara certainly wasn't shy. She had a wide circle of acquaintances, built up over many years as a book-buyer for La Trobe University and had run a successful business in her own bookshop in Carlton.

Like Bert, she was forthright and open-hearted. But she was cautious, or had become cautious belatedly. Looking back later on those years, the last period of Bert's life, she sometimes sadly commented that they had both been too trusting. No doubt she was thinking of Max Joffe, the former art dealer who stole over $2 million worth of paintings from the Tuckers' St Kilda home in the early 1990s, while making an inventory of their art collection. He had been welcomed as a close friend.

Our first real meeting with Barbara, early in September 1999, little more than a year after Joffe's conviction, was full of that sadness, yet also the joy that comes with a sense of renewal. Bert's health had deteriorated during the long police investigation; he could no longer bear to work in the St Kilda studio. The answer was obvious to Barbara. They would go back to the bush, find a place in the hills that resembled Hurstbridge, where they had been so happy in the 1960s and 70s and where—with none of the material resources of the Reeds at Heide—she had created not just a home but a social milieu, full of creative energy, good food and lively argument. Old friendships were nourished, with Nolan and Boyd, for example, and bonds formed with younger painters, such as Fred Williams and Richard Crichton. We did not know

Bert and Barbara then, but we witnessed the rebirth of that earlier milieu at Hoddles Creek, near Yarra Junction after the traumatic Joffe affair. There, surrounded by great groaning gums, Bert was reimagining his 'Explorer Heads' and Barbara was wrist-deep in mountain soil—good enough to eat, she said—creating a beautiful native garden. On the afternoon of our visit the conversation ranged from art to books to people, with Barbara describing the colours Bert saw in the bark of the surrounding trees, Bert asking Harry taxing questions about his latest book, *Representation in Science, Politics and Art*. And somehow the all-important question of friendship, and what can poison it, kept returning.

When our young son was out of earshot, happily installed in a little eyrie under the roof that Bert had built himself, lined with books—the next best thing to a tree-house—the conversation around the table turned to more difficult topics. We all had disappointments with people to share, recent and from long ago, 'betrayals' even. We could laugh about some of them now. As the afternoon light began to slant through the trees, Bert shrugged the memories off with a line from Eliot's 'Burnt Norton': 'But to what purpose/Disturbing the dust on a bowl of rose-leaves/I do not know'. Everyone knew the next line: 'Other echoes/Inhabit the garden ... / Quick, said the bird, find them .../And the pool was filled with water out of sunlight.' It certainly was, but we were in the hills where darkness falls quickly and we had a long drive ahead, so it was soon time to go. Courteous as ever, Bert kissed me on the cheek as we left. A week or so later Barbara called unexpectedly at our place to say how much they'd enjoyed our visit.

This brave new start at Hoddles Creek was cruelly cut short when Bert died of a sudden illness on 23 October 1999. Grief was thus in the background of our friendship with Barbara from the start, and we learned to admire her resilience in dealing with it. This was especially evident during the years immediately after Bert's death. Barbara felt his death had released a certain amount of latent hostility to his art: there were inexplicably censorious reviews; some local institutions were reluctant to display paintings she had donated; she had to resist pressure to authenticate works of dubious provenance, an ongoing problem, as the infamous *Faun and Parrot* case against Christie's Australia for selling a forged Tucker in May 2000 subsequently revealed—and in the midst of all this she was negotiating the terms of the gift of the Tuckers' private collection to Heide. Barbara managed all this with characteristic grace and good humour. But it interfered painfully with the process of mourning her personal loss.

Memories coalesce in grief: our own memories of the people we have lost and the memories they have shared with us of events that predated the relationship. In May 2002 we were living in Paris, where Harry had a visiting professorship, when we received a surprise phone call from Barbara. 'I'll be in Milan next week for an exhibition. Do you think ... could I possibly... come and stay with you?' Tentative as always when asking for what she saw as a favour. We were delighted, especially our son, who already regarded her as family. Here was a chance to distract her from her worries, get her to enjoy Paris, at its best just then, bathed in glorious spring sunshine. On the first morning, over breakfast in our little apartment on the Cours de Vincennes, we discussed what we might do: lunch at an authentic local restaurant, perhaps, or the Louvre ...? 'Well, where did you get that delicious bread?' It was from the farmers' market in the street just below. 'How wonderful, let's go down now.' She returned laden with so many good things, the day's agenda was obvious: a picnic on the banks of the Seine.

And 'Just a wander,' she said, 'perhaps along the left bank, near the back of Notre Dame.'

We had been too slow-witted to realise that it was fifty years exactly since Tucker's first solo exhibition at *Galerie Huit* and Barbara was in Paris above all to revisit Bert's old haunts, especially the site on the riverbank where in 1952 he had lived with Mary Dickson in his now legendary homemade caravan. Barbara located the spot exactly, under a capacious tree, recalling Bert's photos and descriptions. At first she was overjoyed, and spoke warmly of Mary and her importance in Bert's life. But then as we walked away, her mood darkened. 'You know, in late 1948, not long after Bert had arrived in Paris, John Reed showed up here with Sweeney in tow.' Bert had not seen Sweeney for nearly two years and it was an emotional and fateful reunion, because John had demanded that Bert choose there and then: either keep Sweeney with him in Paris, or agree to sign adoption papers. Bert had barely enough to live on. How could he care for a child? He gave in, but he never forgave the Reeds for forcing the issue in this way. Sunday, he believed, had seen Sweeney as her child, with Joy, from the moment he was born. He had tried to explain to Sweeney why he must go back with John and later in life had often repeated Sweeney's protest: 'But I'm Bert's boy, Bert's boy.' Traumatic memories have a life of their own in families. Now Barbara, who had taken on Bert's profound regret over that decision, was gathering all that inherited pain up into her own and treading ever so carefully with it over the cobblestones on the riverbank.

But she never allowed herself to show pain for long. 'Yes, well,' she often said, 'you learn to move on.' She had learned toughness as a child, growing up with her four siblings in 1940s and 50s Croydon, after her brilliant, but occasionally impecunious, film-maker father, David Bilcock, had left their

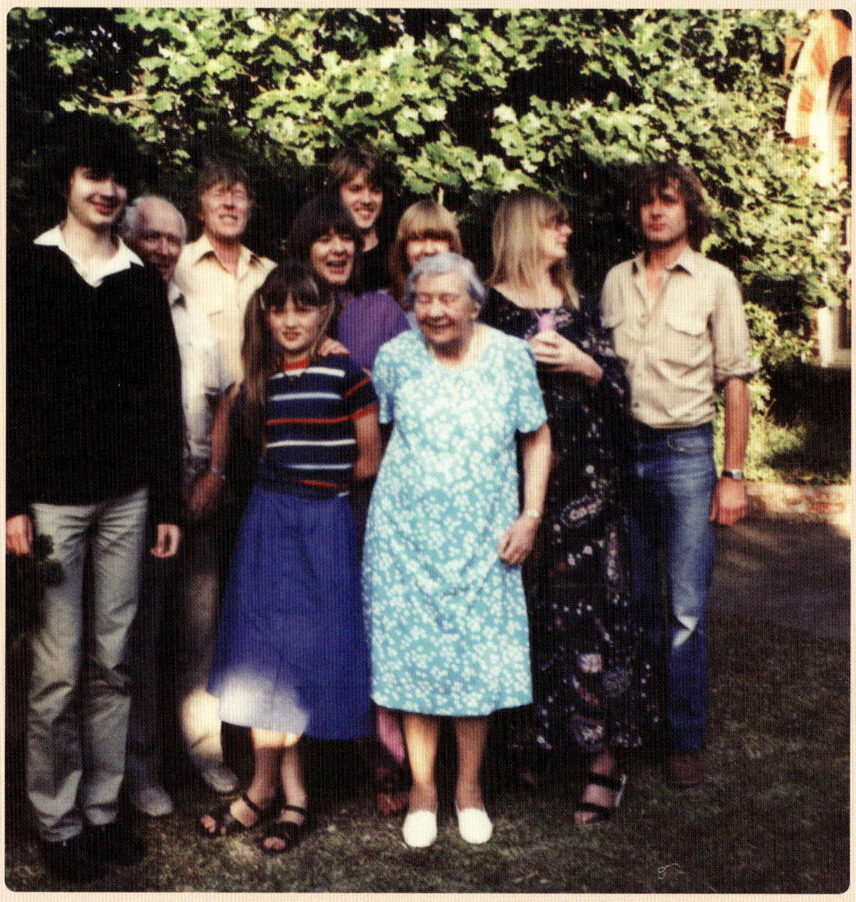

*ANGUS JONES, DAVID BILCOCK SNR, DAVID BILCOCK,
CAITLIN JONES, JOAN JONES, DARREN JONES, BARBARA TUCKER,
JEAN BILCOCK, LINDA BILCOCK AND PETER BILCOCK 1981
Photo by Albert Tucker*

mother and a kind of benign neglect ruled the children's lives. He would pick them all up sometimes, expecting them to jump into the car quickly, and if she was too slow, the door would slam shut leaving her outside. 'Who's not in? Oh, *Barbara*. Well, she's big enough to walk!' This memory came out of the blue once when we were talking about childhood. And then she added: 'We were the poor white trash of Croydon, you know.' This was so incongruous, so obviously the wrong description for her talented bohemian family, that I laughed. And it was just as well. There was a wicked gleam in her eye as she joined uproariously in the laughter. Hard lessons in self-reliance had been learned in Croydon, but she was fiercely proud that the Bilcocks were different.

Humour was one of her main characteristics. And an endearing earnestness that, sometimes coupled with absent-mindedness, caused much mirth. Back at the old house in St Kilda after Bert's death she started another new garden. Looking at my garden: 'What a gorgeous purple iris. Could I possibly have a piece when you divide it?' Then a year or so later in her garden: 'See that purple iris? Can't recall how it got here, but would you like a piece when I divide it?' The iris travelled with her later to the new house in Toorak, where she shocked her neighbours by mowing her own grass and growing pumpkins on her front lawn.

Like most of her friends, Harry, Joachim and I remember her warm hospitality, her way of showing how much she valued us and her talent for grasping the moment and living it fully. These gifts were so pronounced that it is easy to forget she had many others: her love of the Australian landscape and her deep respect for our Aboriginal heritage, amounting in fact to a quasi-religious reverence for the natural environment, which she shared with her husband, and which gave her a unique understanding of his art.

After Barbara's death, at a moving tribute to her life at Heide which was attended by many prominent figures from the Melbourne art world, I was alarmed by a comment from a guest historian: 'Well, I suppose she must have known *something* about art!' Should I have mentioned our conversations about the German painters of the 1920s and her precise grasp of how they influenced Tucker's art during and immediately after the war? Or the insight she gave me into one of Nolan's greatest paintings, *Kelly and his Armour* (1962)? As I stood before this work, deeply moved by its Shakespearean vision of 'unaccommodated man', Barbara gestured toward the prisoner's stripes, formed by bars of yellow light crossing the naked figure and binding him to the harsh landscape; it was a clue to Nolan's uniquely Australian vision of human vulnerability. But no, I didn't answer the historian; perhaps it was only a stray thought, which would quickly be disowned. I did as Barbara would have done, just shrugged and turned away. Very few people in that gathering would have entertained such an idea. But I was pained for her, nevertheless, knowing how hard she had had to fight immediately after Bert's death for the respect from the experts, which she eventually enjoyed.

Perhaps occasional lack of appreciation was the price Barbara paid for not flaunting her knowledge and for protecting Tucker's privacy and her own. In his well-known interview with Robert Hughes in 1994, Bert remarked: 'I couldn't live or work in a place I haven't made my own.' He should perhaps have said 'we' rather than 'I'. But he was intent on refusing to be drawn about his marriage, sidestepping Hughes' persistent questions about Barbara, no doubt out of respect for her independence—knowing how forcefully she could speak for herself, if she wanted to. However, he did allow himself to tell Hughes how lucky he felt he'd been in his third love relationship. His photograph of a delicately beautiful young Barbara (see page 26) tells us more about his love for her then than any statement elicited by an interviewer could hope to do. And anyone wondering what sustained their long relationship should perhaps consider the sense of wonder and the wicked humour that he shared with her and with other key figures in his life—Nolan and Boyd, for example. One of Boyd's paintings, made during a visit to Hurstbridge in 1968, evokes both qualities wonderfully. It shows Barbara disappearing into the bush, red hair streaming behind her, under a gothic arch of turquoise foliage, with her brother David's heavily pregnant dog Ella lolloping behind.

Barbara's niece Caitlin recalls her saying that Boyd was so determined to capture the moment he attacked the canvas with immense energy and used up all of Tucker's oil paint in the process. This may have occasioned some mock-indignation, but Bert would hardly have objected to the result: a painting of Barbara completely at one with the natural world, the jewel-like surface of the paint glowing with her laughter and love of life.

It was an image to hold onto during her long illness, though I found the tender Springbrook photograph also came to mind often in the last months of her life. I glimpsed that young girl more than once in the tired face on the pillow where she lay resting on a high hospital bed, hemmed in now by safety rails. The gracious hostess occasionally reappeared, too. On her good days, when brilliant autumn sunlight streamed through the hospital window, visitors were welcomed with aplomb and she delighted in small gifts, like a vase of slow-blooming deep magenta tulips from her closest collaborators at Heide. Then, it was as if Barbara had never been ill.

Most of us fear death; Barbara, too, probably. There were certainly days when she fought the demon with all her might. But what Harry and I found truly memorable was the deep calm that came over her in the presence of beloved family members, a joyful tranquillity that carried her beyond fear. If she was anxious about anything in the last few days—or so it seemed to us, in the precious time we spent with her then—it was about disappointing those she cared for. Sometimes, struggling for consciousness, she would literally will herself awake to greet a friend, all the energy she could muster gathered up into a smiling 'hello'. The sheer effort expended, to acknowledge each and every kindness, showed how much she valued friendship. And how generously she extended it to those whose lives she touched. ¶

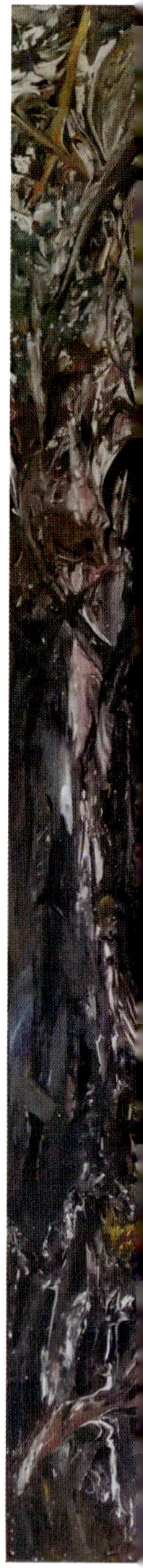

ARTHUR BOYD
BARBARA AT HURSTBRIDGE *1968*
OIL ON COMPOSITION BOARD
91.5 × 91.5 CM
PRIVATE COLLECTION
ARTHUR BOYD'S WORK REPRODUCED WITH THE PERMISSION OF BUNDANON TRUST

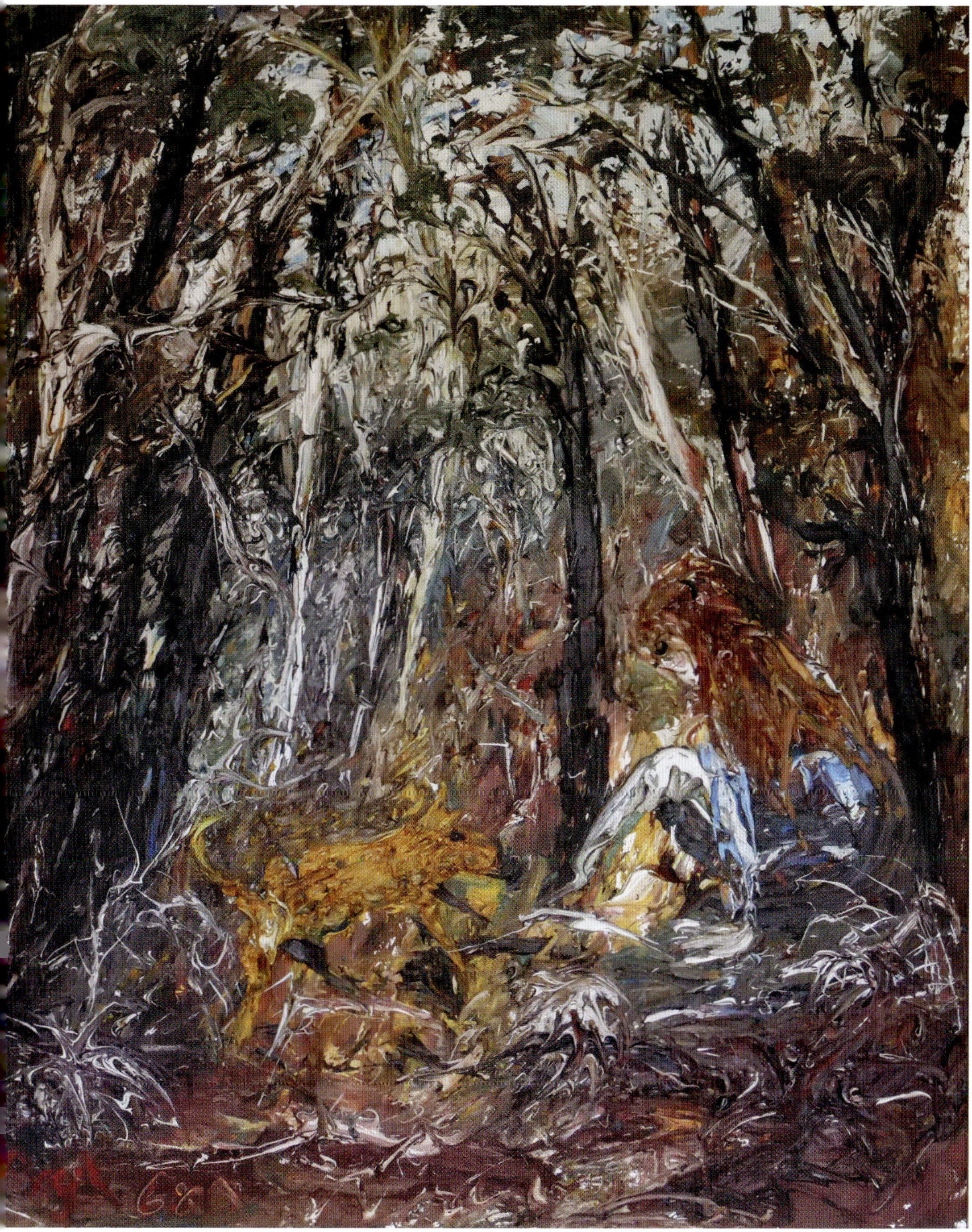

MISSING BARBARA

JINX NOLAN

I first met Barbara in the 1960s in New York when she and Bert came to stay in the Chelsea. My parents moved into the penthouse, where Brett and Wendy Whiteley and his mother, who was ubiquitous, had lived.

My parents and I settled there and I was working as a clerk at the United Nations. I remember Barbara walking into my room, red hair and smiling. We immediately hit it off. While Sid and Bert went downstairs to reserve a table at the El Quixote restaurant next door, Barbara, Mum and I chatted. Bert called Sid 'Ned', for obvious reasons.

Alas my memories of Barbara and Bert in the Chelsea are remote. I was miserable at that juncture of my life and forgot a lot of what went on. Only that it was lovely to have the friendship of Barbara and Bert while there.

I visited Barbara in Australia over the ensuing years. My parents went to stay with her and Bert in the country. Mum always claimed that Barbara centred Bert and provided a stable and loving milieu in which he could paint. She was very organised.

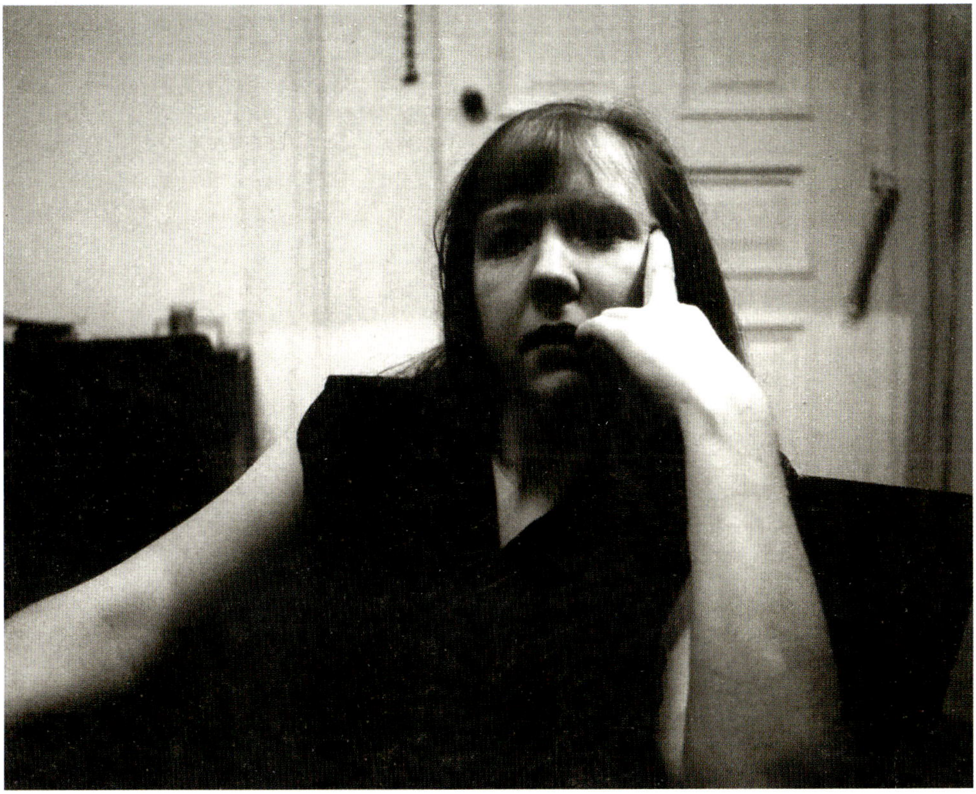

BARBARA TUCKER IN THE CHELSEA HOTEL C. 1963
Photo by Albert Tucker

After Bert died I stayed with her in her lovely house in St Kilda. It was winter and a bit chilly. It was there that I first saw Bert's painting of Barbara in a mango grove, yellow flowers in her hair.

One weekend she drove my husband Bob and me to her small house situated amongst trees by the sea. We walked to the rockpools, where everyone swam except for me. I thought it was too cold. Bob took a beautiful photo of Barbara emerging from a rockpool, glistening with water.

The last time I saw her was in her new house. We went shopping. Barbara confidently drove down the centre of the road.

I called her my sister. I will always miss her. ¶

BARBARA *AND THE* RIDDLE *OF THE* UNIVERSE

BRENDA SMITH

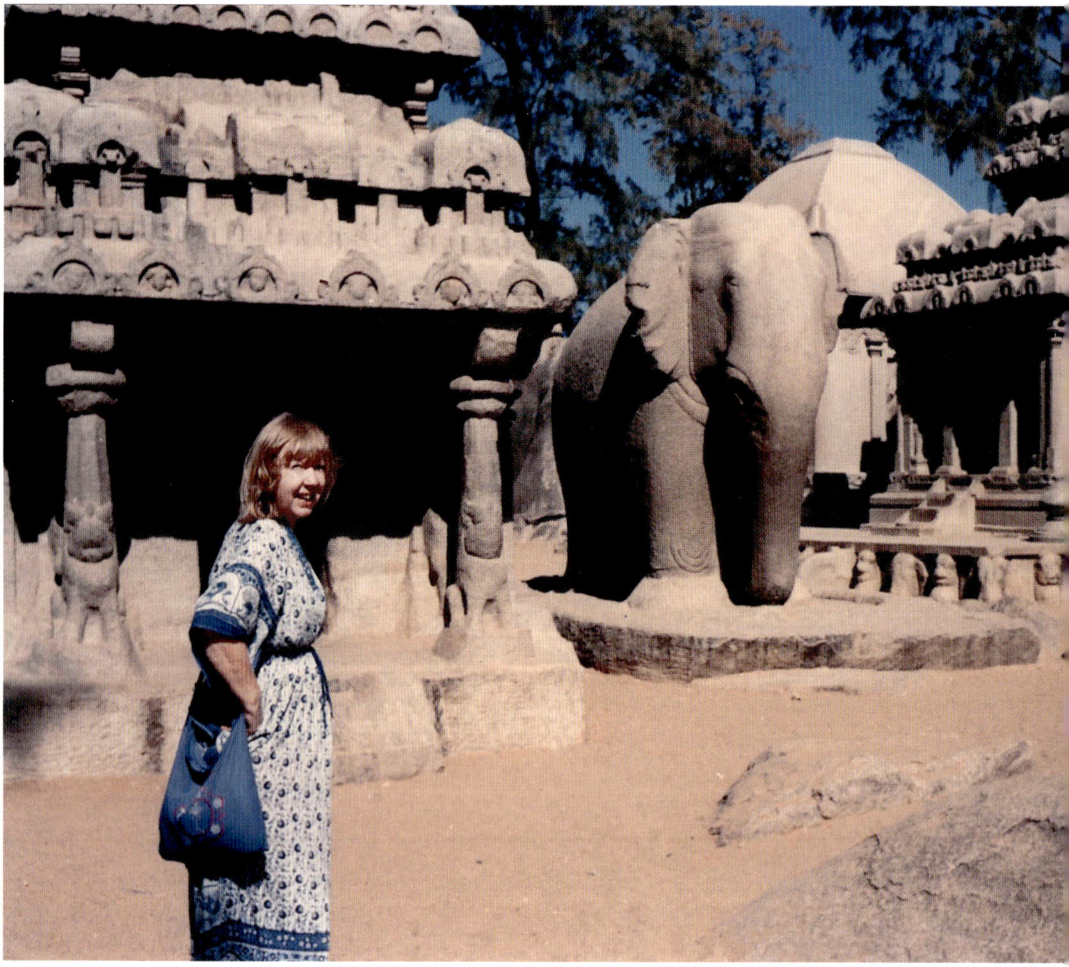

BARBARA TUCKER AT THE TEMPLES OF MAHABALIPURUM, INDIA 1990
Photo by Brenda Smith

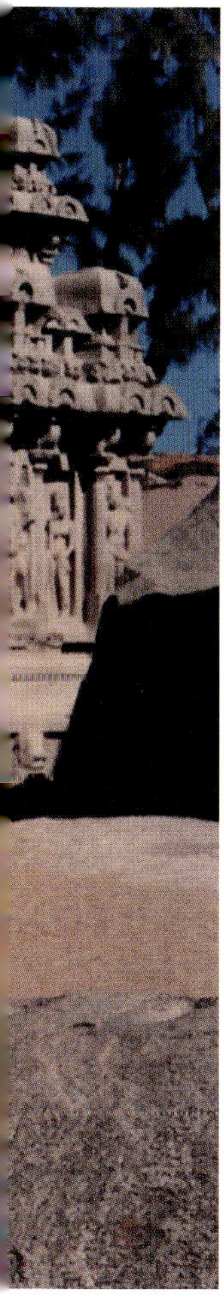

When you got to know Barbara you understood that she had a vision of the world that involved the unity of all things—or to change the emphasis, the connectedness of all things. It was marked by an openness to thinking about how 'reality' might be constituted as well as a refusal to countenance any straightforward division between physical or emotional or spiritual realities.

This was grounded in a genuine humility about her own importance. Barbara never took Albert, or her sisters and brothers and their families, or friendships, for granted. Each relationship had meaning, a specific meaning and she 'attended' to each of us.

She loved the insights gained through meeting, connection, knowing—and accepting. While she was interested in psychological insight like most of us born in the twentieth century, I'm sure she didn't feel this was sufficient. She wanted insight that reached into the metaphysical, stretching into the world of mysticism, that world of visionary connection.

Yet the Barbara Tucker I got to know when she began supplying educational books to several high schools in the 1980s I saw simply as being practical, efficient and reliable. She worked then from her offices at La Trobe University. I was the Social Science Co-ordinator at Eltham High School and I felt her to be an excellent colleague. I thought she was, in fact, the consummate business-woman. Barbara would let me know about the new publications, journals and speakers. All orders for history, geography and text books on politics were delivered promptly. I soon became aware that her reliability was tinged with an unexpected sense of humour. So it was that over the many orders we became friends.

I was so impressed by the organised, business-Barbara that I did not understand at the time that there was another side of Barbara, the one who sought understanding of what I might call 'the riddle of the universe'. If you're a sceptic, as I am, someone else's interest in the mystical can make you uncomfortable. Only later did I come to see that Barbara was drawn to the mystical, perhaps because of the space it offered for reflection, perhaps for its quiet refuge for the soul in a city-centred world buzzing with egos and the traffic of the material.

The dawning of my understanding of this aspect of Barbara began one morning as I was sitting having my tea break when she asked if I would like to join a small group going to visit the ashram of Bhagavan Sri Sathya Sai Baba. They would leave on Boxing Day and return after a month around Australia Day, 1990.

Barbara's sister Joan and her younger sister Linda had organised the two weeks at the ashram and then a tour of southern India to visit the major Hindu temples in Mysore, Tanjore and Pondicherry. I taught Indian history at VCE level and was fascinated with a culture so different from our own. Here was a chance to see it all at first hand.

All I could think of was that I had arrived at a very new stage of life and if my adult children did not mind me flying out immediately after Christmas Day, then this was feasible. It was almost as if I had been waiting for something like this to happen, and Barbara's invitation had opened new possibilities.

The rest of the year was a chaotic tumble. There were visas, injections and organising my rather too enthusiastic family who were happy to see me departing on such an adventure. What joy to be able to visit and see the Chola Temples and Pavlava Empires of Southern India to experience this ancient and complex culture at first hand.

Landing in India for the first time, I felt I was on a film set. I stared at camels and sacred cows wandering around the streets; wooden bullock carts transported loads three times their size. I stared at the women in magnificent saris and men in dhoti, who created the most colourful vision I had ever seen.

We were taken to the ashram by local taxi through Andhra Pradesh to Puttaparthi. The journey went through rural villages, along dusty, bumpy roads. Towards the end of the afternoon we were driven through a valley to the basin of the surrounding hills. We eventually arrived at the gates to the ashram. The entrance revealed many buildings, all of them in pastel marshmallow colours. Before us lay an avenue of ashoka trees, leading to a white shimmering temple. Before we could enter we were welcomed, along with several others. Men were immediately separated from women.

Barbara's sister Joan whispered to me to follow her to the female dormitory. At the edge of the ashram were several long sheds. Each held about a hundred visitors. As we entered the dark space, I was overwhelmed by the contrast with the lightness outside. Immediately we were asked to make up our mattresses and lay them along the floor of the dormitory. Our luggage was to be placed on the floor alongside. There was a stone shower block and hole-in-the-floor toilet at the far end of the building. I thought it a little basic, and even our leader Joan seemed in agreement on that. There was no mention of food.

It appeared that the most important thing for our party was to be ready at sunset for Darshan, the time of being in the presence of a Holy Man. With half an hour to go, we quickly joined the hundreds of devotees making their way to the Temple. Women dressed in saris were gliding in and out of the crowds. We were asked to sit cross legged and make ourselves spiritually ready for the arrival of Sai Baba. Gradually a stillness filled the air. It appeared that everyone around me was straining to receive the blessing and be in the presence of this adored Guru.

I saw a figure in an orange robe walking towards us from the Temple. Gradually as his halo of dark curls became visible, I could see that we were in the presence of Bhagavan Sri Sathya Sai Baba. There was muted Vedic chanting filling the air as the figure approached the hundreds of followers. Many kissed his feet. Those further back passed letters to him, which Sai Baba read, nodded and then passed to his followers, who walked behind. Slowly he worked his way along the huge circles of devotees.

During that first week, Barbara was pleased to show me the new hospital, the university and the students quarters paid for by the many international followers and devotees of Sai Baba. I enjoyed spending the days with her. There were many workshops—dancing, practising weaving, visiting the schools are only a few of the ones I can remember.

By the second week I was restless. As a non-devotee—a sceptic—I was finding the time dragging. I was looking forward to leaving the ashram and its practices and travelling to see the ancient towns and villages of Southern India.

I saw less and less of Barbara. She and her sisters attended the chanting of the Vedic Scriptures as dawn broke. They walked in procession round the ashram with other devotees at daybreak. Later in the morning she would do yoga and she'd read in the library in the hottest part of the afternoon.

In our last week our leader announced that as Australians we might be asked to Sai Baba's residence after Darshan. Two of us, the non-devotees, did not expect to be included but we were told that we were to be together as a visiting group. On our penultimate evening we were brought out of the crowd at Darshan and invited to an audience with Sai Baba. I immediately decided not to speak and followed respectfully to the cool verandah of the inner temple to sit with the Swami. There was an Indian family and the seven of us. Remembering that the devotees believed him to be the reincarnation of God, I decided to keep my head down, too, and hoped he would not notice a non-believer. We were, perhaps, in the presence of a Divine One.

After a prayer Sathya Sai Baba spoke to us all in excellent English. The conversation was informal and friendly. Finally he turned to our leader. His presence was exotic to me and yet strangely calming. 'What would you like me to do for you?' he asked our leader Joan.

'It is enough to be in your presence, Swami,' she replied.

Barbara was next. 'Being with his holiness is sufficient,' was her clear reply.

She said that the meeting had changed her life. Looking at Barbara's face full of intensity and radiance, I suddenly realised she, Joan and Linda had been following their own spiritual path.

The Holy Man turned to me, and asked the question again. Silence was not an option. What could I say? I was slightly embarrassed and thought that maybe I should ask for something but not for myself. I asked that my son's hearing problem could be helped. Sai Baba quietly assured me that it would and passed on to the Indian family.

The Hindu mother asked for Vibhutti, sacred ash. Sai Baba was renowned for his ability to materialise this holy substance and with a swirling of his hand he produced the grey ash in the palm of his left hand. Gently he gave it to the mother, while chanting a Vedic prayer. Had this minor miracle really happened?

Eventually, we were escorted beyond the temple's gardens, bidding farewell and thanking Swami. We bowed and walked away through the temple arches.

We began our tour of the Chola Temples of Tamil Nadu the next day. Despite much reading and studying reincarnation, I still did not understand fully the beliefs of the followers of Sai Baba. My scepticism was intact.

What I did observe, as we moved south, was that India was a very spiritual country, the birthplace of both Buddhism and Hinduism. Sathya Sai Baba was revered not only in India but throughout Europe and America. His beliefs were syncretic, as much Christian as Hindu. Barbara and her sisters had embraced his teachings. Had she been looking to explore more about the life of the spirit for long? I envied her closeness to her sisters and their shared odyssey.

For Barbara the Puttaparthi visit was to influence her life. She altered the garden of her Blairgowrie cottage retreat to resemble the gardens of the ashram. It became a quiet oasis on the ocean side of the Mornington Peninsula. Barbara seemed to embrace nature there in the gardens, in the rockpool walks, in swimming in the surf and reading. She found regeneration of the spirit in that landscape.

About this time Barbara established her own bookshop in Rathdowne Street called simply The Terrace Bookshop. Albert designed the colour scheme for the interior of this gracious Victorian building. Melburnians enjoyed the retreat the Tuckers had created together. Readers savoured the selection of books Barbara made. They sat turning pages by the fire on cold days; they curled up with their children in a corner devoted to younger readers. Everyone who visited could tell that Barbara loved books, the imagination, the creativity within them. The Terrace Bookshop flourished.

Not all that long after our return to Australia Barbara phoned us from the Epworth Hospital. She had been diagnosed with a brain tumour. It seemed unbelievable as good health and high energy always radiated from her. She was booked in for surgery. Eventually we were allowed to visit her at the Epworth. As I entered the ward, there was Barbara sitting up in bed, smiling. She said she had prayed to Sai Baba. The surgeon could not believe that the tumour had simply disappeared.

Later, I read that Barbara had spoken of a visionary moment to the English writer Colin Wilson, who called her 'the remarkable Australian mystic Barbara Tucker, wife of the painter Albert Tucker', and who recorded a vision she had told him she'd had while sitting quietly in the midst of a party.

> All the people round me were laughing and chatting and doing all the things people do at parties—and then, again, I suddenly saw all the connections between these people—how they all interconnected, how all this show that was going on was not, in fact, idle chatter. It was all interconnecting into their relationships with one another in the most extraordinary way.

It would have been impossible for Barbara and Albert to know the difficult times that lay ahead in the world of Australian art. So often loyalties were broken, trust destroyed, relationships disconnected. It was Barbara's composure and her conviction about the life of the spirit, her certainty in the interconnectedness of all things that enabled her to support her husband and to bring them both through times of great difficulty. She was her own person but importantly, she was muse and companion for Albert, for the artist. Albert was, with Barbara's support, able to continue his creative life as a major Australian artist.

To the rest of the world Barbara was outgoing, full of warmth, energy, wisdom and wit. Her spiritual strength embraced all who knew her. Her final generosity was the Tucker Gift to the Heide Museum of Modern Art. It is fitting that the memorial to Barbara at Heide is a black walnut tree in its gracious and extensive gardens. The gardeners searched throughout Melbourne to find this rare tree. It was chosen because it linked her and Albert to their first home together in Hurstbridge. There they shared a love of nature and through it the regeneration of the spirit.

The memorial service for Barbara Tucker ended with family and friends circling the tree, which stands near a path running towards the Yarra in Heide's gardens. Our quiet thoughts that day were a remembrance of Barbara's spiritual legacy.

I think that she felt that if there was not, perhaps, a universal *plan*, there was, certainly, an interconnectedness of all things and a connection to the immensity of our universe that we ignore too easily in the glare of bright lights on busy city streets. ¶

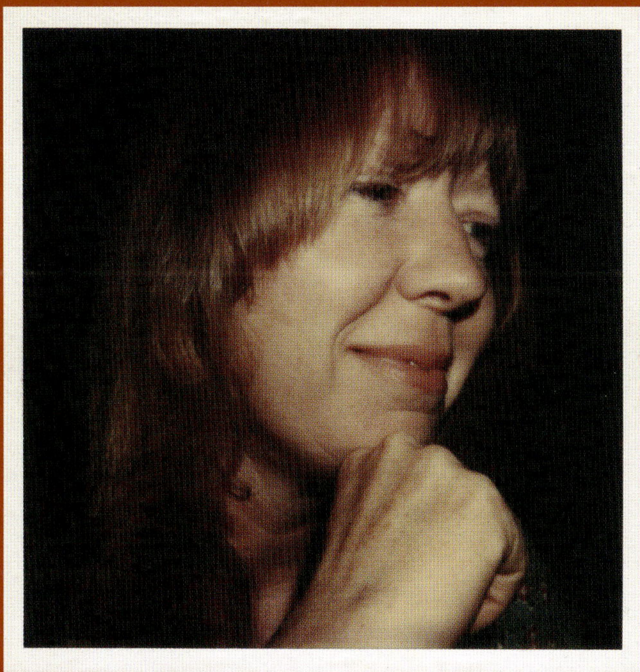

BARBARA TUCKER Photo by Abert Tucker

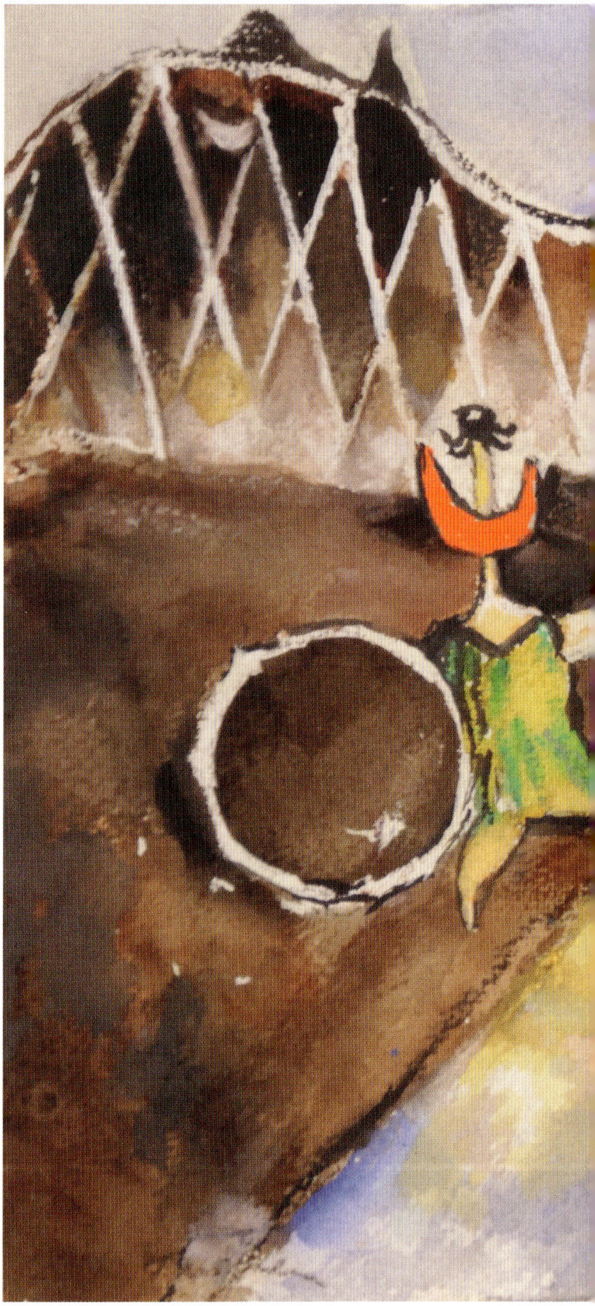

ALBERT TUCKER
LUNA PARK *C. 1986*
WATERCOLOUR AND PASTEL ON PAPER
25.5 × 35.5 CM
PRIVATE COLLECTION

COURTESY SMITH & SINGER FINE ART

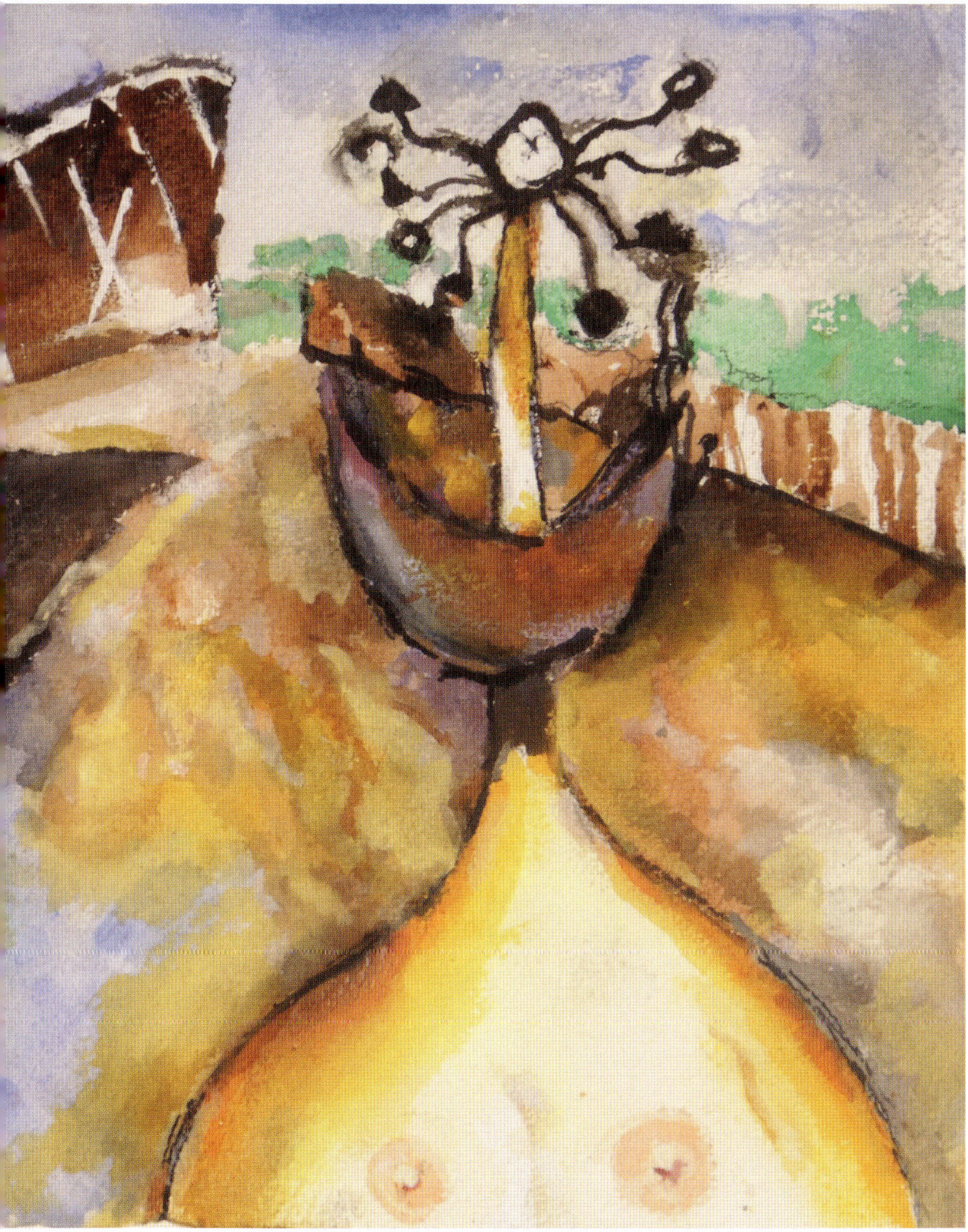

ELEGY *for* BARBARA TUCKER

HERMINA BURNS

The way you lived
warmed by parrots on
an easel at Hurstbridge

hot tea ready on that
scrubbed table littered with
shortbread crumbs

brushed from a recipe
given by your mother for
buttery life

fat with goodness
as we all sat at Hoddles Creek
around the way

you ate with gusto,
linked and talking easily
with great gums dripping bark

as Bert arrived from painting
outside into life hot with the
taste of soup and relish

catching a trim beard,
your hand stirring sonnets of love
made big in that old pot

punctuated by rosemary and
pepper, potatoes and leeks
eloquently stressed.

We knew your architecture
of a crimson rug over wood-grained
arms and green velvet as

lived art ready to cushion
bottoms of great men, lesser men,
great women, girls and a nephew

tumbling on deep-worn sofas
at St Kilda. And a bunch of chives
chopped into submission

sprawled on a board waiting for
what you will as rain falls
in brief squalls and sun

alerts fauns on
random lawns. You bathe
naked in a stream

running free into
scribbly gums scrabbling
southern land.

Nothing is without merit
yet it must be striven for,
hard-earned, even so, you thought

possums gnawing into
the eaves at Blessington Street
who won a home were

a blessing of sorts and a curse,
of course, for electrics and one
weeping elm out front.

You found a loose smile
somewhere in it all—
greenhoods and geraniums

picked early for your vase found
art squatting on a kitchen sill
still when you left us

near or remembering as we
planted for you, at Heide,
a solid black walnut tree.

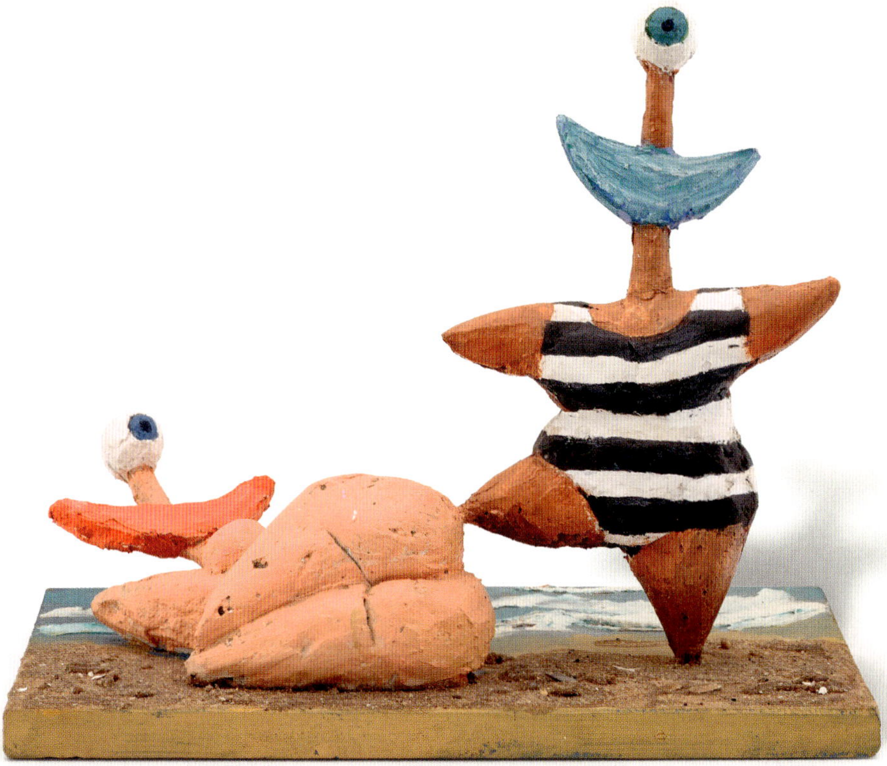

ALBERT TUCKER
FLIRTATION *1974*
MIXED MEDIA
30 × 35 × 21 CM
PRIVATE COLLECTION
© ALBERT & BARBARA TUCKER FOUNDATION
COURTESY SMITH & SINGER FINE ART

ACKNOWLEDGEMENTS

This book would not have been possible without the support of Darren Jones and Caitlin Graham-Jones, nephew and niece of Barbara. From the start, as directors of the Albert & Barbara Tucker Foundation, they supported the idea of gathering the speeches from Barbara's funeral and her memorial service at Heide into a little festschrift volume. The idea grew into a larger project, with more contributors. I deeply appreciate the way they actively sustained the project, suggesting a larger range of contributors, and were flexible and responsive to unexpected suggestions. Importantly, they provided the funding for the book's publication. I would also like to thank Jill Redner for her vital liaison in the early stages of getting this project off the ground.

I am immensely grateful to all contributors: Peter Bilcock, Shane Carmody and Jock Murphy, Florence Crichton and Richard Crichton, Gavin Fry, Caitlin Graham-Jones, Kirsty Grant and Lesley Harding, Darren Jones, Ian Jones, Jinx Nolan, Justin O'Brien, Judith Pugh, Jill Redner, Gary Singer, Brenda Smith, Geoffrey Smith and Lyn Williams. Their willingness to contribute their time and memories, and in some cases, photographs and letters, was informed by their sense of Barbara's significance.

I wish to thank the following people for their work on the book: David Burns for revisions to the introduction; Darren Jones for title suggestions; Cathryn Smith, Senior Editor/Custom Publisher at Miegunyah Press, an imprint of Melbourne University Publishing, for her enthusiasm, guidance and organisation, Trisha Garner for her design and the team at MUP. ¶

INDEX

PAGE NUMBERS IN BOLD INDICATE ILLUSTRATIONS

Albert & Barbara Tucker Foundation 1, 193
Albert and Barbara Tucker Gift 2, 45–6, 83, 198, 216
Albert Tucker (Fry) 83–4, 87
Angry Penguins journal 47
'artist's wife' role 75–7, 89, 140, 162, 165–6, 192, 202, 206
artworks *see* Tucker, Albert (Bert): works
Australian Consulate, New York 75
Australian Gothic (Burke) 83
Australian Painters of the Twentieth Century (Klepac) 82
Australian War Memorial collection *82*
authenticity *see* copyright and authenticity

B

Bard, Stanley 96, **96**, 99
Beechworth area, Victoria 168–70
Bergner, Yosl 46
Bilceaux, Joan 5, 167; *see also* Jones, Joan
Bilcock, Barbara *see* Tucker, Barbara
Bilcock, David **113**, 146, 153, 186, **200**
Bilcock, David Snr 1, 199, **200**, 201
Bilcock, Jean 1, 167–8, 186, **200**
Bilcock, Joan *see Jones,* Joan
Bilcock, Linda **113, 138, 148**, 168, 177, 179, 186, **200**, 210–14
Bilcock, Peter **113**, 142–57, 168, 186, **200**
Blairgowrie, Victoria 25, 37, 108, 139, 150–1, 189, 214
bookshops
  La Trobe University 76, 188, 196, 210
  The Terrace Bookshop, North Carlton **194**, 214–15
Boyd, Arthur 46, **49, 69, 166, 196**
  Barbara at Hurstbridge (1968) 203, **205**
Boyd, Yvonne 88
Boyds' place (Murrumbeena) 144
Bridgehampton, New York 115, 123
Burke, Janine 46
  Australian Gothic (book) 83
Byrnes Gully, Beechworth area, Victoria 169–70

C

camping trips and picnics 102–7, 168–73, 179, 188, 189
Carlton, Victoria, Rathdowne Street bookshop **194,** 214–15
Carmody, Shane 56, 57
Chelsea Hotel, New York 30, 75, **95–9**, 114–15, 206
Christie's Australia 198
Christmas Hills, Victoria 150
colleagues' memories of Barbara and Bert 45–63, 81–9
copyright and authenticity 60–3, 83, 198
Craftsman House proposed book on Tucker 82
Crichton, Richard and Florence **91, 95, 96, 100, 102–5, 107–11, 190,** 196
  family **91, 95, 97–103**
  letters from Barbara and Bert 114–25
  memories of Barbara and Bert 90–113, 186–93
  Richard's works **93**, 166

D

Dickson, Mary 4, 74, 84, **85**, 87, 189, 199
Diggins, Lauraine 50, 83, 87
donations *see* gifts and donations
Dunmoochin, Cottles Bridge, Victoria 69, 77

E

Eye of the Beholder exhibition, 1998–2000 50

F

family (Barbara's) 1, 5, 130, 142–57, 167–8, 177, 179, 186–8, 192
family memories of Barbara and Bert 130–79
Faun and Parrot case 198
food and cooking 56, 139–40, 180 , 183, 186, 187–8
friends' memories of Barbara and Bert 67–78, 180–2, 195–216
friendship 3–4, 6, 188–9, 192
Fry, Gavin 4, 81–4, 87–9
  Albert Tucker (book) 83–4, 87

G

gifts and donations 2–3, 45–59, 161
  Albert and Barbara Tucker Gift 2, 45–6, 83, 198, 216
  see also Heide Museum of Modern Art; State Library Victoria; Tucker, Albert (Bert): legacy (Barbara's custody of)
Graham-Jones, Caitlin *see* Jones, Caitlin
Gritten, Henry
  Jackson's Creek, Sunbury (1857) 57

H

Haese, Richard 76–7
Harkness Fellowships 114–15
Hart, Deborah 135
Hayes, Gerard 55

Heide Museum of Modern Art 89, 134, 135, 161, 193
  Albert and Barbara Tucker Gallery 50, 51
  Albert and Barbara Tucker Gift 2, 45–6, 83, 198, 216
  Tucker visual and literary archive 2–3, 51, 53, 58
  see also Reed, John and Sunday
Hester, Joy 46–7, 48, 51, 70, 77, 84, 87, 92
Hit Parade (Channel Seven television) 167
Hoddles Creek, Victoria 56, 111, **111**, 112, **113,** 151, 153, 196–7
homes *see* Blairgowrie, Victoria; Hoddles Creek, Victoria; Hurstbridge, Victoria; New York; Springbrook, Queensland; St Kilda, Victoria; Toorak, Victoria
Hughes, Robert 46, 202–3
Hurstbridge, Victoria 11–12, 31, 48, 76, 81, 90, 92, 94, 122, 152, 189, 203, 216

I

India 7, 210–14

J

Joffe, Max 196; *see also* theft of Bert's art
Jones, Angus **200**
Jones, Barry **68**
Jones, Caitlin 134, **138, 1**39–40, 177, **200**, 203
Jones, Darren 130, **132**, 133–5, **148**, 177, **178**, **200**
Jones, Ian 5, 165–79, **174**
Jones, Joan **107**, 130, **138**, 142, 145–6, **148**, 149, 167–71, 177, 179, 186, **200**, 210–14
Jones, Linda 142, 145–6, 149
Jung, Carl 162

K

Kelly Gang 169, 170–2
  Ned Kelly's rifle 5, 56, 172–3
  Nolan's *Ned Kelly series* 57, 202
Keon, Aurora **108**
Keon, Michael **108**, 108, 150, 195–6
Klepac, Lou 82, 83

L

La Trobe University bookshop 76, 188, 196, 210
Lawlor, Adrian 81
legacy see gifts and donations; Tucker, Albert (Bert): legacy (Barbara's custody of)
Lennie, Yvonne 88

M

McCaughey, Patrick 57
May, Stephen 90
memories of Barbara and Bert
  colleagues' 45–63, 81–9
  Crichtons' 90–113, 186–93
  family's 130–79
  friends' 67–78, 180–2, 195–216
Mexico 123, 165–7, 168
Murphy, Jock 56
Museum of Modern Art, New York 4, 87

N

National Gallery of Australia 45, 57, 135, 182
New York **95–101**, 123
  Australian Consulate 75
  Bridgehampton 115, 123
  Chelsea Hotel 30, 75, **95–9**, 114–15, 206
  Museum of Modern Art 4, 87
Nolan, Cynthia 6, 206
Nolan, Jinx 206–7
Nolan, Sidney 6, 31, **31**, 46–7, **49**, 69, 196, 206
  correspondence with Bert 57
  Ned Kelly series 57, 202

O

O'Brien, Justin 134, 160–2, 188

P

Paris 198–9
Police Caves, Victoria 170–2, **174–5**
Pugh, Clifton 69, 75, 77–8
Pugh, Judith 69, **72**, 73–8

R

Redner, Jill and Harry 195–204
Reed, John and Sunday 46–8, 51, 54–5, 58, 77, 87, 199; *see also* Heide Museum of Modern Art
Reed, Sweeney 48, 51, 77, 81, 84, 199
Reeder, Warwick 56, 82–3
Reedy Creek, Victoria 169–73
Reid, Barrett 55, 161
Reilly, Dianne 56–7
royalties 3, 62–3

S

Shelton, Esau 173
Singer, Gary 63, 70, 134, 180–2, **181**
Singer, Leisl 57, **108**
Smith, Brenda 208–16
Smith, Geoffrey **61,** 70, 134, 182

Sorrento, Victoria 25, 37, 150, 157, 180
Springbrook, Queensland 21, 69, 154–5, 189
St Kilda, Victoria 82, 88, 109, 153, 177, 196, 201, 206–7
State Library Victoria 3, 51, 54–9, 161

T

The Terrace Bookshop, North Carlton, Victoria **194, 214–15**
theft of Bert's art 151, 193, 196
Toorak, Victoria 153–4, 192, 201
Tucker, Albert (Bert)
  books about 4, 82–4, 87–8
  character and personality 76, 77, 88, 188
  correspondence 57, 58, 114–25
  death 197–8
  health 187, 196
  Heide and the Reeds 46–8, 51, 55, 58, 77, 84, 87, 199
  legacy (Barbara's custody of) 2–3, 60–3, 70, 88–9, 132, 140, 157, 192–3, 198, 202
  library, papers and visual archive 2–3, 51, 53, 54–9, 83
  marriage to Barbara 11, 48, 94, 165–6, 192–3, 202–3, 215–16
  marriage to Joy Hester *see* Hester, Joy; Reed, Sweeney
  memories of *see* memories of Barbara and Bert
  photographs of **xiv, 55, 86, 93, 97, 100–11, 141, 164, 174, 178, 182, 190**
  studios 11, 75, 82, 90, 94, 109, **109**, 122, 151, 153, 166, 196
  travel and life overseas 47, 84, 87, 95–101, 114–21, 123, 165–7, 168, 188
  women in his life 84, 87; *see also* Dickson, Mary; Hester, Joy; Tucker, Barbara
Tucker, Albert (Bert): photography 50–1, 58, 76–7, 81, 100, 107
  exhibitions 50
  portraits of Barbara 24–5, **26–39, 49, 52, 80, 147, 151, 152, 156, 207**
Tucker, Albert (Bert): works
  Antipodean Heads 162, 176
  Aspendale (1984) **128–9**
  Blairgowrie (1974) **136–7**
  Blairgowrie (1982) **Vi–Vii**
  Blairgowrie Headland (1982) **131**
  Convict Dreaming (1969) **18**
  Convict Dreaming (1972) **19**
  Convict in Swamp (1971) **8–9**
  copyright and authenticity 60–3, 83, 198
  creative process 46, 169–70, 216
  exhibitions 47, 199
  Explorer (series) 152
  Explorers (1967) **43**
  Faces I Have Met (portrait series 1976–1985) 10–11, 55, 58, 88–9
  Flirtation (1974) **222**
  Flirtation (1954) 63
  Girl and Convict (1971) 17
  Image of Modern Evil 24 (1945) 170
  Image of Modern Evil (1977) **228–9**
  Images of Modern Evil (series) 57, 81
  Luna Park (c. 1986) **218–19**
  Lunar Landscape (1957) 4
  ownership dispute with John Reed 58
  Portrait of Adrian Lawlor (1939) 81
  portraits of John and Sunday Reed 58
  presence of Barbara in his works 10–23, 88–9
  resale royalty 3, 62–3
  River Dreaming (1971) **ii–iii**
  self-portraits 11
  Sorrento scenes 157
  Springbrook (1973) **22–3, 158–9**
  theft of 151, 193, 196
  The Watcher on the Balcony (1945) (*Image of Modern Evil 24*) 170
  Trees (1965) **xii–xiii**
  wartime works 82
  Woman and Parrot (1965) 12, **12–13**
  Woman Bathing (1970) 12, **14, 15**
Tucker, Barbara
  appearance 24, 139
  'artist's wife' role 75–7, 89, 140, 162, 165–6, 192, 202, 206
  'Barbaraganoush' 180–2
  birth 160
  character and personality 24–5, 74–8, 83, 130, 133–4, 140, 145–6, 149–50, 157, 160–3, 176, 182, 188, 196, 201–4, 215–16
  custodian of Bert's legacy 2–3, 60–3, 70, 88–9, 132, 140, 157, 192–3, 198, 202
  death 1, 134
  elegy for 220–1
  family 1, 5, 130, 142–57, 167–8, 177, 179, 186–8, 192
  friendships 3–4, 6, 188–9, 192, 194–216
  gifts by *see* gifts and donations
  health 177, 203–4, 215
  homes *see* Blairgowrie, Victoria; Hoddles Creek, Victoria; Hurstbridge, Victoria; New York; Springbrook, Queensland; St Kilda, Victoria; Toorak, Victoria
  letters to Crichtons 114–25
  marriage to Bert 1, 11, 20, 48, 94, 160, 165, 192–3, 202–3, 215–16
  marriage to first husband (Sam) 20, 144–5, 165
  memorial tree 53, 216

memories of *see* memories of Barbara and Bert
photographs of **xiv, 42, 44, 55, 61, 66, 68, 71, 72, 79, 95, 97, 100, 102–8, 111, 113, 123, 132, 138, 141, 143, 155, 161, 164, 181–2, 190, 194, 200, 208, 217**
portraits by Bert 24–5, **26–39, 49, 52, 80, 147, 151, 152, 156, 207**
presence in Bert's works 10–23, 88–9
spirituality 7, 146, 162–3, 209, 210–16
travel and life overseas 6–7, 114–21, 165–7, 188, 198–9, 210–14
work 75–6
Tucker Gift (Albert and Barbara Tucker Gift) 2, 45–6, 83, 198, 216

U

Underhill, Nancy 54–5

V

Vassilieff, Danila 46
Vaughn, Gerard 135

W

Westh, Pamela 84
Whelan, Oliver 109, **109**
Whiteley, Arkie 97–9, **97, 98**
Whiteley, Brett 97–9, **98, 99, 115**
Williams, Fred **66**, 67–70, **68**, **104**, 196
Williams, Lyn **66**, 67–70, **104**
Wilson, Colin 163, 215
wood block print books 58
Woolshed Valley, Victoria 169–73, 173, 179

ALBERT TUCKER
IMAGE OF MODERN EVIL *1977*
WATERCOLOUR AND PEN ON PAPER
27.5 × 38 CM
PRIVATE COLLECTION
© ALBERT & BARBARA TUCKER FOUNDATION
COURTESY SMITH & SINGER FINE ART

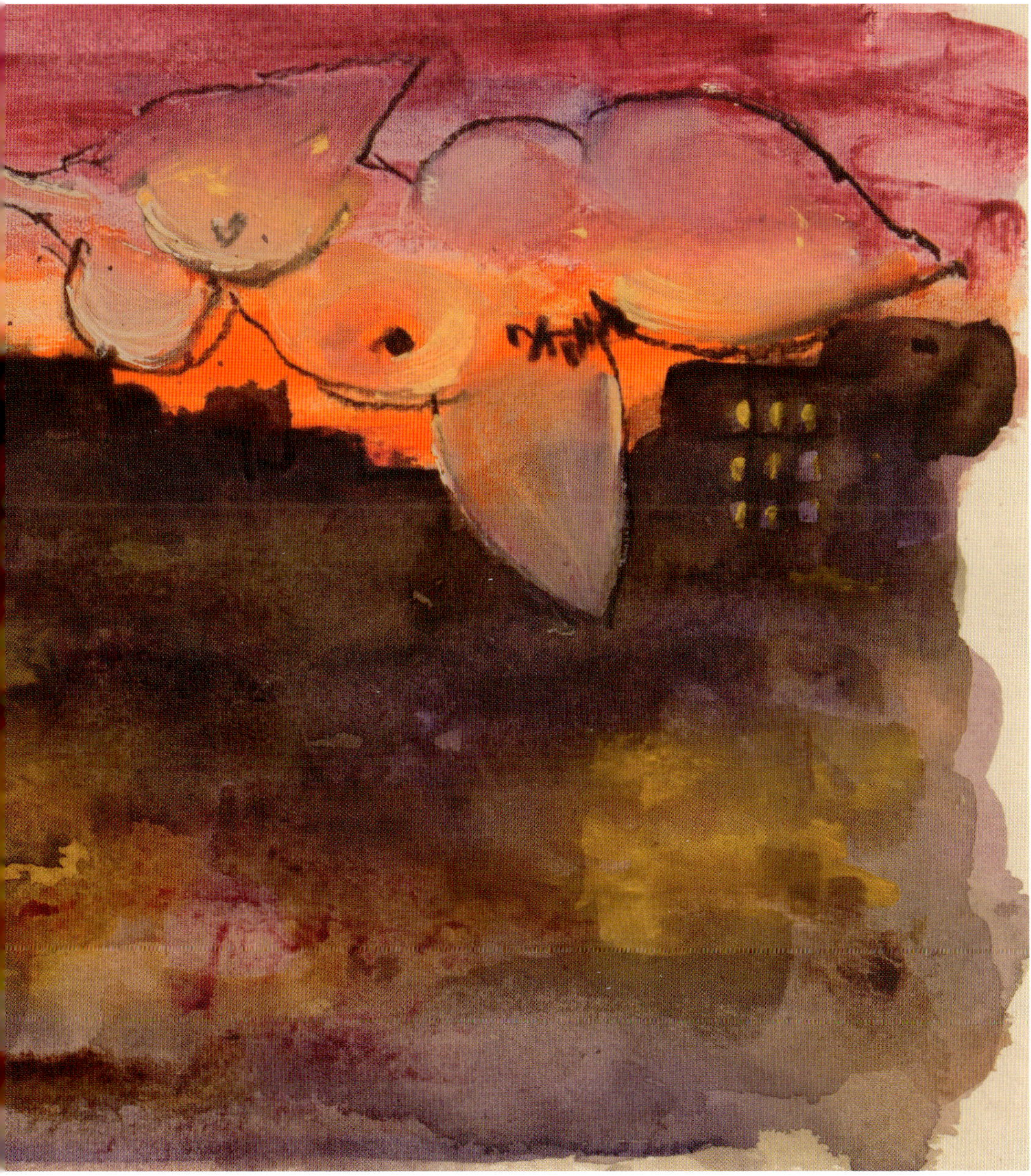

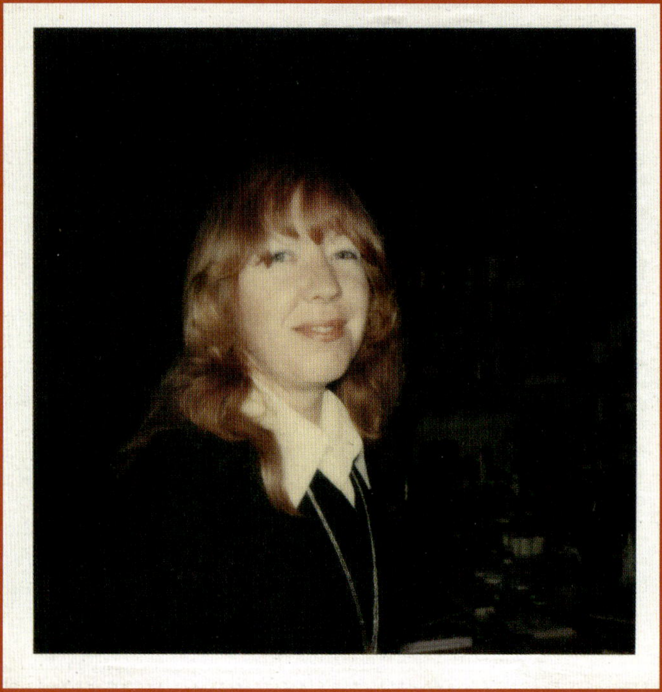

THE MIEGUNYAH PRESS
This book was designed and typeset
by Trisha Garner
The text was set in Sentinel Light
with 16 points of leading
The text is printed on 128gsm Matt Art
This book was edited by Cathryn Smith

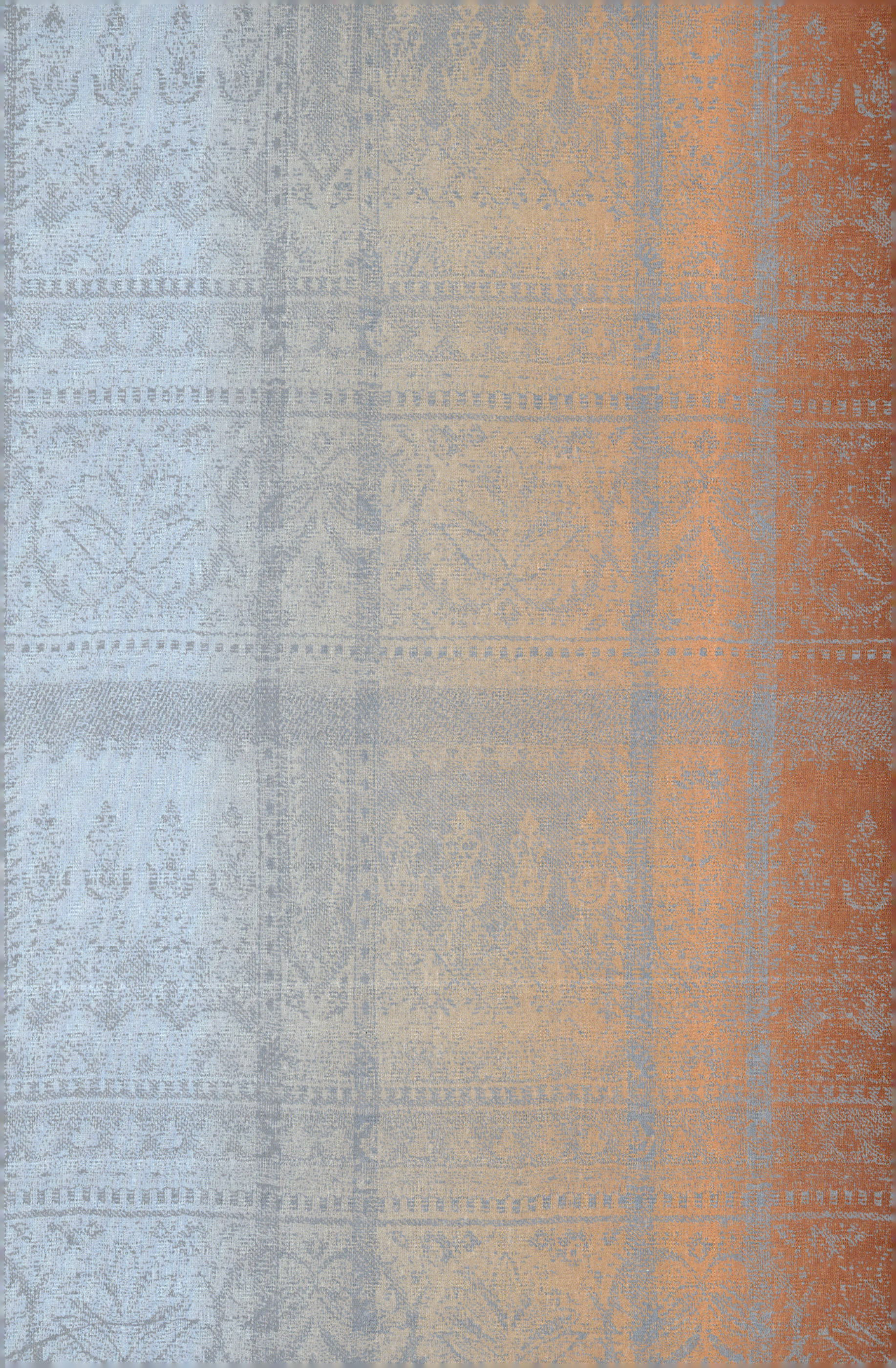